ANTHROPOLOGICAL PAPERS OF
THE UNIVERSITY OF ARIZONA
NUMBER 66

Beyond Chaco: Great Kiva Communities on the Mogollon Rim Frontier

Sarah A. Herr

THE UNIVERSITY OF ARIZONA PRESS
TUCSON
2001

About the Author

SARAH A. HERR began work in the Mogollon Rim region of Arizona in 1993 with the Silver Creek Archaeological Research Project and the University of Arizona Archaeological Field School. Her continuing research in the area, with the S.R. 260–Payson to Heber Archaeological Project, focuses on understanding the social and political organizations of regions dominated by small settlements. Dr. Herr received an A.B. degree from Bryn Mawr College in 1991 in Anthropology and Classical and Near Eastern Archaeology, and earned Master's (1994) and doctoral (1999) degrees from the Department of Anthropology, University of Arizona, Tucson. In 1999 she became a senior project director at Desert Archaeology, Inc., a Cultural Resource Management firm in Tucson, Arizona.

Cover: Plan and photograph of the great kiva at Tla Kii Pueblo, east-central Arizona (adapted from Haury 1985d, Figs. 20, 21; *see* Fig. 4.16). Original photo by Emil W. Haury, 1940 (Neg. 560, courtesy Arizona State Museum). Composite graphic by Geoffrey Ashley, Photographer, Arizona State Museum, University of Arizona, Tucson.

THE UNIVERSITY OF ARIZONA PRESS

Copyright © 2001

The Arizona Board of Regents
All Rights Reserved

This book was set in 10.7/12 CG Times
∞ This book is printed on acid-free, archival-quality paper.
Manufactured in the United States of America.

2012 11 10 09   5 4 3 2

Library of Congress Cataloging-in-Publication Data

Herr, Sarah A.
  Beyond Chaco : great kiva communities on the Mogollon Rim frontier / Sarah A. Herr.
    p. cm.-- (Anthropological papers of the University of Arizona ; no. 66)
Includes bibliographic references and index.
  ISBN 0-8165-2156-5
  1. Pueblo Indians--New Mexico--Chaco Canyon Region--Migrations. 2. Pueblo Indians--Relocation--Arizona--Mogollon Rim. 3. Pueblo architecture--Arizona--Mogollon Rim. 4. Kivas--Arizona--Mogollon Rim. 5. Land settlement patterns--Arizona--Mogollon Rim. 6. Mogollon Rim (Ariz.)--Antiquities. I. Title. II. Series.
  E99.P9 H39 2001
  979.1'3301--dc21
                    2001005084

Contents

FIGURES

TABLES

Preface

Frontier: in popular usage, the word is evocative. To some, the frontier is the *Call of the Wild*; to others, it is "cowboys and Indians," Hadrian's Wall, "space–the final frontier," Kennedy's "New Frontier," the wireless internet, or biogenetic advances. Can the social sciences stake a claim in the broad realm of meaning expressed by dictionary definitions: an international border, the area along an international border, a region just beyond or at the edge of a settled area, an undeveloped area or field for discovery or research? Place, physical or metaphorical, is an integral part of the definition. On the physical landscape, the spatial aspect of the frontier definition has real ramifications for people living there. The course of daily life is different on frontiers than it is in more populated or central places. Thus, it is within the realm of anthropology and other social sciences to attempt to understand those experiences.

Even though every settler and every frontier has a history linked to a local history that has come before, there is an underlying structure to frontiers that makes the living processes in these regions similar around the globe. As such, the frontier is a valid construct for studying the organization of people who live beyond the margins of populated areas. From the patterned behaviors enacted on historic and modern ethnographic frontiers, it is possible to build theoretical models that extend the concept into the past and use archaeological methods to reconstruct former frontiers.

The Mogollon Rim region of east-central Arizona, in the eleventh and twelfth centuries, is an ideal place to study frontiers. In this time and place, the region was situated between three highly populated areas with strongly organized societies: the Ancestral Pueblo, the Mimbres, and the Hohokam. Politically, the Mogollon Rim region was marginally situated on this landscape, but the definition of a frontier does not end with place alone. Processes associated with frontiers, including migration, integration, and attempts to create communities in areas with low population densities, are also apparent. Demographic reconstructions based on settlement pattern surveys show that even after a migration into the region in the eleventh century, population remained extremely low. Migrants living in small settlements formed communities around large structures of ritual architecture called great kivas. In addition to providing a public focus for the community, this architecture was imbued with meaning by the strong political or ritual organization centered in Chaco Canyon. Although migrants brought their past with them (from the Chacoan region and elsewhere), the course of history in the Mogollon Rim region does not parallel Chacoan history. Ultimately, these communities were noticeably different from communities in the homeland, both in outward manifestations and in their sociopolitical organization.

This research explores the Mogollon Rim frontier, not from the perspective of the many who lived at Chaco Canyon, but from the local perspective of the few living on the Mogollon Rim. Survey and excavation data provide information about how the households and communities were organized. By comparing the daily circumstances of these people with those of modern people living in frontier situations, it is possible to perceive the identities, values, and experiences of the eleventh-century Mogollon Rim pioneers.

Chapter 1 describes the juxtaposition of material culture on the Mogollon Rim: small settlements, abundant great kivas, and artifact assemblages that do not fit easily into existing categorical schemes. I argue that these material patterns can be understood as frontiers and differentiate these patterns from those of core areas. By examining the qualities of ethnographic and historic frontiers (Chapter 2), it is possible to create an archaeological model applicable to areas with the material patterns that characterize frontiers. Before applying the model to the Mogollon Rim region, the evidence for those regional characteristics that define a frontier (migration, integration, and community organization in an area of low population density) are examined (Chapter 3), as is the situation of the region on the social landscape of the eleventh and twelfth centuries A.D. This period is one of significant political change and population mobility across the northern Southwest, but when compared with the Chacoan, Mimbres, and Hohokam regions, the material culture of the Mogollon Rim region is most like that of the Chacoan region. Thus, I propose that at least the fringes of Chacoan settlement were the homelands of many of the settlers of the Mogollon Rim. From the regional picture provided in Chapter 3, the focus narrows, first to communities in Chapter 4, and then to households within communities in Chapter 5. The settlement pattern and excavation data from the Mogollon Rim region are synthesized into discussions of community scale and structure that reveal the way residents of households and communities interacted with the material world through production, distribution, transmission, reproduction, and co-residence activities. Finally, the interrelationships between the activities of households and communities are brought together to explore how social and political organizations were constructed on the Mogollon Rim (Chapter 6). Recognizing the frontier as a type of sociopolitical organization has implications for reconstructing the many paths to power across the prehispanic Southwest.

Acknowledgements

From fieldwork, to laboratory analyses, to use of archives and collections, to data analyses, to writing and publication, in virtually every way this research was the result of group efforts past and present. Foremost among these, it is a product of the Silver Creek Archaeological Research Project (SCARP) and the University of Arizona Archaeological Field School. A descriptive report (Mills, Herr, and Van Keuren 1999) combines the results of five years of technical reports and artifact analyses by numerous graduate students and professionals, and since that publication includes a complete listing of contributors to the Project, I do not repeat them here.

Financial support for portions of this research was provided by the National Science Foundation (SBR–9507660, SBR–9507661, SBR–9633771), the Wenner-Gren Foundation for Anthropological Research, the University of Arizona Department of Anthropology, the Social and Behavioral Sciences Research Institute, and the Society for American Archaeology Fred Plog Memorial Fellowship. Additional funding was provided by the Apache-Sitgreaves National Forests through cooperative agreements coordinated by Forest Archeologist Linda Martin. A National Science Foundation grant to the Laboratory of Tree-Ring Research at the University of Arizona funded the interpretation of samples from Hough's Great Kiva and Cothrun's Kiva. Department of Anthropology staff, including Norma Maynard, Lynn McAllister Bell, Cathy Snider, and Ellen Stamp administered these grants. William H. Doelle allowed me to use resources at Desert Archaeology, Inc. to produce several of the figures.

The Silver Creek Archaeological Research Project (SCARP) is directed by Barbara Mills and she has created an intellectually exciting research environment with an ambitious field and laboratory team. The excavations at three great kiva sites (Hough's Great Kiva, AZ P:16:160 ASM, and Cothrun's Kiva) resulted from five summers of field work conducted with University of Arizona field school students, volunteers from the Passports in Time (PIT) project of the U.S. Forest Service, and the incomparable staff of SCARP: Scott Van Keuren, Susan Stinson, Eric Kaldahl, Joanne Newcomb, Elizabeth Perry, Trenna Valado, Jenny Horner, and Kristen Hagenbuckle. Additionally, Jeff Clark, Dave Gregory, Ruth Van Dyke, Jan Peterson, Pat Bauer, and Frank and Hannah Sherman worked as volunteers. It is through this group of individuals that many of my ideas have been developed, encouraged, and critiqued.

All the SCARP sites investigated to date are in the Sitgreaves National Forest. Linda Martin, the Forest Archaeologist, provided us with excavation permits, helped organize two PIT projects that helped collect information from Hough's Great Kiva Site and Cothrun's Kiva, and, most importantly in the long term, arranged for these sites to be protected by site stewards. We were ably assisted by Bruce Donaldson and Heather Tamietti in the district offices, as well.

The Laboratory of Tree-Ring Research cross-dated tree-ring samples from Hough's Great Kiva site and provided species identification for samples from Hough's Great Kiva and Cothrun's Kiva sites. Lisa Huckell identified samples from Cothrun's Kiva for AMS radiocarbon dating. Douglas Donahue and Rosemary Maddock of the Accelerator Mass Spectrometry Laboratory at the University of Arizona Department of Physics processed the samples and provided the initial interpretation of the results and a student discount on this expensive experiment.

The ceramics and archives of previously investigated sites are housed at the Arizona State Museum (ASM) in Tucson, the Field Museum of Natural History in Chicago, and the Museum of Northern Arizona in Flagstaff. Mike Jacobs, assistant curator of archaeology at ASM, orchestrated many loans and permissions concerning work with the Tla Kii and Forestdale Valley collections. Lisa Zimmerman and Elaine Hughes helped process and compile the loans. Alan Ferg (ASM) provided access to the Museum archives and told stories about Haury's work in the Forestdale Valley and Mogollon Rim region. Kathy Hubenschmidt (ASM Photo Archives) furnished photos from the 1940 and 1941 excavations in the Forestdale Valley, which provided valuable information about field methods that was unavailable in published texts or field notes. Beth Grindell (ASM) provided information from the site files. Tla Kii Pueblo materials were collected from excavations on the Fort Apache Indian Reservation and I thank John R. Welch (White Mountain Apache Tribe Historic Preservation Officer) and the White Mountain Apache Tribe for permission to work with these artifacts.

At the Field Museum of Natural History in Chicago, Jonathon Haas gave permission to use the Carter Ranch collections and Wil Grewe-Mullen made arrangements for me to study them, Janice Klein directed my use of the archives, and Steve Nash quickly and efficiently fielded more recent questions about the Paul S. Martin collections. David Wilcox of the Museum of Northern Arizona permitted me to work with the FLEX (Goodwin) and FLEX (Show Low II) collections and the archival materials from the Sundown Site. Tracy Murphy and Nolan Wiggins assisted with the collections and site records. George Gumerman and Alan Skinner provided details about the personnel of the Highway Salvage project that excavated the Sundown site.

Michael A. Adler and John R. Welch reviewed the manuscript and their comments were careful, constructive, and thought-provoking; their efforts have resulted in a better presentation. I have also benefited from numerous intellectual exchanges with personnel at Desert Archaeolology, Inc. Permissions for publication of certain figures were obtained from the following authors, presses, and institutions: the University of Arizona Press; Ricky Lightfoot, Tobi Taylor, and Ron Towner (*Kiva*); Joanne Newcomb, Charles Adams, and the Arizona State Museum (*Arizona State Museum Archaeological Series*); Steve Nash, Jonathan Haas, and the Chicago Museum of Natural History (*Fieldiana*); and David Wilcox (Sundown Site, Museum of Northern Arizona). Several figures were prepared by Susan Hall, Doug Gann, Ellen Herr, and Rob Ciaccio.

Special thanks go to University of Arizona personnel Dirk Harris, Support Systems Analyst, and his assistant Eric Hanson, who provided computer support with scanning and figure production; Geoffrey Ashley, former Photographer at the Arizona State Museum, who designed and composed the graphic for the cover; and María Nieves Zedeño, who translated the Abstract into Spanish. I greatly appreciate Carol Gifford's decisive editing and kind guidance that transformed the manuscript into a book.

Finally, I am grateful for the closeness of family and friends. Jeff Clark is my sounding board and my greatest supporter. Thank you to my parents, Bruce and Ellen Herr, for their friendship and for having faith in the greater things in life, and to my sister, Rachel Herr, who entertains us with her great adventures that keep the imagination alive.

CHAPTER ONE

Material Patterning in the Archaeological Record: The Weak and The Strong

During the late eleventh and early twelfth centuries A.D. in the Mogollon Rim region of Arizona, residents of communities with ceremonial great kivas experienced life from a perspective accorded to few of their contemporaries. These early settlers lived on the edge of the Ancestral Pueblo world. This frontier was a place beyond and between the great Puebloan and Hohokam organizations of that time. Here, flexibility was crucial to survival and creativity was rewarded. The great kiva, an architectural form brought from their homeland, was first a familiar symbol to families living on a rugged new landscape but it took on fresh meanings on the frontier. In the process of settling the area, migrants with diverse histories transformed the values from their homelands and created new, if temporary, social formations.

Today, in the twenty-first century, this region poses a contradiction to the archaeologists who study it. Demographic reconstructions demonstrate that populations in the region were never large. Habitation sites are small, other types of sites are even smaller, and all are scattered across the landscape. Remains of expedient technologies and diverse artistic styles make artifact classifications unwieldy. Exotic trade items are absent. Yet this region, on the far southwestern edge of the Puebloan world, has one of the densest clusters of great kivas in the Greater Southwest.

The circumstances of daily life on a frontier are different from those of people who live in stable population centers. The individualistic behaviors of early settlers do not leave uniform patterns of material culture on the landscape. Conscious of their marginality relative to core homelands, the early settlers of the frontier acted in ways that expressed their changing identity and values. The spatial patterns of material culture they left behind are not just archaeological puzzles waiting to be explained, they signify real differences in the experiences of individuals and societies of the past.

In the ancient Puebloan Southwest there were geographic areas such as the Mogollon Rim region in which population was sparse and social formations were transitory. A paucity of material culture makes sociopolitical organizations in these areas difficult to reconstruct. However, areas of sparse settlement gain meaning when considered in relation to population centers. The economic, social, and political institutions of these centers strongly affect the experience and behaviors of their residents. Outlying areas of low settlement density may be frontiers, beyond the hegemony of core areas but connected by a common heritage. The frontier model provides an explanatory framework that can clarify the implications of migration into areas of low population density.

WEAK AND STRONG PATTERNS OF MATERIAL REMAINS

Fred Plog (1983, 1984; Tainter and Plog 1994) noted the different ways in which the remains of past societies were distributed across the landscape, describing areas of "strong patterns" and "weak patterns." He argued that areas of ceramic and architectural homogeneity, or "strong patterns," were created by the day-to-day behavior of members of a society. These behaviors were structured by centralized economic and political powers at large settlements, and the dominion controlled by these centers was an "alliance." Weak patterns, on the peripheries of strong patterns, were interpreted as areas of expedient and resilient behaviors (Adams 1978). He thought the autonomous households in these areas had less access to the "culture" of large settlements. After setting up this dichotomy, Plog concentrated on strong patterns and alliances and did not devote much attention to explaining social and political organizations in areas with weak patterns. The frontier model I use here provides a powerful tool for integrating areas of weak patterns into discussions of cultural processes.

Weak patterns occur in areas composed of small sites characterized by cultural remains that demonstrate unspecialized production, the use of local materials, wide ceramic variability, expedient and varied architecture, limited quantities of exotic trade goods, and evidence for egalitarian and diverse social organization (Tainter and Plog 1994: 169). By contrast, strong patterns are identified in areas with centralized sites that reveal specialized production, active trade, clear ceramic type distinctions, homogenous architectural styles, prestige goods, and vertical or strongly modular social organization. Although this definition of strong patterns masks local variability, it does identify normative behavior (Plog 1983). Evidence of patterns of normative behavior is more difficult to find in areas of weak patterns.

Because strong patterns can seem so obvious, they are sometimes described in detail rather than explained. Weak patterns present even more of a challenge to archaeological interpretation. Recent work on organizational complexity emphasizes the need to look at old problems in new ways. Waldrop (1992: 325) describes an analogous paradigmatic shift in the study of economics in the late 1980s:

> They sensed that the conventional neoclassical framework that had dominated over the past generation had reached a high water mark. It had allowed them to explore very thoroughly the domain of problems that are treatable by static equilibrium analysis. But it had virtually ignored the problems of process, evolution, and pattern formation—problems where things were not at equilibrium, where there's a lot of happenstance, where history matters a great deal, where adaptation and evolution might go on forever.

Although there are material patterns that can be conveyed through description and mathematical relationships, more understanding can result from contextualizing the question within studies of small and large scale dynamic models.

Archaeological research in the American Southwest has concentrated on areas of strong material patterning, but weak patterns are not weak merely because they are understudied. Strong patterns reflect some kind of societal "structure"; weak patterns represent more individual actions. Behaviors that are strongly affected by political organizations leave behind identifiable redundant patterns. On the frontier, individual behaviors are not regulated by embedded institutions and the creative and flexible behaviors necessary for survival do not leave behind the repetitive patterns indicative of controlled behavior. This fact does not mean that those living outside these political systems lived on an apolitical landscape; it means that they experienced politics differently.

Table 1.1. Examples of Strong and Weak Settlement Patterns in the American Southwest

Large sites	Small sites
Strong patterns (centuries)	
Chaco Canyon (10th–12th)	
Mesa Verde (9th–13th)	
Mimbres region (10th–12th)	
Phoenix Basin (8th–14th)	
Rio Grande (14th–15th)	
Weak patterns (centuries)	***Weak patterns*** (centuries)
Flagstaff (11th–12th)	Acoma (10th–12th)
Mesa Verde (7th–9th)	Black Range Mimbres (12th)
Rio Grande (13th–15th)	Mogollon Rim (11th–12th)
	Rio Grande (6th–12th)

From the Phoenix Basin to Chaco Canyon to the Rio Grande, archaeologists find examples of strong patterns of material culture throughout the American Southwest (Table 1.1). The settlements in these regions are often interpreted in sociopolitical models of alliances, confederacies, peer polities, and tribes, but these political and economic models are often inappropriate for areas with small, dispersed sites that show no evidence of social differentiation.

Settlement patterns dominated by small sites do not necessarily show "weak" material patterns. Small sites are spread throughout the Greater Southwest. In areas of strong patterns they surround large sites; areas of weak patterns are composed only of small sites. Thus the interpretation of areas of weak patterns is tied to that of small sites. However, small sites are not well integrated into most common archaeological models of sociopolitical organization. In some cases, these sites are not considered; in others, they are consciously excluded. For example, in alliance theory (Upham and others 1994) large settlements are identified as the past residences of managerial elites, and thus they are the only sites appropriate for the study of political organizations between A.D. 1300 and 1630. Adams and others (1993) demonstrated that inclusion of small sites in the analysis of the distribution of those "prestige goods" used to identify the Jeddito Alliance significantly changed the evidence for exchange of Jeddito Yellow Ware vessels and thus the political implications of the model. Often when patterns at large sites define the organization of an area, small sites are excluded due to their more limited visibility. Seemingly omnipresent, small sites are treated as background noise to the "real" question or are uniformly ignored. When ignored, so too are the details of the daily life of the inhabitants of the region.

Small sites are not usually considered in aggregate (although see Nelson 1999), and rarely are they deemed essential to understanding regional social or political organization. Instead, political history is written from the perspective of the population centers. The largest problem with the study of small sites is the level of generalization and the economic determinism applied to this variable class of sites. The residents of small settlements did not live as purely economically motivated individuals whose sole source of meaning came from direct and rational interaction with their environment. Social and political circumstances, if only weakly identifiable in the archaeological record, also guided their life choices. There are small sites in areas of both strong and weak material patterns, although much of the small site research has been conducted in areas of strong patterns. Some small sites are remnants of habitations and others indicate a more limited range of activities, but to fully understand the behaviors and relationships of households and communities, small sites need to be returned to models of social and political action in all areas.

SOCIOPOLITICAL ORGANIZATION

Strong and weak patterns of material culture depict an ancient Southwestern landscape imbued with social and political meaning. Certain organizations such as households were ubiquitous, but larger and more powerful sociopolitical organizations may have provided opportunities for or obstacles to individual action. Throughout the past, there were many types of sociopolitical organizations, and even more archaeological models have been developed to describe them.

The characteristics described by Tainter and Plog (1994) that identify strong patterns are often considered indicative of vertical or modular social organization. Generally, these characteristics are associated with groups that had more labor than land, where acquisition of land and material items (including exotic pieces) was a path to wealth and prestige. Accompanying the higher value of material items was a developed territoriality that protected local resources and identities, leading to spatial clusters of large settlements bounded by vacant land. Individuals in these groups gave up some of their freedom to create cohesive institutions that made decisions for the community. Homogeneity in public architecture and in symbolic systems may be indicative of this institutionalization of meaning.

Weak material patterns in areas of dispersed small sites are associated with mobility, short occupations, expedient behavior, less formal political organization, and low population density (Tainter and Plog 1994: 169). Patterns of variability are important, as they indicate areas with alternative forms of social organization, including, but not limited to, frontier organizations.

Archaeological analyses of weak patterns start with the most basic reconstructions of the behaviors that produced the artifacts and architecture found in small sites. The provenance of artifacts provides information about the social context of production, distribution, and consumption. Anthropological theory and ethnographic and historic accounts provide social and political analogies.

The predominant perspective for understanding political organization is a top-down rather than a bottom-up approach. Although there are exceptions (Bayman 1994; Windes 1987), attempts to reconstruct social and political structures at a regional scale often precede clear articulation of the organization of households. When communities are examined, the public structures are the focus of study. When the focus is on the individual, it is often through studies of the agency of individuals that became leaders (Kantner 1996; Sebastian 1992b). Augmenting what is known of community and regional organization with research on domestic organization provides a more complete picture of the scale, structure, and durability of social institutions.

The approach that I take to understanding social organization is one that focuses on the relationship between the individual and society. Households and communities are the foundation of regional social and political organizations. Dissecting the public and private activities of households and communities allows institutions and leadership strategies to be evaluated at a number of scales.

In situations where labor is readily available, land and material wealth are highly valued. Where land is abundant and labor scarce, people are highly valued as mates and workers. The base of leadership and power differs in such societies. Dual processual theory (Blanton and others 1996; Feinman 1995; Mills 2000) is a means of examining various strategies used to gain leadership. Because of its theoretical flexibility, it is applicable to a variety of political formations and is ideally suited to interpreting the forms of social organization that existed outside core areas. It differentiates two ends of a continuum of leadership strategies. Archaeologists commonly define a leader as an individual who commanded the allegiance of others, primarily through achieved status and wide personal networks materially signified as control of resources and prestige artifacts. Legitimation may have come through his or her descent group. The dual processual model also considers an alternative form of leadership, the corporate group, in which authority was acquired from the local group, legitimation was more broadly based, and command over shared resources such as labor and ritual was important. This distinction between strategies allows researchers to move away from the historically derived models of pueblo egalitarianism without necessarily embracing hierarchical models of leadership. The lack of "either–or" pronouncements makes room for the heterarchical articulation of economic, social, political, and ritual organizations within the society.

The ethnographic derivation of dual processual theory provides a relativistic approximation of leadership strategies used by societies with a wide range of demographic compositions. While recognizing conventional models of land-poor and labor-rich societies in which leadership is based on control of material resources, the theory also acknowledges leadership based on the acquisition of people and of specialized knowledge. The model provides material correlates of different types of political strategies, examining the context of acquisition and consumption, the concentration or dispersion of power, and the value of materials, labor, and knowledge. The archaeological data do not need to be converted into the proxy measures of prestige associated with other models (Artifact A = Status 1, Artifact B = Status 2, site settlement pattern A = Status 1). The theory articulates well with precapitalist organizations where the social and political are inextricably intertwined. Emphasis on the different expressions of power within communities and societies provides a way to understand the variability of social relations visible in the archaeological record. Ultimately, understanding the dynamics within and between political organizations is important for reconstructing macroregional patterns and processes.

Macroregional analyses reveal strong and weak patterning of material remains across the Southwest. Ultimately, considering weak patterns together with strong patterns will help us understand the distribution of political power. For example, the Chacoan region was likely the homeland of the Mogollon Rim frontier migrants. The Chacoan sociopolitical organization, one of the strong patterns on the Colorado Plateau, is defined primarily by distinct forms of architecture and settlement. Great houses and great kivas formed the public nuclei around which communities of unit pueblos clustered. Roads may have connected these communities. The topographic situation, arrangement of internal space, and construction technology of Chacoan public architecture were also distinctive (Lekson 1991; Powers and others 1983; Van Dyke 1998). Some definitions of "Chacoan" include the presence of Gallup Black-on-white pottery, exotic items such as macaws, and ornaments of turquoise, shell, jet, and quartz crystal (Judge 1991: 28; Tainter and Plog 1994: 171). Considering the extensive distribution of Chacoan material culture, there is a relatively high degree of homogeneity at this time, causing archaeologists to think about what institutions and leaders regulated the behaviors of members of the Chacoan communities. However, Chacoan outliers were not all similar, and settlements beyond the edges of the Chacoan organization reveal weak patterns (Tainter and Plog 1994: 173).

How would the history of the Colorado Plateau change if the Chacoan organization was considered together with less archaeologically visible organizations? Interpretations of Chacoan history are often based on conspicuous patterns; few reconstructions include the contemporaneous smaller sites (although see Vivian 1990).

The production, distribution, and consumption behaviors of large and small settlements within a core area organization can be compared, because the economic choices made by households and communities were not necessarily determined by their social, political, and ritual choices. In all areas, households may have had differential access to overarching institutions. Households at small settlements may have participated in religious and political institutions differently than households at large population centers. Often the fate of households was not tied to that of the overarching political structure. As is demonstrated so many times in history, political regimes come and go, but families endure. The occupants of small habitations in areas of weak patterns probably did not behave like the residents of large communities in areas of strong patterns, but did they behave like the residents of small habitations *within* the areas of strong patterns? Eliciting the behaviors of residents in small habitations through time and space can tell us a great deal about how households experienced sociopolitical organizations.

Although there is certainly room for more work on understanding the activities of households in areas of strong patterns, here I attempt to integrate weak patterns into questions of regional organization. In particular, I use a frontier model to interpret small sites and patterns of material variability and imbue marginal areas with social and political meaning. This model provides a framework for exploring the relationship between local expressions of the frontier and regional demographic, economic, social, and political processes.

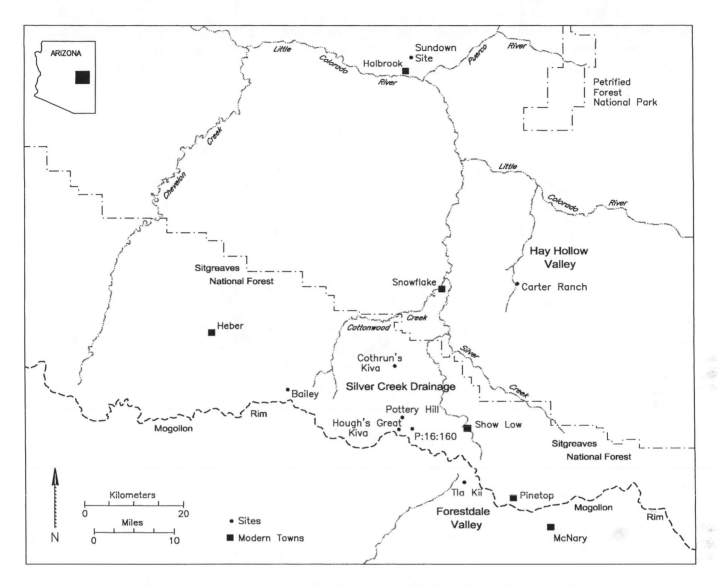

Figure 1.1. The Mogollon Rim region of east-central Arizona and sites mentioned in the text. (Graphic by Susan Hall.)

THE MOGOLLON RIM REGION AS A CASE STUDY

The Mogollon Rim region is a good example of an area with a weak pattern of material culture. Herein, the region is defined as the portion of east-central Arizona that includes the Silver Creek drainage (which in turn drains into the Little Colorado River), Sitgreaves Forest outside the drainage, Hay Hollow Valley, and Forestdale Valley (Fig. 1.1). The Mogollon Rim is a prominent geographic feature that marks the southern edge of the Colorado Plateau. To the south the "sub-Rim" area is a mountainous transition zone between the mesas and washes of the Colorado Plateau and the basins and ranges of southern and central Arizona.

Between A.D. 1000 and 1150, the Mogollon Rim region lay outside of, but adjacent to, three strong cultural patterns of this period, Chaco, Mimbres, and Hohokam (Tainter and Plog 1994: 173). Many of the current sociopolitical models for the Southwest that attempt to explain these core areas do not apply to the Mogollon Rim region during this time period. Weak patterns across the Southwest are not uniform, and their interpretations vary case by case.

The Mogollon Rim region was the home of Ancestral Pueblo peoples. Despite the shared moniker "Mogollon," the name of the region does not mean it was a part of the "Mogollon culture area." Prior to the second half of the eleventh century, population was sparse and people may only have occupied the area seasonally. In

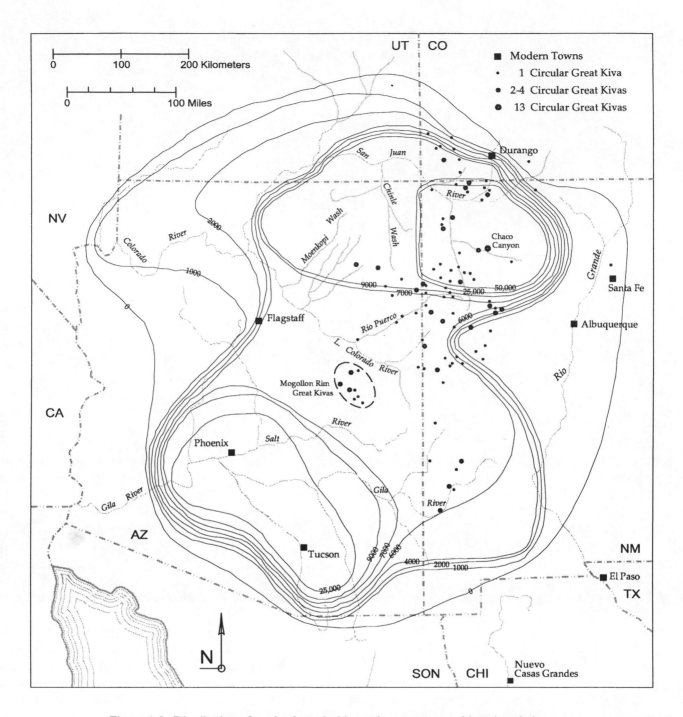

Figure 1.2. Distribution of tenth- through thirteenth-century great kivas in relation to regional population distribution at A.D. 1100; contour lines indicate population density. (Adapted from Dean, Doelle, and Orcutt 1994, Fig. 4.15; graphic by Susan Hall.)

the late eleventh century, groups expanded across the Southwest moving into a number of different areas, including the Silver Creek drainage. Even after these migrations, the population was numerically low and dispersed (Newcomb 1997, 1999), although some portion remained in year-round residence. These migrants lived lightly on the abundant land, occupying small settlements, often for no more than a generation. However, the area was overbuilt with great kivas, a form of ritual architecture associated with the Chacoan organization at this time. Compared to other areas in the Southwest during the same period, the density of great kivas in the

Mogollon Rim region was high (Fig. 1.2). There was much variability in the size of these structures, and Hough's Great Kiva was one of the largest great kivas in the Southwest (Herr 1994). What were these few people doing with so much large-scale integrative architecture? This apparent paradox is the crux of this investigation.

Similar co-occurrences of migration, integration, and low population density happen around the world, and the frontier model I describe is built on these cross-cultural commonalities. The archaeological identification of similar frontiers has been more limited (Bogucki 1988), but the Greater Southwest provides an excellent region in which to apply this model as a case study. The high level of chronological control in the Mogollon Rim region and across the northern Southwest, often at a scale finer than that of a generation, makes it possible to apply a process-oriented model that identifies temporary social and political formations, such as the frontier.

Frontiers are integral parts of the social whole, existing as one of several possible counterparts to core areas. As is demonstrated later, the history of the Mogollon Rim region is tied to that of the contemporaneous Colorado Plateau. Recent research on the Chacoan organization demonstrates that the "Anasazi Regional System" (Doyel 1992; Kantner and Mahoney 2000) was not a monolithic polity; it encompassed wide variability in regional and temporal participation in the creation of Chacoan communities (Meyer 1998; Van Dyke 1998). Through the study of the frontier it may be possible to evaluate the relationship between the Chacoan organization (if it is indeed a cohesive entity) and Mogollon Rim households and communities beyond its control, thus integrating those individuals living on the frontier into macroregional discussions of power, identity, and experience on the prehistoric Southwestern landscape.

Past researchers of the Mogollon Rim region grappled with the variability of the region as they crafted synthetic histories from their culture historical and processual theoretical positions (Haury 1985b; Lightfoot 1984; Longacre 1970). I use and evaluate the data collected by these scholars, but explore the same patterns with different models and methods. Two approaches distinguish the current study from those that came before. First is a consideration of the "place" of the Mogollon Rim region communities. For various reasons previous researchers presented the region as the center of the organization they were describing. Interpretation changes if we step back and view the region not as a sociopolitical center, but as an area beyond and between more cohesive organizations. Then boundary, periphery, and frontier processes become available as analogies. Second, I augment standard archaeological approaches to the region with ethnographic and historic analogies. Although ethnohistoric matches to the Mogollon Rim region do not exist, detailed case studies (Kennedy 1978; Netting and others 1989; Stone 1996) provide excellent analogs of frontier processes within certain environmental and social settings. More generalized accounts of frontiers indicate ranges of behavioral variability and demonstrate that such processes can occur under widely differing conditions around the globe.

Information about the households and communities of the Mogollon Rim region comes from nearly one hundred years of archaeological exploration. Excavations by the Silver Creek Archaeological Research Project (SCARP) between 1995 and 1997 recorded architectural, artifactual, and subsistence data from three sites with circular great kivas: Cothrun's Kiva Site, Hough's Great Kiva Site, and AZ P:16:160 (ASM). The modern field methods used by the excavators complement the wider architectural exposures and larger collections of artifacts recovered from past excavations at Tla Kii Pueblo (Haury 1985d) and Carter Ranch Pueblo (Martin and others 1964). Each of these sites had a circular great kiva and was defined as a community center. Five cultural resource management excavation projects collected vital information about the residents of 24 small settlements, and 27 surveys provided information from 823 sites about the functional and spatial composition of communities.

Residents of the great kiva communities of the Mogollon Rim region lived in a land-rich and labor-poor environment. Their past behaviors challenge archaeology's conventional models that were built to help explain areas of strong material patterning where labor was abundant and land both scarce and highly valued. At a macroregional scale, the Mogollon Rim was outside contemporaneous organizations, and the inhabitants experienced a sociopolitical marginality that affected their behavior. Interpretations of that marginality must come from a new perspective.

CHAPTER TWO

Frontiers

*Or might it be that place is something special, with
its own essential structures and modes of experience?*

(Casey 1996: 13)

Time and space are "the twin preoccupations of modern thinking in the west" (Casey 1996: 36). In the early part of the twentieth century, culture historians attempted to fit material culture into neat boxes organized by space and time. Each box represented a culture in its entirety during a certain period. Beginning in the 1960s, processual archaeology took issue with this normative depiction of culture to focus on adaptive systems and processes. In many early social models, time was treated as the axis of change with contingent effects on space. Postmodernism, with its emphasis on relativism in research, also treats space as a vector of change. In the late 1980s and 1990s, anthropologists began to study how humans experience space at a number of scales, from local to global (Feld and Basso 1996). We are beginning to understand that the meaning of human experience can change in relation to placement on the landscape and that social processes are intimately tied to places. Archaeological sites are not the passive remains of past activities; they were not only acted upon, they were part of the action. What we now bring to anthropological understanding is a better sense of how place affects value and identity.

Frontiers at and beyond societal boundaries provide an excellent opportunity to examine the articulation of place and social process. In the study of boundary areas, assumptions about the "isomorphism of space, place, and culture" (Gupta and Ferguson 1992: 7) erode. Spatial context is essential to substantive reconstructions of past lives, and we can use the strong and weak material patterning in the archaeological record (Chapter 1) to differentiate the experiences of those who lived in various circumstances. The frontier model treats weak patterns as the remains of political landscapes by examining the distribution of archaeological remains at multiple scales of analyses.

PRODUCTION AND LABOR

Evidence of production and labor can be used to reconstruct the activities and social contexts that created the weak patterns of the archaeological record. Although "production" is an abstract construct, labor is an individual or collective action, and as such it is measurable. Architecture and artifacts provide direct evidence of technology and manufacturing processes. Placing architecture and artifacts in their archaeological contexts reconstructs distribution and consumption activities. The organization of production is both created by and affected by social and political organization (Calagione 1992; Calagione and Nugent 1992). Thus, once behavioral patterns of production have been discerned, social theory, economic models, ethnographic research, and historical documentation can be used as comparative guidelines for understanding the sociopolitical significance of past relations between people and material objects.

Production can be described according to four criteria (Bernbeck 1995: 7): the number of tasks in the production sequence, the number of people needed for each task, the repetitiveness of the task, and the number of tasks that must be executed simultaneously *versus* sequentially. These criteria can be addressed relatively, if not quantitatively, to evaluate and compare the availability and coordination of labor. Productive choices are heavily influenced by the flexibility or rigidity of culturally imposed labor rules, which affect the ability of farmers to deal with unusual circumstances, benefiting or damaging chances of economic success (Linares 1997).

The economic, social, and political aspects of human life are expressed through production and labor. Labor is the means by which people extract their livelihood in their environment (Marx 1906: 197). It is the way people relate to each other through the material objects they make, exchange, and consume, and the control of a person's labor is one avenue toward power. The value of materials, labor, and knowledge is constantly being negotiated in the social and political relations that accompany the production, distribution, and consumption of artifacts inside and outside the workplace.

One of the primary characteristics of the frontier is the low availability and high value of labor. The frontier is distinct from many other types of sociopolitical organizations because here the classic capitalist model of value is inverted. Many archaeological models of political systems are built on the premise that land was scarce and labor abundant; thus, control of land was the key to wealth and power. On frontiers, land is cheap and labor is expensive, and households and communities strive to attract people.

Political models that examine areas beyond the edges of strong patterns are often core-centric. The dualistic distinction between core and areas beyond, whether they be borders, peripheries, or frontiers, has a reality, but researchers often ascribe an implicit "dependence" of marginal areas on a core (or multiple cores) that disregards any agency the inhabitants of the frontier might have. Although migrants to a frontier have a "tool kit" from socialization in the homeland, frontiers have their own processes and are not simple replications of the core area. Weak patterns are not poor demonstrations of strong patterns; they are shaped by different material conditions and different experiences.

Pioneers describe themselves as active participants in and not passive recipients of change (Jeffrey 1998), contradicting those archaeological treatments in which the experience of frontier residents is contingent on actions of core area residents. The processes of migration, integration, and community formation in a situation of low population density create a social and economic environment in which previous structures and ideologies are transformed. Regional scale processes have local implications.

I use an activity-based approach to create a frontier model applicable to archaeological research. The initial conditions of frontier settlement diverge from those in core areas. It is through action that the world is experienced and social meaning is created for frontier households and communities. These choices and actions have different consequences in new physical and demographic environments. The model described and implemented here and in the following chapters examines the frontier places and processes from a frontier perspective.

DIMENSIONS OF VARIABILITY: DEFINITIONS OF FRONTIERS

The frontier is not a monolithic experience shared by all who live beyond and between political boundaries. It is many experiences shaped by places, processes, and local histories. The popular history of the American West conceptualized the frontier as an untamed wilderness overcome by civilization and virtue. In magazines of science and technology it is that place beyond the boundaries of knowledge and control, a place for individual expression, exploration, and exploitation. It has a metaphorical quality as a place, real or imagined, where social transformations can be negotiated. The vivid images conjured up by this popular definition lie in direct opposition to the difficulty of creating an academic definition. Defining the frontier specifically is problematic. Researchers from a variety of disciplines, economics, geography, history, sociology, and anthropology, use the term, and it is defined to meet a similar variety of research interests and methods.

Consider, for instance, the license plates of Alaska. Alaska is a state with an enormous amount of unpopulated land, but, by the same token, it is a state where the vast majority of the people live, not outdoors in nature, but in cities. In that very urbanized state, each automobile sports a license plate with the words, "Alaska: The Last Frontier." Not a single one of these drivers, I am willing to bet, understands this to mean, "Alaska: The Last Zone of Cultural Interpretation and Contested Hegemony" (Limerick 1994: 79).

Frederick Jackson Turner was one of the first American anthropologists to grapple with the frontier, and some recognition of frontier diversity came in response to his work. Even now, more than 100 years after his memorialization of the closing of the American frontier, historians directly or indirectly address Turner's thesis. His 1893 paper (Turner 1972), "The Significance of the Frontier in American History," has been called the most important piece of writing in American history for the interest it aroused in popular audiences (Limerick 1994) and the controversy it aroused in academic circles. Turner (1972) preferred an elastic to an explicit definition of the frontier. His definition can be paraphrased as the continual reorganization and simplification of society through the pioneer processes of conquest and innovation as necessitated by the demands of inhospitable lands. Thus, the American's rugged individualism is derived from the spirit of man's conquest of adverse environments rather than from any connection with the European or capitalist past. This romantic theory has been contested for its perception of "free land," for its environmental determinism, for casting off the European connection, for its historical inaccuracy, and for its racism and sexism. As frontier literature is reviewed throughout this chapter, anthropological discussions of agency and experience, place, gender, and ethnicity augment the frontier model, but the partial truths of Turner's definition remain essential starting points for a modern definition of the frontier.

The variability of frontiers world wide can be unnerving. A common theme in frontier definitions is their spatial, temporal, demographic, or economic variation. Frontiers are founded by small independent groups of settlers from one or many areas and have been associated with foragers, pastoralists, farmers, and nation-states. They have been differentiated as internal and external, temporary and permanent, political and settlement, primary and secondary, exploitative and agricultural, and cosmopolitan and insular (Kopytoff 1987b; Prescott 1978; Steffen 1980). These definitions demonstrate many important dimensions of frontier regions. They address variation but often attribute explanatory primacy to only one aspect of the frontier and thus do not provide a comprehensive definition.

If nothing else, frontiers are spatial phenomena. Most discussions address place, but vary in the amount of consideration they give it and the determinative effects they attribute to it. Frontiers can only exist in opposition to core areas. However, once frontiers (or other types of marginal settlements) have been associated with a particular core area they are often treated as one and the same social entity as if drawing an analytic boundary around the entirety of an area makes the behaviors within equivalent. Most frontier models describe the effects of the frontier from the perspective of the core area, rather than describing the dynamics of the frontier (Lightfoot and Martinez 1995: 476).

"Internal" frontiers are formed in the sparsely populated "no-man's lands" between organized polities, as opposed to the "beyond the boundaries" external locations that are the more frequent American perception of frontiers. They have been identified across Africa and in northeastern Arizona (Kopytoff 1987a; Schlegel 1992). Otherwise, few frontiers have been described specifically as "internal," and, in part, the distinction may be a product of the scale of the analysis. Interior frontiers appear more in macroregional analyses than in discussions of the frontiers of specific societies.

Macroregional scale analyses identify frontiers as the leading edges of contact and change between cultures (Rice 1998). In such scenarios, they are the transparent membranes of societies and the first places through which culture contact occurs. In ecological models, frontiers are "regulators" for the maintenance of social and ecological equilibrium in otherwise closed systems (Green and Perlman 1985; Mitchell and others 2000). Those living on frontiers are perceived as the passive recipients of core area norms or the submissive transmitters of external "influence" into core societies (Lightfoot and Martinez 1995).

Frontiers have also been defined economically as exploitative or agricultural. Vast areas of supposedly "free land" were exploitable territories to the pioneers (here and elsewhere, pioneer is defined literally as "early settler"). The extensive or intensive nature of use distinguishes "exploitative" and agricultural frontiers (Nugent 1989), a distinction that has demographic, economic, and sociological implications for the subsequent development of the area. If there is a temporal sequencing of frontier organizations, the exploitative frontier generally comes first, but it is not a prerequisite to other economies. Exploitative frontiers are primarily associated with state-level, market-oriented economies. Economic pursuits are extractive, mining, trapping, ranching, and land speculation, and those participating in these industries are mostly young men. This is an unstable demographic situation, even when supporting businesses move into the area. Sustainability is attained when an influx of pioneers invest in the long-term development of the area by introducing agriculture. With agriculture comes a division of labor that depends on families, alleviating the age and gender imbalance of the frontier. Many of the frontiers across the world are agrarian, and this type of frontier organization is most common in nonstate societies. The distinction made between "insular" and "cosmopolitan" frontiers addresses the political consequences of frontier economies (Steffen 1979). The cosmopolitan frontier, another name for an exploitative frontier, is created by those pursuing short-term economic gain and who invest little in the development of local institutions. What institutions are present are brought from the homeland, no matter how far distant. The insular frontier has the economic diversity associated with long-term settlement and develops local institutions distinct from those of the homeland.

Demographic situation and temporal durability distinguish political from settlement frontiers (Prescott 1978: 33). Whereas settlement frontiers are habitable lands that are quickly populated, the political frontier is often environmentally, economically, or socially undesirable, and thus is characterized by lower density populations. The "wretched Bedde pagans, who lived in the swampy areas between the Kingdoms of Sokoto and Bornu in the western Sudan" (Prescott 1978: 40), are an example of the poor quality of life on a political frontier.

Most frontiers derive population from the multiple political organizations that surround them (Eidt 1971; Hudson 1979). The diversity noted in frontier demographics is attributable to the various origins of recent migrants and to the prior occupants who lightly occupied the land before colonization. However, diversity is expressed in many ways. Sometimes frontier communities are composed of people with mixed origins, competing and cooperating. Other times communities are uniform, as migrants from afar move to the same settlement as relatives and friends, but each community is unlike its neighbor (Ostergren 1998).

Frontiers are often, although not always, temporary social formations. The nature and durability of frontiers are affected by both changes in the core area and internal changes. A frontier may be incorporated into a nearby polity or its members may form their own government. Sometimes, through passive or active processes, habitable but less desirable areas may remain frontiers. The passive frontier will grow or shrink with the territorial expansion of nearby states and may be avoided or exploited for its resources by one or many organizations. A frontier zone may also be actively maintained as a buffer zone between states in conflict (Prescott 1978: 46).

Spatial, economic, demographic, and temporal dimensions are critical to the definition of the frontier. Each dimension differs in its core area and frontier expression. This study attempts to find the underlying circumstances that make frontiers distinct from core areas in order to achieve an integrated model of the frontier as a sociopolitical organization that leaves a weakly patterned material signal on the landscape of the past.

PLACE AND PROCESS

The frontier is "a geographical region with sociological characteristics" (Kopytoff 1987b: 9). Place is an essential aspect of the frontier, but location alone does not provide a sufficient explanation. Process encompasses the individual opportunities and decisions that retain the status quo or change behaviors and institutions. Process adds a temporal dimension to a spatial

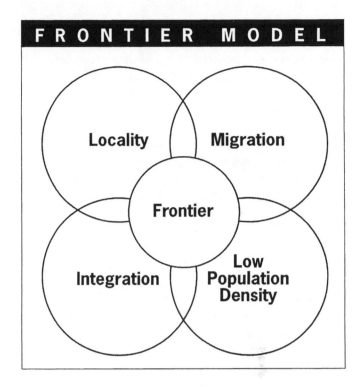

Figure 2.1. Venn diagram demonstrating the relationship between locality and the processes of migration, integration, and low population density. At the center, on the frontier, place and process coincide. (Graphic by Ellen Herr.)

situation. To this end a dualistic definition is used here to create a model in which the frontier is both a place and a process (Lewis 1984; Limerick 1994; Prescott 1978). These two aspects of the frontier are complementary.

A general model of process can be derived from archaeological and ethnographic accounts of the frontiers of foragers, farmers, and states, past and present. The following discussion emphasizes frontiers with agricultural economies, but the processes described are also applicable to the exploitative frontiers of capitalist societies. Four themes underlie the discussion of process on the frontier: locality, migration, integration, and the organization of communities with low population density. No single process alone defines the frontier; all are commonly associated with nonfrontier circumstances, but together they characterize a frontier organization (Fig. 2.1).

The frontier model of place and process accommodates historical contingency and provides a means for interpreting regional reorganizations associated with population movement and the establishment of communities in sparsely populated regions. By recognizing similar social constructions of immigrant populations in areas characterized by high land-to-labor ratios, the application of the term *frontier* provides a sociopolitical explanation for these patterns.

Place

Space plays an important role in shaping social processes. Place "goes beyond physical location to include the cultural values and political meanings which are actively encoded in these locations" (Fox 1996: 483). The effects of place create general patterned and locally particular social organizations. The fact of being at or beyond a political boundary creates a sociocultural phenomenon that can be identified cross-culturally as a "frontier." The frontier is not an imaginary or arbitrary line across a political landscape. It is a place shaped by people conscious of their position relative to other sociopolitical organizations and by the behaviors described here as frontier processes. Recognizing the fact of being in a frontier has long term effects on the psychology and social memory of the inhabitants of such regions (Nugent 1991, 1993).

The term frontier is often used synonymously with "boundary." However, frontiers are a specific type of boundary. Marginal positioning is an important aspect of all boundaries, but there are important differences between types of boundaries and the processes associated with their formation, their location in relation to "centers," dependency on these centers, their population characteristics, and their effects on the identity of their inhabitants.

The place aspect of the frontier is familiar to archaeologists. Sometimes "frontier" is used to delimit the farthest extent of a certain style of material artifact or architecture. It is not unusual for cultural historians to identify the ambiguous boundary between the "Mogollon" and "Anasazi" culture areas as a frontier. Other times, "frontier" is used to describe the place where different types of identified organizations (often economic) meet and interact. The case of the interface zone between Mesolithic foragers and Neolithic agriculturalists in Europe is commonly called a frontier (Bogucki 1996; Moore 1985: 94).

When frontiers are described as "zones of interaction," they are arenas for the processes of acculturation, boundary maintenance, and the creation and recreation of identity. In the American Southwest, the Virgin Anasazi area was where the mobile populations of the Great Basin met the more sedentary Pueblo populations to the east (Lyneis 1984), and portions of the Rio Grande were zones of interaction between Plains and Pueblo peoples in the late prehistoric period (Spielmann 1991).

The frontier is a place beyond or between political entities (Kopytoff 1987b). Political divisions may also approximate other boundaries, such as ecological zones. The Great Wall of China, which separates the Chinese from the outer provinces of the Mongols, roughly follows the line dividing loess and steppe environments and wet-rice and dry-rice agricultural production (Lattimore 1940: 58). Space, ecology, and organization of production vary on either side of this wall.

Often, "place" is the only aspect of the definition of the frontier that is addressed archaeologically. If this were all there was to the definition of the frontier, frontier studies would be synonymous with the study of borders and the associated studies of boundary maintenance and the creation of community identity. Because of these interpretive limitations, the concept of "frontier" has not lived up to its full anthropological potential. But since the frontier is a region (Prescott 1978: 22) with its own processes and organizational parameters, a frontier model can address social and political organization and transformation on a macroregional scale.

Migration

The frontier may be temporary or permanent, but initially it is created by a long distance movement of people from a homeland into an area with sparse or nonexistent population. This movement must cross beyond the area controlled by the homeland. The frontier is formed by small groups of people in search of "land and freedom" (Nugent 1993). These people want to escape the hegemony of the dominant political organization and choose to break their preexisting economic and social ties. The destination area is usually economically attractive (Bowman 1931) and is beyond the bounds of most government controls.

In the aggregate, the frontier is often depicted as the creeping extension of the core area (see Jordan and Kaups 1989: 13) or the "glacially slow but sure advance of civilization into the wilderness" (Hudson 1976: 255), but this is not an accurate depiction of how households get to the frontier. The archives from the WPA Historical Data Project, which collected questionnaires and autobiographies from Dakota pioneers, show that people were not creeping to the Dakotas at all; the distances traversed were large. Those migrating from closer homelands could retrace their route and return seasonally as labor requirements dictated, but others, including immigrants who had come directly from Europe, had limited options for return migration (Hudson 1976).

Integration

Integration is the process by which migrant groups, who have broken most previous ties, come together to create permanent homes. On a frontier, the challenge is to sustain a community in a situation of low population density. Integration is enacted in every production, exchange, and ideological activity, linking people at multiple levels from household to community to region (Kroeber 1917: 185). Ideally, agriculture and craft production and physical and social reproduction are enacted by the co-residing members of the household. The feasts, trading events, alliances, competitions, and rituals that attract people from the region are organized at the community level.

Ritual is one of the most commonly identified integrative activities, but not the only one. Legends from ancient Mexico demonstrate the importance of integration on a traditional frontier. Fox (1996: 485) wrote that these legends:

> identify the construction of the ballcourt as an event linked symbolically to the creation of a social and sacred place. After the Mexica had reached Coatepec and established their villages and the temple of their patron god, Huitzilopochtli, they were instructed by that god to build a ballcourt. In these migration legends, the transformation of wild, uninhabitable spaces into controlled, social places was partly accomplished through the imposition on the landscape of public, ritual architecture.

A shared system of meaning provides an ideological meeting ground through which immigrants can create communities (Kopytoff 1987b). Charles Henry, a Western Apache, recalls how his ancestors came to the land and how naming places made the landscape a shared and familiar "picture they could carry in their minds" (Basso 1996: 12). In the fourth century B.C., Hellenistic sanctuaries on the Cretan frontier were physical symbols of self-representation (Alcock 1999) and provided an identity to both individuals and landscapes. When the Wixárika of Mexico set up a new residence, whether in their own community or in a new place, they symbolically establish it and connect it to the world of the ancestors by making ritual treks from their houses to sacred temples and emergence sites. They "relive how their ancestors moved there from an authentically

sacred site" (Liffman 2000: 136). These symbolic names, behaviors, and spaces provide a "culturalization" or "sacralization" of physical space (Stoddart 1999), creating familiar reference points for individuals on a new landscape.

Integration is the "coevolutionary dance of cooperation and competition" (Waldrop 1992: 292). Conflict and competition are as common as cooperation and sharing on the frontier. The initial migration to the frontier, as a place, provides an escape from social and economic troubles in the homeland (McNeill 1983: 59). Strained relations with indigenous populations whose local settlement dynamic is disrupted, or with the homeland, continue on the frontier. Chronic conflict is one of the most difficult types of behavior to recognize archaeologically. Material patterns indicating overt warfare and defensive settlement locations may indicate the certain presence of conflict, but the absence of these patterns does not imply the absence of conflict. Continuing residential mobility and common second-step migrations, examples of "voting with your feet" (Netting 1993: 276), indicate that conflict is part of the dialectic of daily life. Intense episodes of conflict are the sources of irrevocable changes in the course of local and regional histories.

Low Population Density

Migrants to the frontier move from an area with a low land-to-labor ratio to one with a higher ratio, such that the frontier is characterized as land-rich and labor-poor. As the relationship between availability of land and labor changes from the core area to the frontier, so too do values in these sparsely populated regions. It is difficult to recreate the social and political organizations of the homeland. Core area patterns of political organization and leadership do not travel intact to the frontier. Social contracts are pared down as pragmatism overwhelms complexity (Hine 1980: 80). In areas of low population density, multitudes of political or religious roles are unnecessary (Brumfiel 1992). Here, people have more difficulty filling multiple social roles demanded by the many levels of horizontal or vertical integration associated with more complex social organizations. Consequently formalized institutions, especially political ones, are not typical on frontiers and the need for order can often be filled by ritual associations.

The acquisition of people and labor becomes an important goal of the family and the community. Further deterring the ready adaptation of previous political organizations is a change in social values, such that labor becomes at least as important as the products of labor. On capitalist frontiers, the conflicting value of materials and labor was expressed in extreme form, where slavery and indentured servitude were once means of resolving labor shortage problems in competitive productive environments (McNeill 1983: 18–25). In less extreme scenarios, society may value knowledge and skills differently on frontiers and in core areas. On a frontier, the knowledge of a specialist is less valuable than the generalized skills of a flexible and creative worker. Large pioneer families attest to the value of the labor of men, women, *and* children. Frontier women and men challenge conventional gender roles and stereotypes. Both had to assume work they might not have otherwise, although it was not always easy to shed the moralities of the homeland (Jeffrey 1998).

The easy mobility of households also detracts from the creation of strong social and political organizations. Neither families nor institutions are firmly rooted in frontier communities. The promise of something new or better, or the retreat to the familiar, constantly factor into decisions made by frontier families. However, there are situations when residential stability is rewarded.

The earliest settlers to a frontier, the "firstcomers," are highly valued in some societies. The first Goba immigrants to their current land on the Zambezi River valley (Kopytoff 1987b: 54; Lancaster 1987: 110) are considered to be the royal lineage, although they were dissidents in their homeland. The Hopi, recounting their migratory past, accord ritual respect and the right to judge to the Bear Clan, the first settlers of the current Hopi region (Schlegel 1992: 385). Firstcomers in Costa Rica had early access to resources in areas where the frontier was rapidly populated subsequent to initial colonization (Sewastynowicz 1986), giving them economic priority. Latecomers have decreased rights to increasingly valuable land and may be accorded positions of lower status, to the point that they may work the land of the firstcomers (Schlegel 1992).

Historical Contingency

Frontiers are a combination of what is drawn from the homeland and common responses to conditions of migration and subsequent life in a situation of low population density. Even in societies as diverse as the American Midwest in the last half of the eighteenth century (Jordan and Kaups 1989), the modern Jos Plateau in Nigeria (Stone 1996), sixteenth-century Argentina (Guy and Sheridan 1998), prehistoric Alaska (Odess

1998), and north-central Europe (Bogucki 1988), processes on the frontier are similar whereas the specific histories and consequences of the frontier are diverse.

Structural transformations and historical contingencies make each frontier unique. Migrant settlements are not the simple replications of home institutions in new environments. Instead, they are altered by the intersection of individual consciousness, human agency, local history, and macroregional processes. Roseberry (1988: 172) has discussed the transformative dynamic of structure and agency as "the activity of human subjects in structured contexts, that are themselves the products of past activity but, as structured products, exert determinative pressures and set limits upon future activity." The individual acts upon the structure and the structure upon the individual, and the initial situation does not necessarily determine the course of action or the condition of the society at any given time. When structuralist methods are embedded in considerations of local history (Sahlins 1981), they can be an important tool for comparisons and for discussing dramatic social and institutional changes such as the upheavals created by migrations into sparsely or fully populated regions.

For those anthropologists with the luxury of documented history, it is not just relations between land and labor that are critical to the frontier experience, but the perception of these relations (Calagione and Nugent 1992; Merchant 1989: 5). The individual's consciousness of the changed land-to-labor relationship makes the "cookie cutter" societal replication after migration unlikely. The migrants' perceptions of the new area and the actions that they take thereafter create a new and unique history in relation to all that has gone before. The historical process unfolds as a continuous and reciprocal movement between the practice of structure and the structure of practice (Sahlins 1981: 72).

Nugent (1993: 7) illustrates the role of consciousness and the creation of identity of residents of Namiquipa, Chihuahua over the past two centuries. Their consciousness of their place on the military frontier of eighteenth-century New Spain and their position as defenders against the Apaches play a role in their modern revolutionary fights against the Mexican government to defend their land as capitalism is introduced into the region.

It is thus possible to explain both the unique and patterned processes we associate with the coeval processes of migration and community organization on the frontier. We can attribute to these processes the innovation and versatility that is often associated with frontiers (Gilpin 1998; Steffen 1979: 99).

METHODS FOR ANALYZING HOUSEHOLDS AND COMMUNITIES

The frontier is part of a politicized landscape (Green 1991). In this archaeological application, sociopolitical is defined as the dynamic and patterned relationships between households and communities on a regional scale. The expression of the frontier characteristics of place and process has local implications for households and communities.

Wilk and Netting (1984) offer an activity-based means of describing households that helps us reconstruct the organization of labor and production. Five main activities (Table 2.1) affect household size and structure: production, distribution, transmission, reproduction, and co-residence. The "phenotype" of the household varies with changing circumstances, and negotiation and compromise are a continuing process.

The study of production and labor is the basis of much of our understanding of the experience of frontier households. Subsistence production can be examined through botanical and faunal assemblages, storage facilities, and water control and other field features. Craft production and distribution, particularly of ceramics, have been systematically investigated throughout the Southwest (Mills and Crown 1995a, 1995b). Reproduction is demonstrated by changes in household size as reflected in architectural and ceramic variables. Socialization is indicated through the presence and use of "enduring symbols" and more qualitatively by exploring the changing values of individuals and their labor in a frontier setting. Transmission is a difficult topic to address archaeologically, although some variables such as property ownership can be inferred. The size of cooking and service vessels may be used to address the size of the eating group (Vint 1998), but it is difficult to assess how both co-residential and eating groups articulate with the activity-based definition of the household (Mills 1999). It is possible, however, to use architectural and artifactual data to reconstruct the activities occurring within individual rooms to verify that a household participated in the defined activities.

Household studies (Flannery 1976; Hegmon and others 1998) moved archaeologists away from normative views of culture change and brought attention to the role of domestic organization, which in turn allowed archaeologists to reenter anthropological discussions by evaluating behavior at the same scale as ethnographers. However, considering households without considering communal facilities gives only a partial understanding of community organization. The issues of production, distribution, reproduction, co-residence, and transmission are of concern not only to the individual household but to interacting groups of households. The community can be evaluated along the same parameters, differing mainly in scale. Local social and political organizations can be discerned by comparing those situations when household and community interests and responsibilities complement each other and when they diverge (Magness-Gardiner and Falconer 1994). It is only after patterned relationships between households and adjacent communities have been explored that the fundamental processes of regional social and political organization can be understood.

Information from analyses of community production, distribution, reproduction, transmission, and co-residence can be used in several other models that interpret organizations at a larger scale. Although Costin (1991) originally intended to analyze craft production, her variables, context, concentration, scale, and intensity, are applicable to the study of production more generally. Scale is the size of the production unit (number of individuals) and the means of labor recruitment and its flexibility or lack thereof. Intensity refers to the time spent at the production activity and is essentially an issue of scheduling. Costin adds a spatial dimension to the model by assessing the concentration of production. Context, short for "sociopolitical context," is the relationship between production, distribution, and consumption: is production for the producer, for unrestricted exchange with others, or for a specific group, particularly an elite class? These producers, usually specialists, are referred to as either independent or attached. Each variable lends insight into productive relations among interacting households and communities.

The formality of distribution to those outside the household varies. The social power of exchange relationships is discussed by Mauss (1967) and reiterated by Levi-Strauss (1969) in terms of the obligations to give

Table 2.1. Activities of the Household and Community
(After Wilk and Netting 1984)

Activity	Definition
Production	Division of labor, organization of labor
Distribution	Distribution of products of labor
Reproduction	Physical reproduction and socialization of the succeeding generation
Transmission	Inheritance of property, status, knowledge
Co-residence	Sharing of domestic space

Table 2.2. Expectations of Household and Community Organization on the Frontier

	Household	Community
Production	Extensive agriculture and residential mobility Craft production for household use	Few labor intensive constructions No community craft specialization Importance of situational work groups or organizations
Distribution	Households with widespread social networks	Redistribution at communal ceremonies
Reproduction	Large household sizes? Continuity of traditional technologies Division of labor may change in response to new environment	Duration of community centers Communal architecture as shared institution Little evidence of political uniformity Few formalized organizations
Transmission	Little evidence of ownership Usufruct strategy of land use	Unmarked and flexible community boundaries
Co-residence	Single family households Few "men's houses" or other places of eating and sleeping	Dispersed communities

and to receive. In a capitalist society, quick monetary transactions replace the social ties created by delayed exchanges of other economic organizations. But those items acquired through exchange direct a certain prestige to the individual who receives such a gift, and more so to the giver who can afford to bestow such an offer (Sahlins 1994). Delayed exchange transactions create relationships between individuals, and their families that are temporally open-ended.

The specifics of exchange relationships are more difficult to reconstruct. Patterns of exchange can sometimes be predicted based on certain environmental conditions. In periods when the spatial variability of productive resources is high, wide geographic interaction or residential mobility may be ways of alleviating risk (Plog 1984). The distribution of local and nonlocal items for mundane or prestigious use can be evaluated against this environmental backdrop. However, as food and other perishables may play a role in these exchanges, what is materially visible in the archaeological record today may not fully represent the most common intercommunity exchanges of the past.

Transmission, reproduction, and co-residence at the community level are evaluated in much the same way as they are at the household level, differing mainly in scale. Instead of evaluating the relationships of individuals within a single household, the relationships among households within a community are examined. Transmission relies heavily on concepts of proprietary use and ownership, and community boundaries may be marked or unmarked, as are individual fields. The physical reproduction of the community relies on the physical reproduction in the household. Socialization occurs through

institutions and rituals that reinforce community values, ideals, and cohesion. Successful reproduction of the community is not necessarily the exact replication of social institutions, but instead is the assurance that a range of desirable options is available in the succeeding generation (Bogucki 1996: 307). Co-residence is the spatial relationship of households within settlements and settlements within communities, dispersed or aggregated.

EXPECTATIONS FOR THE FRONTIER MODEL

With this model of household and community activities, it is possible to derive expectations for a specifically frontier organization. Migration, integration, and low population density are interwoven into the experience of frontier households and communities (Table 2.2).

Production

Despite the fact that movement to the frontier is a breaking away from home institutions, the frontier is not an institutional *tabula rasa* (Kopytoff 1987b: 12). Immigrants are never free of their homeland and their most basic ideas of domestic production and ideology will likely be brought to their new homes (Kopytoff 1987b: 19). New farms are formed with family labor; however, in the new environment, the division of labor within the family may change. We do not expect the perfect replication of core area social forms on the frontier.

Small populations are not usually socially or economically diverse. Labor intensive activities and economic specialization are uncommon. "A larger group makes possible specialized skills, discrepancies in wealth and class structure. A smaller group generates participation . . . [and] . . . makes possible frequent, primary, face-to-face contacts . . . ." (Hine 1980: 23). Europeans moving to the North Dakota frontier at the turn of the twentieth century found creative ways to use their specialized training, and flexibility was the key to survival. Hudson (1976: 262) describes a man who owned a portable cook shack, barn, and a blacksmith shop, in addition to supporting himself as a carpenter. Another man used his team of horses for farm work and for grading the railroad. When Euroamerican officials in North Dakota alienated Sioux women from their traditional roles as horticulturalists, the women earned extra income by learning to quilt and to make lace (Jeffrey 1998: 244). The social roles of men, women, and children on the frontier are affected by the changing rhythm of labor and differ from those of the homeland.

Instead of intensifying agricultural production in response to changing resource availability, widely available frontier land is used extensively for agriculture and foraging (Jordan and Kaups 1989: 3). Foragers roamed the prehistoric frontiers of Europe (Dennell 1994). The pastoralists of the Mongolian frontier use land more extensively than the wet-rice farmers immediately across the Great Wall (Lattimore 1940). In the low populated area occupied by the Ushi of Zambia, gardens are relocated frequently and residents can farm or gather wild foods anywhere (Netting 1993: 161). In the mid-eighteenth century, South Carolina farmers extensively farmed grain crops in the backwood frontiers away from coastal rice plantations (Lewis 1984: 73). Marjorie Rawlings (1942: 49) describes the Florida back country, "I could not understand how folk could settle in the bare piney-woods, when here were uninhabited hammock acres, rich of soil, magnificent of vegetation. But the work of clearing hammock is heavy, and land easily cleared and already open is tempting to migrants."

Dry-farming is never an easy pursuit, and on the frontier available labor is at a premium. On agricultural frontiers, where households are dispersed across the land, certain tasks may be too large or too tedious for a single family. Outside help may be necessary for large tasks, especially those that must be performed quickly, such as harvesting and storing crops. Multiple families also participate in nonagricultural tasks, sometimes building family homes, most often building communal structures, in events similar to an Amish barn-raising (Hostetler 1980: 246). Among the Susu of Sierra Leone

(Nyerges 1992), a patron-client system is used by materially wealthy families to attract men to their communities, initially through the creation of bonds of loyalty and dependence and ultimately by bonds of marriage. The creation of fictionalized kinships serves the same purpose (Kopytoff 1987b: 38).

The conversion of material wealth to "wealth-in-people" characterizes the temporary associations for agricultural and building projects. Among the largest of the agricultural organizations are the work parties known to the Kofyar of Nigeria (Stone and others 1990; Stone 1996) and the Tarahumara of Mexico as "beer farming" (Kennedy 1978). The Tarahumara convert stores of corn into "tesuigno," a protein-rich corn beer; the Kofyar brew a millet beer. A party is announced, and a day or two later families come together to help with the agricultural task at hand and to help consume the beer. Labor is exchanged for beer and the entertainment provided by competitions, dances, and friendships makes it a social event. Perhaps more importantly in the long term, the labor of the guest is exchanged for labor of the host. Should the occasion arise, the host must participate in "beer farming" on other farms.

Small-scale work groups are also prevalent. In Baghestan, Iran work groups milk their animals together and share threshing floors (Horne 1994). Pueblo farmers share the responsibility of maintaining irrigation canals (Lange 1959: 81–83) and cleaning springs (Parsons 1966: 109). Individuals in small farming groups rotate systematically among members' fields. Membership in both forms of association is situational and may be seasonal, disbanded and recreated as needed.

Communal work groups are practical and necessary, even as they serve an important integrative function. Agricultural work and communal building projects are intimately tied to the social and ritual aspects of life. In an area of contemporary New Guinea that is just beginning to enter the capitalist economy, hundreds of Ilahita Arapesh men of all ages engaged in a once-per-generation construction of the Spirit House of the Tambaran cult. This massive enterprise unified men throughout the village with the spirit world, which was called upon to help with the most precarious aspects of the construction. The laboring group was much larger than that commonly used for agricultural and domestic construction jobs. Participants had to be extremely careful to avoid upsetting the spirit, Nggwal. Anything that went awry during the two months of construction was analyzed by the village to determine whether or not the spirit was upset and how to appease him if he was. Arguments were quickly pacified, and an unexpected cloud burst invoked a village meeting to decide responsibility for this unlucky event. In this communal society, individual behaviors were cautiously monitored so as to benefit the communal goal. The shared participation in labor and obedience strengthened the community (Tuzin 1980: 116–167).

It would be incorrect to assume from this discussion that the division of labor is egalitarian on frontiers. Although generally true of many small-scale agricultural societies, it is not the rule for all frontiers. Simple but highly vertical social hierarchies formed on colonial and capitalist frontiers.

Distribution

Households from a multiplicity of homelands have diverse ties outside the community and may retain these connections as a risk reducing strategy. When the local population is not sufficient to ensure community viability, social ties may be widely spread. This situation is not often discussed by ethnographers but has been documented for the dispersed settlements of prehistoric agricultural frontiers. Ceramics provide evidence of extensive relations of inhabitants of the eastern edge of the Black Range among the post-Classic Mimbres (Hegmon and others 1998; Nelson and Hegmon 1996, Table 1). Ceramics, flaked lithics, and in particular *Spondylus* shell show a similar pattern on an early frontier of north-central Europe (Bogucki 1988: 126). Odess (1998: 426) suggests that "far-flung networks of interaction," as indicated by lithic raw materials, characterized the period of initial colonization of the Frobisher Bay Dorset people. In each example, individual households, not communities, were participating in this long distance exchange. When exchanging with areas of higher population density, such as core areas, frontier households are expected to provide wild and natural resources in exchange for manufactured products (Bogucki 1996: 301).

Redistribution and exchange at the scale of the community is expected on the frontier, although they may not be institutionalized. It is likely that unrestricted group-oriented food sharing occurs at rituals, feasts, work events, and other occasions. Competitive reciprocity of individuals is not expected.

Reproduction

The physical reproduction of the household and community is important, especially in situations of low population density. Not only will the natural birth rate be of concern, but it is expected that attempts will be made to recruit people to the community, for marriage and child bearing as well as for labor. The African groups that attempt to attract men into patron-client relationships and ultimately to marriage (described above) are particularly illustrative (Nyerges 1992). More generally, all evidence of large scale aggregation is considered as creating potential mate selection opportunities.

The social reproduction of households and communities is through social and ideological constructions, some real and some fictive, that give history and identity to pioneers in their new homes. Traditional symbols provide a focus for meaning and the socialization of succeeding generations. Ritual provides a liturgical and formalized education to participants and observers (Gluckman 1955; Hegmon and Lipe 1989; Leach 1977) and promotes participation in a shared ideology.

Appeals to shared identity or ethnicity can also encourage group cohesion. At a societal level there is a creation of a "fictive kinship" that at once acknowledges the inhabitants of the frontier as "outsiders" while maintaining ties to a motherland. Claims by modern African frontier societies of political kinship with great past states such as Great Zimbabwe, Mali, Ghana, and Benin (Kopytoff 1987b: 72) are supported by emulation of the mother society. The dispersed 'Ubaid period communities of Northern Mesopotamia were not politically unified, but across the region tripartite structures that were part of a tradition longer than any single community served as ritual places (Akkermans 1989). Rituals, such as those associated with tripartite shrines in Mesopotamia, are a particularly strong means of integration. As symbols, they invoke the whole religious and symbolic system and the place of the individual in it.

Transmission

In situations where land use is extensive and population is low, residential mobility is high and the principles of land ownership are undeveloped. Where resources are abundant, as on the frontier, usufruct rights are expected, meaning the farmer possesses the products of the land, but not the land itself. This strategy works well when populations are low and mobile, and land is readily available. Land tenure rules become more complex as resource scarcity increases and allocation of resources is more likely to be contested (Adler 1996c). The development of strong rules of inheritance within the frontier family or community is unlikely (Netting 1990: 46).

Frontier mobility patterns do not encourage the labor investment required of owned property. It is common for a second migration to follow shortly after the first, particularly when the initial attempts to settle in a new environment have less than ideal results. In the seventeenth century, when the Delaware Valley could still be considered a frontier, the Finns and Swedes clear-cut farmland and burned the forest, but left tree stumps in their fields. When field productivity declined after three to five years, the Scandinavians moved on and let their German successors invest greater labor in the land (Jordan and Kaups 1989: 100).

Co-residence

Although small-scale demographic data are difficult to reconstruct archaeologically, they are an important part of the definition of the household and community structure on the frontier. They play a key role in understanding the frontier process and provide the best data from which to draw implications about household organization. Frederick Jackson Turner (1972: 4), who (understandably) hesitated to commit to any specific definition of the frontier, borrowed U.S. Census Bureau demographic statistics to define a frontier as less than two persons per square mile. Although this specific statistic is useless in cross-cultural examinations of the frontier, demographic characterizations of frontiers are essential. Because studies of frontier demography require accurate data across several generations, the diversity of cross-cultural discussions is limited to areas with census documents and detailed record keeping.

Complicating the reconstruction of frontier demography is the fact that the pioneers did not simply settle in one area to live out the rest of their days; they were easily mobile: "There is a fever in our blood. We have itching feet. Here today and gone tomorrow. Let's go. Scuse our dust" (Pierson 1973: 7–8 as cited in Hine 1980: 22). Some individuals and some families moved onward to newer frontiers, some retreated while staying in frontier and other rural environments, and some moved back to more populated areas, as did their children (Hudson 1979).

The typical perception of frontiers is that they have a large proportion of single young men (Nugent 1989: 402) or large families with many children. Demographic data show that both situations are common. The pattern of single young men characterizes exploitative frontiers and early agricultural frontiers (Hudson 1979). In 1860, Colorado was an exploitative mining frontier where 97 percent of the population was male, and 94 percent of the males were between 15 and 44 years of age. The agricultural frontier at this same time period was in eastern Kansas, where the males made up 55 percent of the population and the age distribution was slightly more natural; the 15 to 44 age group comprised 57 percent of the population and the infant to 14 age group comprised 42 percent of the population (Nugent 1989: 402). Like the Kansas frontier, more mature agricultural frontiers in general have a more even distribution of the sexes. There is some evidence to suggest that fertility was higher on the frontier, contributing to larger families as the number of young people was high in virtually all frontier population curves. However, American historians have difficulty sorting out the coincident effects of ethnicity and a nationwide decrease in American fertility at the end of the nineteenth century (Coombs 1993; Hudson 1979: 47).

It is rare for archaeological sites to yield enough mortuary information to reconstruct the specifics of family compositions. Historical data provide an array of statistics from the American frontier that help us envision the families and communities that may have inhabited the prehispanic frontiers. These data show that early or exploitative frontiers may once have been populated by young men and that agricultural frontiers may have been populated by young families. Although comparable data are rare, similar demographic siuations have been identified in the Kofyar region of Nigeria and in Buenos Aires, suggesting that frontier population patterns may not be unique to the U.S. frontier.

THE COMPOSITE FRONTIER

To understand the social relations of production, archaeological evidence is augmented by anthropological theories and ethnographic analogies that demonstrate the articulation of economic pursuits with social, political, and ideological life. Each household or community activity that is identified in the archaeological record adds to our understanding of the division of labor on the frontier. The composite picture of the frontier created by ethnography and history can be characterized as the physical place and social processes in which land is plentiful and labor is scarce. The constraining variable to production on the frontier is population. The greatest challenge facing frontier social and political organizations is integrating a small and dispersed population into a corporate entity. The household is the strongest organization on the frontier, but it is too small to be self-sustaining. Other social institutions are present, but are often weak and transitory. Labor is at a premium, particularly during intervals when scheduling is important. One solution is the creation of informal organizations, such as the work group, that help with planting and harvesting. Work groups also provide an opportunity for social interaction: children play, adolescents compete and flirt, and adults catch up on local gossip. These occasions are important contexts for household interaction and exchange of material goods and information. Women, as cooks, produce the feast that feeds the work party, thereby enhancing the status of male kin and marriage partners.

The roles played by gender and status in production within core areas survive in altered yet recognizable form on the frontier. The relationships between the organizations of production and sociopolitical institutions differentiate frontier processes from those of core areas. Labor, not land, is most desired by early settlers. On the frontier, social experiences and cultural values are reinterpreted to reflect this transformation of economic priority.

CHAPTER THREE

Local Expressions, Regional Organizations

Sociopolitical organizations are created by the patterned and dynamic relations between households and communities in a region. It is possible to move from the archaeological record, in this case the weak patterns of cultural remains, to regional political systems by interpreting the patterns of material culture on a regional scale. Sociopolitical systems are part of the total human experience, as they affect and are affected by changes in the relationships between individuals, households, and communities. Individuals, not regions, enact behaviors, so it is necessary to look at how individual agency and practice are expressed in the households and communities within regional organizations. The way to make the interpretive transition from the Mogollon Rim as an archaeological weak pattern to the Mogollon Rim as a frontier on a political landscape is to examine, layer by layer, the behaviors responsible for creating these material patterns, a "bottom-up" approach.

Reconstructing sociopolitical organization from the bottom up is a multiscalar means of examining the relationships among households, communities, and regional organizations, such as the frontier. These layers of analysis are mutually informative. The effects of regional characteristics, such as frontier places and frontier processes, are visible on local communities (Chapters 4 and 5) and on households (Chapter 5). In Chapter 6, the layers are reassembled to demonstrate how the Mogollon Rim frontier experience was expressed in the daily life of the pioneers.

This chapter focuses on the relationship of the Mogollon Rim region, as a frontier, to the surrounding political landscape of the late eleventh and early twelfth centuries. By examining the juxtapositions previously noted (for example, the 'flash in the pan,' short-lived association between too few people and too many great kivas on this southwestern edge of the Ancestral Puebloan world), past economic, social, and political organizations in the Mogollon Rim region emerge from the archaeological patterns.

On a local level, small sites and a diversity of artifacts in the Mogollon Rim region form an archaeological weak pattern (Table 3.1). However, when landscape analysis is at a macroregional scale, areas of weak material patterns and strong material patterns can be explained by social and political behaviors. Stronger patterns are formed by societal "structure" or "norms," weaker patterns by individual "action." Institutional structures are strongest in core areas, or homelands. Where structure is less institutionalized and less enduring, behaviors are subject to more variability, and the archaeological record reflects this diversity. Frontier behaviors are variable because each frontier derives its personality from characteristics of the homelands that were brought by migrants, from the extant population (if any) in the destination area, and from adapting to the environment.

The frontier model identified the universal characteristics of life on the frontier, at that place beyond or between and affected by the processes of migration, integration, and low population density, and defined frontiers as areas with an identity distinct from that of the homeland. Although personal histories and socialization of the pioneers may have been tied to their ancestral homes, their domestic economy and political organization were not. Mogollon Rim region communities had an identity distinct from that of their homelands. To understand the historical significance of the Mogollon Rim frontier, I examine the possibility that the Chaco, Mimbres, and Hohokam regions could have been homeland areas for the migrants who created the frontier.

PLACE

In this volume, "local" refers to the Mogollon Rim region, including the Silver Creek drainage and the Hay Hollow and Forestdale valleys (see Fig. 1.1). The behavioral patterns described, however, are not necessarily limited to the arbitrary boundaries of the study area. General patterns of migration, integration, and settle-

**Table 3.1. Attributes of Strong and Weak Archaeological Patterns
Compared to the Mogollon Rim Region**

Attributes	Strong Patterns	Weak Patterns	Mogollon Rim Region
Site characteristics	Some large, planned, centralized sites	Predominance of small sites	Predominance of sites with fewer than 10 rooms
Ceramic production	Specialized, localized; much trade	Unspecialized; mainly local use	Unspecialized; diffuse; mainly local use
Ceramic pattern	Clear association of types and areas	Much variation through time and across space	Ceramic diversity
Architecture	Homogenous styles at large sites	Expedient, diverse	Expedient and diverse architecture
Trade goods	Substantial quantities at large sites; many exotics	Limited quantities; mainly utilitarian	Limited quantities of utilitarian and exotics
Agriculture	Intensive	Extensive	Extensive
Social organization	Vertical or strongly modular	Egalitarian, diverse	Egalitarian, diverse

After Tainter and Plog 1994: 169

ment in areas with low population density extended into the eastern Chevelon drainage to the west and the Petrified Forest region to the northeast. To the south, the pattern ends just below the Mogollon Rim.

Archaeological projects in the eastern Chevelon drainage have identified four circular great kivas that represent the westernmost edge of the distribution of circular great kivas in the Southwest, although there is a gap in great kiva distribution in the intervening area between Pinedale and Heber, Arizona. No circular great kivas were built in the western Chevelon drainage and ceramic assemblages there were dominated by paddle-and-anvil manufactured brown ware and Little Colorado White Ware. The boundary between the eastern and western drainage appears between A.D. 1000 and 1200 (Gregory 1992b).

The Petrified Forest area has been identified as "beyond and between" the Puebloan and Sinagua regions (Stewart 1980: 54). The area had a larger baseline population than the Mogollon Rim region (Burton 1993a: 6), but settlement pattern data revealed a ten-fold increase in settlements between the Pueblo II and Late Pueblo II–Pueblo III periods (Stewart 1980: 116). This immigration was contemporaneous with the population growth in the Silver Creek drainage. The new settlements were small; most had fewer than ten rooms (Stewart 1980: 104), and across the region regularly distributed settlement clusters were centered on circular or rectangular great kivas (Burton 1993a).

McCreery Pueblo (A.D. 1087–1125) is unique within the Petrified Forest park boundaries but is similar in several ways to the great kiva sites of the Mogollon Rim region. The great kiva was shallower than kivas in the Mogollon Rim region, and of slightly different con-

struction, but was more similar to the Mogollon Rim great kivas than to those in the Chacoan area. The room block had at least five large rooms and was enclosed by a courtyard. Unlike the Mogollon Rim region pueblos, the courtyard wall enclosed a small kiva. Other features included a trash midden and the remains of ephemeral buildings and surfaces (Burton 1993b).

In the Grasshopper region south of the Mogollon Rim, few sites have been identified dating before the thirteenth century. The area may not have been used for permanent residence until the end of the thirteenth century, when this well-watered but cool area became more attractive to those escaping the effects of the Great Drought (Reid 1989).

MOGOLLON RIM LOCAL HISTORY

History is a record of those changes in the relationship between humans and nature that have economic and social consequences (Bottomore and others 1991: 399; Marx 1973 [1857: 409–410]). Changes in degree of residential mobility, resource use, population, and the organization of labor for subsistence and craft pursuits are apparent in the sequence presented below. The Mogollon Rim region research of Haury (1985c), Longacre (1964b, 1966, 1970), and Lightfoot (1984) provided the chronological baseline for all current survey and excavation projects (Fig. 3.1).

After limited use of the region in the Paleo-Indian and Archaic periods, occupation of the Mogollon Rim region became more substantial around A.D. 300. At the Bluff Site (Haury and Sayles 1985), pit houses excavated into a bedrock ridge above Forestdale valley provided evidence of the earliest substantive occupation in

Year (A.D.)	Haury (1985b)	Longacre (1970)	Plog (1974)	Lightfoot (1984)	Mills and Herr (1999)	Woodbury (1979)
1400	Canyon Creek	Phase VII: Large Towns – Full Convergence		1250-1475	Region Unoccupied	Pueblo IV
1300	Pinedale		Phase VI		Canyon Creek 1325-1390	
					Pinedale 1275-1325	
1200	Linden	Phase VI: Established Towns – Beginnings of Convergence			Linden 1200-1275	Pueblo III
				1100-1250	Late Carrizo 1150-1200	
1100	Carrizo				Early Carrizo 1080-1150	
1000	Dry Valley	Phase V: Beginning of Planned Towns	Phase V	900-1100		Pueblo II
900	Corduroy					
800		Phase IV: Established Village Farming	Phase IV	700-900		Pueblo I
700	Forestdale					
600		Phase III: Initial Sedentary Agriculturalists	Phase III			Basketmaker III
500	Cottonwood			300-700		
400		Phase II: Incipient Agriculturalists	Phase II			
300	Hilltop					Basketmaker II
200						

Figure 3.1. Concordance of chronologies for the Mogollon Rim region.

the region. The great kiva there, the earliest known in the puebloan Southwest, signaled the development of a new form of suprahousehold organization. The settlers practiced maize agriculture and used ceramic containers, but on a more limited scale than in later periods.

In the Hay Hollow Valley (Martin and others 1964), pit house settlements dating to the sixth century were located in areas overlooking valleys and perhaps agricultural fields. People in the sixth century did not reuse the locations of previous settlements, and the few

Table 3.2. Late Eleventh-Century to Early Twelfth-Century Circular Great Kivas in the Silver Creek Drainage

Site	Diameter (meters)	Circumference (meters)	Area (square meters)	References
Surveyed Area of Silver Creek Drainage				
AZ P:11:55 (ASU)	17.0	53.4	227.0	Lightfoot 1984
AZ P:11:124 (ASU)	16.0	50.3	201.1	Lightfoot 1984
AZ P:11:130 (ASU)				Lightfoot 1984
AZ P:11:157 (ASU)				Lightfoot 1984
AZ P:12:76 (ASU)	13.0	40.8	132.7	Lightfoot 1984
AZ P:12:99 (ASU)	10.0	31.4	78.5	Lightfoot 1984
AZ P:12:105 (ASU)	13.5	42.4	143.1	Lightfoot 1984
AZ P:16:90 (ASM)	13.0	40.8	132.7	Dosh and Maloney 1991
AZ P:16:112 (ASM), Hough's Great Kiva	24.0	75.4	452.4	Hough 1903; Dosh and Maloney 1991
AZ P:16:153 (ASM)	11.0	34.6	95.0	Neily 1991
AZ P:16:160 (ASM)	15.5	48.7	188.7	Neily 1991
Unsurveyed Area of Silver Creek Drainage				
AZ P:12:277 (ASM), Cothrun's Kiva	16.5	51.8	213.8	Mills and others 1994
Mogollon Rim Region Outside Silver Creek Drainage				
AZ P:16:2 (ASM), Tla Kii	18.2	57.2	260.2	Haury 1985d
AZ Q:13:1 (ASU)	10.0	31.4	78.5	Rice 1980
Carter Ranch	17.3	54.3	235.0	Martin and others 1964

sites from this period are not patterned on the landscape. However, after A.D. 700 it is possible to identify the spatial clustering of sites (Longacre 1964b: 209, 1970: 13). Great kivas continued to be the primary form of integrative architecture, as indicated by the lobed, "turtle"-shaped structure at Bear Ruin (Haury 1985a: 175). Brown, red, and gray utilitarian wares were manufactured locally, but painted wares were imported. In the earlier centuries, imported ceramics were produced in the Phoenix Basin, but increasingly trade was with areas to the north and east. Throughout the pit house period, population was low. Haury (1985b: 377) argued that the Forestdale Valley pit house settlements were occupied year round based on the labor invested in the construction of deep pit structures at the Bluff Site, but the question has not been addressed with studies of botanical and faunal assemblages and remains uncertain (Lightfoot and Jewett 1986).

The late eleventh century was a period of social and political reorganization in the Mogollon Rim region, as indicated by changes in domestic architecture, settlement pattern, local ceramic production, imported ceramics, and integrative architecture. Despite the evidence for a significant population increase in the tenth and eleventh centuries, the absolute number of people in the Silver Creek drainage was still low. The dispersed settlements had access to agricultural land,

because they were usually situated near small drainages. People occasionally resettled in old locations but built new masonry surface structures. Communities containing room blocks of up to 20 rooms sometimes included one or more circular great kivas that formed the center of dispersed settlements of small one-room masonry or jacal structures. Eleven circular great kivas have been located and recorded by survey in the Mogollon Rim region (Table 3.2), not including the Chevelon Canyon area, the westernmost cluster of such structures. Utilitarian vessels continued to be sand-tempered brown ware. Locally produced decorated wares included Cibola White Ware, in both light paste and dark paste varieties, and Puerco Valley Red Ware. The variety of imported ceramic wares increased, although the quantity of such pottery remained low. Red Mesa Black-on-white (A.D. 880–1040), Reserve Black-on-white (1100–1200), Snowflake Black-on-white (1100–1275), and Black Mesa Style Cibola White Ware (about 1000–1150) are the most common diagnostic ceramics used to identify sites from this period.

The pattern of dispersed communities in the late eleventh and early twelfth centuries endured for 75 to 100 years. Small habitations were abandoned between A.D. 1150 and 1180 (Mills and Herr 1999). Then people moved to small aggregated pueblos in new locations on valley bottoms or ridges and hilltops overlooking minor drainages. These settlements, too, may have reused previous settlement locations. Room blocks partially enclosed plazas. Room block kivas and rectangular great kivas were added to the canon of ritual architecture, and circular great kivas were no longer used. This period is commonly described as transitional (Haury 1985b) between the dispersed communities and the large aggregated communities of the late thirteenth and fourteenth centuries. Ceramic assemblages were also transitional, both in variety of wares and in ceramic style.

Recent work at Bryant Ranch, occupied in the last decades of the thirteenth century, showed relatively short term occupation of small habitations prior to the period of largest aggregation (Mills, Fenn, and others 1999). After approximately A.D. 1290, people lived in increasingly aggregated, but unplanned, plaza-oriented pueblos such as the one at Bailey Ruin. Late thirteenth- and fourteenth-century settlements were located closer to permanent sources of water (Longacre 1964b: 209–210; Mills 1998: 66–67). There were few field houses dating to this period; presumably agriculture was practiced close to the pueblo, in the well-watered valleys. Increased variability of room functions indicated changes in the way activities were organized. Ritual architecture included kivas, room block kivas, enclosed plazas, and open plazas (Mills 1998: 70). Diversity continued to characterize ceramic assemblages, but imported ceramics came almost exclusively from areas north and east of the Mogollon Rim. Locally produced decorated wares recovered from Bailey Ruin included: Cibola White Ware, Roosevelt Red Ware, Puerco Valley Red Ware, and White Mountain Red Ware, as well as the decorated brown ware type, Cibeque Polychrome. Changes in ceramic manufacture demonstrated that people migrated into the Mogollon Rim region in this period, but demographic reconstructions do not show an increase in population (Newcomb 1999). The identification of Mogollon Rim ceramic technologies in nearby regions, such as the Tonto Basin, suggests that as migrant households moved into the Mogollon Rim region, other households moved out (Mills 1998; Stinson 1996). The last tree-ring date in the area is A.D. 1384, from Show Low Ruin. Permanent settlement in the area ceased in the 1390s, although the area continues to be used differentially by modern Puebloan and Apachean groups.

This historical sequence provides evidence for several periods of reorganization: from the Archaic procurement sites to the ephemeral pit house occupations, from the light use of the area to dispersed great kiva focused communities to the uneven development of aggregated settlements. This description of the Mogollon Rim region provides a "closed system" view of the local culture history. But change is not self-generated, and the history and processes of the Mogollon Rim region as a social and political landscape need to be reevaluated in relation to contemporaneous changes and processes across the Southwest.

MIGRATION AND LOW POPULATION DENSITY IN THE MOGOLLON RIM REGION

Migration is a regional process that can dramatically alter the course of local history. In homelands and destination areas, migration creates a situation wherein structure and parochial history meet in the person and the event (Sahlins 1985: xiv). The contact between culture and event has effects that are not entirely predictable. The context of meaning changes, irrevocably revaluing cultural symbols. Migration is also the first step toward the creation of frontiers (Anthony 1990: 897).

Migration is differentiated from other forms of population movement, such as residential mobility. It can be defined as "a long-term residential relocation" by individuals, households, or other social units, "beyond community boundaries . . . as the result of a perceived decrease in the benefits of remaining residentially stable or a perceived increase in the benefits of relocating to prospective destinations" (Clark 2001: 2). Although households are most likely to be more archaeologically detectable, individual scouting missions are part of the structure of migration (Anthony 1990: 903).

To be demonstrated, migration must be differentiated from behavior that can generate similar material culture patterns, including trade, imitation, and social inequality. When sufficient information on regional settlement patterns is available, population modeling can be used to identify population movements. Population increases greater than those explained by natural birth and population decreases greater than those explained by mortality rates provide evidence of migration, particularly when potential contemporaneous source and destination areas can be identified.

In local perspective, every diachronic treatment of the Little Colorado River drainage identifies a population increase around the eleventh and twelfth centuries A.D. (Dosh 1988: 514). In macroregional perspective, the area is a "population trough" between areas of high population density on the Colorado Plateau and in the Hohokam region of southern Arizona. Population density remained low from the earliest settlement until between approximately A.D. 1100 and 1200, when the balance of settlement in the Southwest shifted west (Dean and others 1994: 78–79). Haury (1985d: 16) used survey data to demonstrate a population increase in the Forestdale Valley between A.D. 900 and 1100: 3 sites dating to the Hilltop–Cottonwood–Forestdale phases, 6 to Corduroy, 16 to Dry Valley, 16 to Carrizo, 10 to Linden, and 1 to Pinedale–Canyon Creek, and the last three phases were represented by aggregated pueblos. Population increase was one of the key characteristics of Haury's definition of the Carrizo phase. He suggested that the increase was due to immigration, but not all researchers in the area have agreed.

Longacre (1970) quantified the population increase by using a formula that multiplied the number of sites in his Little Colorado drainage survey area by the mean number of rooms per site for each of seven identified phases. The resulting curve indicated a dramatic population increase beginning sometime before A.D. 700 and increasing until just after 1100. The researchers who excavated in the Hay Hollow Valley viewed change as internally generated. Longacre's interpretation of population trends in the Little Colorado Valley posited that the growth was encouraged by a period of increased agricultural productivity. He postulated two population maxima: one for the entire region peaking around A.D. 1200, and one for the Little Colorado Valley peaking around A.D. 1400, with residential abandonment of the area in the sixteenth century.

In addressing the demographic trends of the entire Southwest, Dean, Doelle, and Orcutt (1994) found that the Little Colorado area, including the Hopi Buttes, Wupatki, Chevelon, Hay Hollow Valley, Snowflake, Pinedale, and Zuni subareas, experienced a significant population increase between approximately A.D. 1000 and 1150. Population increased in the Hay Hollow Valley as early as the ninth century, but the scale of increase was far less dramatic than that of the later period (Dean and others 1994: 63–64).

Newcomb (1997, 1999) has demonstrated that migration was responsible for the population increase in the Silver Creek portion of the Mogollon Rim region. Newcomb's demographic analysis was applied specifically to the 883 square miles drained by Silver Creek. Her database consisted of the 748 sites recorded by 25 surveys that covered an area of approximately 261 square kilometers (101 square miles), or 11 percent of the Silver Creek drainage (Newcomb 1997: 35). By extrapolating site locations based on the soil type and elevation of known sites, Newcomb estimated the population for the entire drainage. She used Schlanger's (1987, 1988) momentary population model, and then evaluated effects of big sites, seasonal sites, and room function interpretations in her estimates. Variables held constant included people per room (N = 3), room rebuilding frequency (N = 1), and life span of living rooms (15 years). Newcomb created 13 population reconstructions for the region, of which three of the most likely are shown in Figure 3.2. The most compelling evidence for migration into the Silver Creek drainage is the comparison of the archaeological evidence for population increase in the region to ethnographically derived statistics of maximum yearly birth rate for prehistoric small-scale agriculturalists and preindustrial societies (Newcomb 1999). Population growth at the rate of 0.30 percent (Cowgill 1975) to 0.52 percent per year (Hassan 1981: 140) is expected among such societies. In the Silver Creek drainage, average yearly population increased between 1.8 and 2.0 percent from A.D. 1000 to 1050 (Newcomb 1999: 74–78). Population growth in the drainage was nearly four times the statistic Hassan considered his maximum, thus demonstrating a migration. At its peak, between approximately A.D. 1000 and 1100, the extrapolated population of the Silver Creek drainage was probably between 774 and 1,670 people (Newcomb 1997: 71).

INTEGRATION IN THE MOGOLLON RIM REGION

Integrative behavior is the "glue" that binds social groups through time and across space. The strongest bonds are created through numerous overlapping and crosscutting interactions. As part of the structuralist paradigm, integration has been criticized as being an overly static concept, but it does not have to be so. Ideally, integrative bonds are the relationships through which meaning is created for the individual and stability is created for the community. Integration is an important aspect of creating a community that is more than the sum of its constituent households. Reconstructing the integrative processes is the first step toward understanding broader patterns of sociopolitical organization and culture change, including those of archaeological "frontiers."

Integrative mechanisms described ethnographically include kinship, kinship metaphors, affinity, patron-client relationships and more general production and exchange procedures, shared group affiliation, institutionalized relations created by a bureaucracy, belief, political systems, and ideology. Often the spatial scale

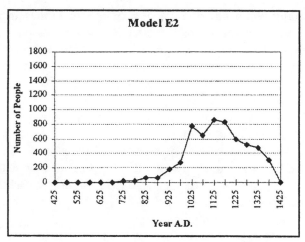

Habitation sites, with 5 or more rooms

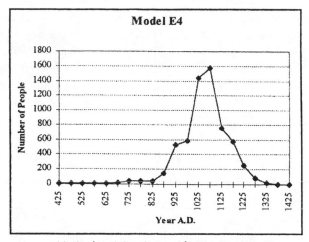

Limited activity sites, with 1 to 4 rooms

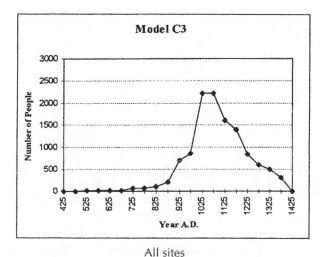

All sites

Figure 3.2. Demographic reconstructions for sites in the Silver Creek drainage (from Newcomb 1999, copyright The Arizona Board of Regents, courtesy of the Arizona State Museum.)

and the strength of these relations varies. Some integrative behaviors and affiliations are difficult to recognize in the archaeological record; others are manifest in special spaces set aside for integrative activities.

Integrative architecture formalizes communal space. Integrative behaviors can also occur in less formal places. Many of the integrative activities of small-scale agriculturalists occur in their fields, as do the work parties described in the previous chapter. Integrative architecture is often simple and formalized. This morphology, like the simplicity, redundancy, and formalization of ritual liturgy, helps impart the ritual message (Hegmon 1989: 6). The message is not necessarily benign. As Leach wrote (1977: 16):

> if anarchy is to be avoided, the individuals who make up a society must from time to time be reminded, at least in symbol, of the underlying order that is supposed to guide their social activities. Ritual performances have this function for the participating group as a whole; they momentarily make explicit what is otherwise a fiction.

These fictions include relationships of power and ideology (Brandt 1994: 16).

Integrative facilities can be differentiated into those used almost solely for ritual purposes (high-level facilities) and those ritual places that are also used for cooking, sleeping, craft manufacturing, and other domestic and secular activities (low-level facilities; Adler and Wilshusen 1990: 135). In the puebloan Southwest, kivas are considered low-level integrative facilities (although see Lekson 1988) and great kivas are high-level integrative facilities.

Great kivas were built in the puebloan Southwest after about A.D. 300, and their number increased significantly between 900 and 1200. By around 900 their distribution centered in Chaco Canyon and the San Juan Basin; later it was centered in the Little Colorado drainage. After around 1100, great kivas were no longer constructed in the San Juan Basin, but were rapidly being built in the Mogollon Rim region, on the western edge of their distribution (Herr 1994: 52).

Chacoan great kivas were defined by Lekson (1991: 36) as round, masonry-lined pit structures that were generally greater than ten meters in diameter. In places and periods that were not "Chacoan," structures fulfilling similar integrative roles within the community were constructed of masonry or earth. It is likely that the rectangular great kivas of the southern and western Pueblo areas embraced a type of ritual dissimilar to that practiced in the circular great kivas (Gregory and Wilcox 1999). Herein, unless otherwise specified, the term "great kivas" denotes circular great kivas.

The morphology of circular great kivas was highly variable (Vivian and Reiter 1960), but Chacoan great kivas were more formal than those built earlier and in other areas of the Puebloan Southwest (Herr 1994). They had a formalized set of floor features, including a hearth and fire screen, vaults or foot drums, pits, and roof support posts. The structure was encircled by a bench faced with a stone veneer. Antechambers and elaborate entrances were common. When the great kiva became part of Chacoan ritual architecture it was subject to a change in meaning. In the San Juan Basin, circular great kivas became more formalized and less variable in size and construction. Great kivas built after A.D. 900 expressed a symbolic connection to Chacoan identity and ritual (Fowler and Stein 1992; Lekson 1991: 42).

There are undeniable differences between the Mogollon Rim region great kivas and Chacoan great kivas, although I suggest that despite differences in form, there were similarities in the symbolic meaning of the ritual structures. Considering the strong ideology associated with the great kivas of the northern Southwest at this time (around A.D. 900–1100), the Mogollon Rim region people, by using such structures, were identifying with the Chacoan organization. They chose this "traditional symbol" as a beacon to attract other pioneers to their communities.

The Mogollon Rim region in the late eleventh and early twelfth centuries was overbuilt with ritual architecture (Chapter 1). The region had a low population density and a relatively large number of circular great kivas per person. The largest masonry circular great kiva in the area, Hough's Great Kiva, had a wall-to-wall diameter of 24 meters. Measurements are available for 10 of the 12 Silver Creek circular great kivas (see Table 3.2). The total area enclosed by the 9 measured great kivas located in the 11 percent of the drainage that has been surveyed is 1,651.2 square meters. The maximum population for the *entire* drainage at this time has been estimated at between 774 and 1,670 people (Newcomb 1997: 71). The point of this numerical exercise is to emphasize that even if some of the structures were used consecutively, the Silver Creek drainage area still had an overabundance of integrative architecture and that enclosing space for communal and ritual functions was clearly a priority of the ancient inhabitants of the region.

Curiously, no small suprahousehold kivas from the late eleventh and early twelfth centuries have been conclusively identified on survey or in excavations in the Silver Creek drainage, distinguishing this period from those that follow. The great kiva was the only type of communal architecture in the region, and there is no evidence for institutions integrating subsets of the population. In contrast, many contemporaneous communities across the Southwest contained numerous small kivas within their settlements.

Communal ritual is an essential element of life on the frontier. Rituals provide the opportunities for shared experiences that foster cohesiveness among households with diverse backgrounds. Great kivas can be evaluated as part of a symbolic system. Symbols in any given context have a value formed by their past history, the current cultural context, and the actions of the individuals who manipulate the symbol. Initially, they may be used to integrate the new local landscape into an existing system of meaning; yet, their value may be transformed in the process. If great kivas were originally built for functional purposes (Vivian 1990: 486), such as attracting new households to the community, they likely acquired stronger meanings as part of the shared frontier experience.

IDENTIFICATION OF A HOMELAND IN A REGIONAL PERSPECTIVE

The history of a frontier cannot be understood apart from its relationship to the social and political history of its homeland or core area. In the Mogollon Rim region, the years between A.D. 1000 and 1150 defined a period of migration and initial community formation. In this same period, three macroregional sociopolitical organizations created strong behavioral patterns that have been identified by archaeologists as Chaco, Hohokam, and Mimbres (Fig. 3.3). The location of each of these regional organizations could have been the homeland for Mogollon Rim migrants.

A summary comparison of some general societal attributes shows the similarity or dissimilarity of the Mogollon Rim frontier with each of these core areas (Table 3.3). Although cursory, it is possible to identify certain areas with greater similarities to the frontier than others because, in the new environment, migrants drew upon knowledge gained through their own socialization and expressed and identified themselves through traditional cultural symbols. Because of the social transformations affected by migration, adaptation to new environments, and new demographic and political landscapes, frontier societies were not "cookie cutter" replicas of their homelands.

Demographics

During the eleventh century, groups of migrants moved into the Mogollon Rim region. Population density in the San Juan Basin was high and "many niches capable of supporting limited numbers of people were filled" (Vivian (1990: 222; see also Sebastian 1992a: 101). People were moving from the San Juan Basin to other portions of the Colorado Plateau, although the most significant drop in population did not occur until approximately A.D. 1250. In the Hohokam region, population was extremely high, was mainly concentrated in major river valleys, was generally stable, and was growing slightly between A.D. 1000 and 1150. Population was not as high in the Mimbres region, but there, too, it was increasing (Dean 1996a: 36; Dean and others 1994: 63, 67). The general picture of declining, stable, and growing populations masks the internal reorganization in each of the three regions between 1000 and 1150, but the declining population and the increased mobility of Colorado Plateau populations provides some support for considering this region the homeland of Mogollon Rim migrants.

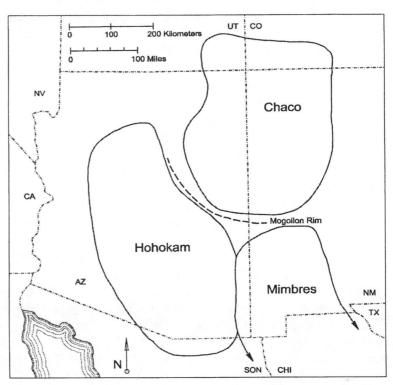

Figure 3.3. Maximum spatial extent of Chacoan (great house and great kiva distribution), Hohokam (ballcourt distribution), and Mimbres (Classic period pueblo distribution) regional systems between A.D. 1000 and 1150. (Boundaries after Doyel and Lekson 1992, Fig. 2–3; graphic by Susan Hall.)

Table 3.3. Comparison of Attributes in Core Areas with the Mogollon Rim Frontier, A.D. 1000–1150

| | Core Areas | | | | Mogollon Rim Frontier |
	Chaco North	Chaco South	Mimbres	Hohokam	
Population	Slow decline		Fast growth	Slow growth	Fast growth
Ceramic form	Coil-and-scrape, corrugated forms	Coil-and-scrape, corrugated forms	Coil-and-scrape Corrugated forms	Paddle-and-anvil	Coil-and-scrape, corrugated forms
Ceramic smudging	No	Only in the Puerco Valley	Only in west-central New Mexico	No	Yes
Wall construction	Full-height masonry walls	Full-height masonry walls	Full-height cobble masonry walls	Adobe, post-reinforced adobe	Full-height masonry walls
Habitation	Compact masonry structure, 6–15 rooms avg.	L-shaped, ⊓-shaped masonry structure, 9 rooms avg.	Masonry structure	Pit house, some compounds	Masonry structure, 4 rooms avg.
Integrative architecture	Great kivas, kivas, triwalls, biwalls	Great kivas, kivas	Plazas, ceremonial rooms, kivas	Ballcourts, platform mounds	Great kivas
Settlement structure	Compact, with kiva, midden	SE oriented room block, kiva-pit house in front, midden to SE	Agglomerative architecture	Household clusters, village segment	SE oriented room block, midden to SE
Community structure	Clustered habitations; dispersed small structures; many soil and water control features	Clustered habitations; dispersed small structures; few soil or water control features	Aggregated pueblos; dispersed limited activity sites; soil and water control features	Linear along canals; elsewhere, habitation clusters; dispersed agricultural features	Clustered habitations; dispersed small structures; few soil or water control features

Technology

Technological style (Lechtman 1977) is the idea that when any number of equally functional choices are possible for the manufacture of an item, the method chosen is the one that has been learned through socialization. Technological styles help locate homelands through the identification of commonalities in learned behavior. Because of their low contextual visibility and thus the conservative rate of change, technological variations have potential to signify differences of social affiliation. Methods learned by socialization include the construction of homes; the layout of structures, settlements, and communities; and the manufacture of ceramics. Emblematic style, which is used in highly visible contexts, signals the public identity or desired identity of the craftsperson or builder.

Technological style has been used to differentiate co-residing social groups (Clark 2001; Clark and others 2000), but it is also possible to use this method to demonstrate links to potential source areas for pioneers. From many excavated sites on the Mogollon Rim there is evidence of local production of utilitarian and decorated vessels. The dominant utilitarian pottery was a coil-and-scrape corrugated ware. Cibola White Ware ceramics were made with local clays, sand and sherd tempers, and mineral paints. Both ceramic technologies were used in areas north and east of the Silver Creek drainage. In the late eleventh and early twelfth centuries, the Mogollon Rim region settlement structure included front oriented ⊓-shaped room blocks (in addition to other, less formal, room arrangements) analogous to those of pueblo groups in the central and southern San Juan Basin. This settlement layout, organized around circular great kivas, was different from that of earlier settlements in the area.

There are few similarities in domestic architecture and ceramic technology between the Mogollon Rim region and the Hohokam region. Hohokam residents lived in adobe pit houses or pit rooms organized around ballcourts, platform mounds, or ceremonial rooms, and they made paddle-and-anvil pottery. Their communities were highly structured and situated along rivers and canals (Gregory and Nials 1985). These strong differences in domestic architecture and ceramic manufacture eliminate the Hohokam region as a source area for Mogollon Rim migrants.

Residents of the Chacoan and Mimbres regions lived in pueblos, stored materials in rooms within their room blocks, and produced coiled-and-scraped corrugated vessels. Although architecture in the Mogollon Rim and Mimbres regions was broadly similar, differences in wall construction and settlement structure make the Mimbres region an unlikely homeland. Mimbres region residents lived in large, unplanned, agglomerative room blocks, whereas the Mogollon Rim migrants lived in dispersed communities. Smudged vessels were not produced in the southern Mimbres region until after the mid twelfth century. However, the settlement pattern of the west-central New Mexico portion of the Mimbres region was one of small, irregularly constructed habitations clustered around rectangular great kivas, and this restricted area cannot be as easily dismissed as a homeland. Potters here made coil-and-scrape pottery and smudged their brown ware bowls.

There are compelling similarities between the Mogollon Rim region and southern Chacoan communities, particularly in the Puerco Valley. Mogollon Rim region wall construction, settlement structure, and community structure were similar to those in the southern Chacoan region, although the suprahousehold kivas common in the Chacoan region have not been identified in the Mogollon Rim region. Tla Kii's occasional identification as an outlier (Fowler and Stein 1992: 103) is due to a single wall in the room block (Room 14) with "Chacoan masonry" (Haury 1985d: 39). Less elaborate single-course, double-course, or compound walls were more common in the small habitation (non-great house) settlements in both regions. Potters in the southern Chacoan and Mogollon Rim regions produced coiled-and-scraped vessels and both smudged some of their brownware bowls.

Integrative Architecture

Between A.D. 1000 and 1150, Mogollon Rim region communities were not organized around enclosed plazas as were communities in the Mimbres Valley, or around rectangular great kivas as in west-central New Mexico, or around ballcourts as in the Hohokam region. Instead, the Mogollon Rim region communities clustered around circular great kivas, like the communities of the Chacoan region. Using ritual architecture to identify enculturative background is problematic, but it does denote the social groups with whom these migrants chose to publicly identify themselves, in this case the groups of the Chacoan region.

In local chronologies across the Southwest, the late eleventh and early twelfth centuries were periods of cultural florescence. The Chacoan regional system was reformulated then, great houses were built in existing communities, and new communities were settled. People moved into the southern portion of the San Juan Basin and the Upper and Middle Little Colorado drainage (Dean and others 1994; Gumerman and Skinner 1968; Lange 1989; Longacre 1970). A.D. 1000 marks the beginning of both the Mimbres Classic and Hohokam Classic periods; these were times of significant transformations in community organization marked by changes in domestic and public architecture.

The affiliation of Mogollon Rim migrants with the Chacoan region is demonstrated, if tentatively, by both low-visibility technologies and a more public identification with a Chacoan form of integrative architecture. However, in such unsettling social and political times, households in all areas were probably mobile. Small numbers of households from the Hohokam and Mimbres regions may have moved across this ancient landscape, undetectable now to archaeologists. Few but intriguing similarities to Mimbres iconography appear in the Tla Kii ceramic assemblage, indicating that the relationship between these two areas warrants further research.

THE CHACOANS OF THE PUERCO RIVER VALLEY

The term "Chacoan region" encompasses a great deal of spatial variability in the eleventh- and early twelfth-century communities of the Colorado Plateau. Moving north and east from the Mogollon Rim region and the Little Colorado River valley, patterns of migration, integration, and population density change. These areas had large population bases before A.D. 1000 and maintained their populations at a relatively high level during the period of interest (Dean and others 1994). Labor was readily available, and land was the sought after resource, a characteristic of core areas (Gumerman and Olson 1968).

The Mogollon Rim region shared greatest affinity with the southern Chacoan area, particularly near the Puerco River valley. The Houck region of the west Puerco River valley parallels Interstate 40 from the Arizona–New Mexico border to Sanders, Arizona, and it is in this area that ceramic assemblages were generally similar to those in the Mogollon Rim. Smudged, corrugated, brown ware pottery indicated technologies shared with areas to the south. However, there is no evidence of a population influx in the tenth and eleventh centuries (Gumerman and Olson 1968). The relatively high population densities (Winter 1994: 251) were apparently due to local growth. The Wide Ruin area of the Puerco River valley was abandoned by approximately A.D. 1200. Suprahousehold rectangular kivas, many of

which had walls painted with simple black-on-white designs (Gumerman and Olson 1968; Winter 1994: 243), were associated with front-oriented pueblos; they indicate an intermediate level of social differentiation between the household and the community that was absent in the Silver Creek area.

Navajo Springs, an outlier on the Chacoan "frontier," was located in the Puerco River valley near Sanders, Arizona, 300 km (186 miles) southwest of Chaco Canyon (Warburton and Graves 1992: 52). This settlement, occupied between A.D. 1050 and 1150, is considered the farthest southwest outlier within the boundaries of the Chacoan organization. Chacoan attributes were associated with the latest occupation of the Navajo Springs locality and included great house architecture, settlement structure, and Gallup Black-on-white pottery. Warburton and Graves (1992: 65) suggested that the Rio Puerco valley was identified by Chacoan people as an area of abundant resources; thus a colony was established to create an economic relationship in which the Navajo Springs area provided agricultural resources and in return became part of the Chacoan ritual system. In some discussions of the extent of Chacoan outliers, this settlement has been identified (Wilcox 1999: 137) as part of a:

> periphery of the great-house peer polity system, and the network of great kivas in [the middle Little Colorado Valley] may have facilitated prestige-good and possibly commodity flows . . . into and out of the great-house systems.

To others, myself included, the Mogollon Rim region was just beyond these boundaries of the Chacoan great house organization. The Puerco River valley was still within the Chacoan organization. As such it may have been a periphery or a boundary zone, but it is likely that just beyond this valley was where the "frontier" began (Warburton and Graves 1992: 52).

The Motivation to Migrate

The causes of migration are often categorized as "pushes" and "pulls" (Anthony 1990). Pushes are reasons to leave the home area, and pulls are incentives to move to a particular destination. These stresses and attractions are analytically identified as economic and social pushes and pulls. Every adaptation is a compromise based on a number of low and high frequency environmental processes and socially motivated factors. Environmental stresses are perceived through social and ideological means of understanding the world and meaning is attached to climatic fluctuations. Changes in precipitation, frost-free seasons, and yields of cultigens and wild foods affect decision-making; rain, fertility, and good harvests are foci of ideology and ritual. In the years before the migration into the Mogollon Rim region, there were few social pulls into the area, but land was readily available. Lacking social incentives in the Mogollon Rim region, disincentives to stay in the homeland were more likely the "cause" of migration.

A summary of environmental trends provides a context for understanding the migration and demographic processes in the Mogollon Rim region and the Colorado Plateau in the latter half of the eleventh century and the first half of the twelfth century. The period was warm and wet and marked an overall expansion of small-scale agriculturalists into new territories across the Colorado Plateau. Increased warmth allowed expansion into higher elevations, and increased precipitation allowed expansion into lower or drier areas (Salzer 2000).

Because the Mogollon Rim is part of a mountainous transition zone between the Colorado Plateau and the Basin-and-Range province of southern Arizona, orographic effects make it one of the areas of highest precipitation in the Southwest (Dean and others 1994: 56). Climatic differences between the Mogollon Rim and the Colorado Plateau vary in scale, the Mogollon Rim region is cooler and wetter, but not in trend (Kaldahl and Dean 1999). The average rainfall just above the Mogollon Rim is 41.2 cm (16.2 inches) per year (range 10.3 to 22.3 inches per year), *versus* 37.4 cm (14.7 inches) per year on the Plateau more generally (range 9.7 to 19.4 inches per year), and 49.2 cm (19.3 inches) just below the Rim (range 14.0 to 30.0 inches per year; Kaldahl and Dean 1999). These statistics become relevant when compared to the 30.5 cm (12 inches) of annual rainfall necessary to grow corn (Hack 1942: 23).

Environmental conditions on the Colorado Plateau during the late eleventh and early twelfth centuries were among the best during the entire prehistoric sequence for the dry farming and water and soil control agricultural systems used by Puebloan groups. In the first half of the eleventh century effective moisture increased and remained high throughout the twelfth century. Only once, in the early A.D. 1120s, did rainfall drop below the Hopi 30.5-cm (12-inch) standard. Summer rainfall was plentiful between 1020 and the late 1080s, and again between 1100 and 1130. Between approximately 1080 and 1100, rainfall dropped slightly below the mean in the Mogollon Rim region, and the Colorado Plateau experienced a slight drought. The 1120s were particularly wet, but a period of 25 consecutive years of below average rainfall began around 1130 (Dean 1988, 1996a; Dean and others 1994: 55; Kaldahl and Dean 1999; Sebastian 1992a).

Movement into the Mogollon Rim region occurred as floodplains were aggrading, indicating that water tables were higher and that floodplain soils were being replenished by overbank deposition (Dean and others 1994: 63). Water tables began to lower only after about A.D. 1130. With the high water tables and the average-to-high levels of precipitation through much of the eleventh and early twelfth centuries, it is likely that the flooding of fields near washes was common. Many settlements were located close to small washes.

Precipitation was not the limiting factor to dry farming agriculture in the moist Mogollon Rim region, but temperature was. In the 55 years of modern climatic data from the weather station (Pinedale, elevation 1,981 m asl) closest to Hough's Great Kiva Site (1,996 m asl) and AZ P:16:160 (1,993 m asl), the average time between frosts is 123 days. At Cothrun's Kiva (elevation 1,908 m asl) the average growing season is approximately 137 days. Temperature trends reconstructed from bristlecone pines in the San Francisco peaks, which are generally applicable to the Mogollon Rim region (Salzer 2000), show temperatures near the long-term average between about A.D. 1050 to 1070 and higher temperatures between approximately 1070 and 1090, until the final years of the eleventh century when temperatures plunged and remained lower than average until almost 1150. The low temperatures probably shortened an already brief growing season. Compared to the standard growing season for Hopi corn, which is between 115 and 120 days (Bradfield 1971: 6; Kaldahl and Dean 1999), the leeway between corn maturation and the onset of the first frosts was probably slim in an average year and was shortened in the cool years at the beginning of the twelfth century.

As population density increased on the Colorado Plateau and populations outgrew their "niches," and as the rest of the Colorado Plateau was experiencing droughts, the Mogollon Rim region presented two economic attractions to eleventh-century farmers considering migration: land was abundant and well watered.

Social Pushes and Pulls

Demographic trends and material culture patterns indicate that the Chaco region was most likely the core area homeland for the Mogollon Rim frontier migrants. During the eleventh and twelfth centuries people moved out of the San Juan Basin, and people moved into the

Mogollon Rim region. Coincidence in timing is one reason the Chaco region is considered a homeland. Similarities in the technological style of domestic architecture, settlement and community structure, and ceramic manufacture support this argument. The direction of exchange demonstrates active relationships were maintained by Mogollon Rim region households with households in areas to the north and east. The circular great kivas of the Mogollon Rim region were part of the system of meaning signified by the distribution of similar structures across the Chacoan region. They marked the ideological affiliation of the Mogollon Rim region migrants with the Chacoan organization.

Potential "pushes" out of the highly populated San Juan Basin are readily apparent. The late eleventh and early twelfth century sociopolitical reorganization, and the years immediately preceding it, can be considered a period of social stress, to which residents of the San Juan Basin and the outliers responded in a variety of ways, including moving (Dean and others 1994: 85; Vivian 1990).

Chacoan influence, as indicated by the number and distribution of great houses and great kivas, did not reach its maximum spatial extent until the late eleventh and early twelfth centuries (Marshall and others 1982: 1231; Van Dyke 1997: 137). Some of the earliest outliers were established in the south and southwestern part of the San Juan Basin in the tenth century (Judge 1989: 217; Vivian 1990: 182), but the period of greatest construction activity across the Chacoan region was between A.D. 1080 and 1130 (Judge 1989: 225). Much of the construction in outlier communities was completed by the end of the 1080s (Powers and others 1983: 252). The roads that created links between outlier communities date to the eleventh century and early twelfth century (Powers and others 1983; Vivian 1997b: 14).

The Chacoan regional system was reorganized between A.D. 1115 and 1140 (Judge 1989: 245). The second massive building program in Chaco Canyon history began at this time (Lekson 1984: 267), and changes occurred in settlements across the San Juan Basin. Outliers were built in the northern portion of the basin as Aztec Ruin and Salmon Ruin became important centers in the twelfth century. Residence may have continued at the southern outliers, but large scale constructions ceased after A.D. 1120 (Vivian 1990: 489). Settlement pattern, great house construction, ceramic style, faunal assemblages, and patterns of trash deposition provide archaeological evidence of significant economic, social, political, and religious changes in this period (Judge 1989; Saitta 1997; Toll 1985). The decline of great kiva construction in the San Juan basin emphasizes a change in ritual organization (Vivian 1990: 488). Changing land use patterns indicate more extensive agricultural strategies, probably in response to a drier environment. Important changes in settlement structure (whose meanings are uncertain) include the addition of a great number of storage rooms in Chaco Canyon great houses and the enclosures of areas in front of room blocks with walled plazas. The significance of this period has been debated. However, the decrease in great kiva construction and the changing function of great house rooms signified a change in the structure of secular and religious leadership (Saitta 1997).

It is tempting to relate the southern Chacoan region and Mogollon Rim region as homeland and destination, but the relationship between the areas was probably not as simple as this overview presents it. The local effects of the reorganization identified in Chaco Canyon had ramifications across the region, one of which was increased population mobility. The rate of new construction provides evidence that people were moving and creating new settlements in the San Juan Basin during the eleventh century and early twelfth century (Vivian 1990). Population movements often cause chain reactions, accounting for steplike patterns in the migratory process. Immigrants may stop, settle, then move again (Anthony 1990; Hudson 1976; Sewastynowicz 1986), or one immigration may cause a subsequent emigration of the indigenous population. Migration to the Mogollon Rim region must be considered in light of the effects of other local and regional scale movements throughout the Colorado Plateau.

Florescence or demise, periods of regional expansion and reorganization were likely to have been stressful for some portions of the population as the scale and structure of Chacoan communities changed. It is this social and political context that the migrants chose to leave behind as they headed for land and freedom in the Mogollon Rim region, and it is this same social and political heritage that the migrants brought with them as they turned the new landscape into familiar territory. But the identification of this migration is not the end of the story, it is the beginning of the frontier.

CHAPTER FOUR

After the Migration: Mogollon Rim Communities

As small groups of migrants entered the Mogollon Rim region, they began to form small-scale agricultural communities. But even with the continuing influx of people, population remained low and land was readily available to the pioneers. The communities created were the largest form of social organization known on the frontier. Fragile institutions bound together the mobile migrants from diverse homelands, if only temporarily. Understanding the composition of frontier households and communities is key to understanding the sociopolitical organization of the Mogollon Rim region in the late eleventh and early twelfth centuries A.D.

In some respects, frontier communities fit neatly into a continuum of agricultural communities ranging from those with high population density and extensive or intensive land use to those with low population densities and extensive land use. Settlers to frontiers inhabit a land-rich, labor-poor environment. Whereas the classic Marxian economy is one where labor is cheap and exploitable, on frontiers land, *not* labor, is cheap and exploitable. The concern with understanding the relationship between labor and society remains relevant, but issues such as maximization are better understood in terms of labor rather than product. This relationship between demographics and agricultural production is one determinant of social and spatial organization on an agricultural frontier.

When farmland is readily available, settlement patterns among agriculturalists are the result of value-laden choices about whether it is worth more to live close to fields or close to other people. In the first case the result is a dispersed settlement pattern; in the second case the result is an aggregated settlement pattern. Factors that weigh on these choices include population pressure, the number and size of fields, defensive needs, the elasticity and availability of labor outside the household, and costs associated with the transportation and distribution of goods (Chayanov 1966; Stone 1996). Frontier fields are often larger than those of more aggregated settlements or more intensive producers, and considera-tions such as the length of the daily walk guide the placement of residences, as does the need for labor. Such considerations are apparent in Mogollon Rim frontier communities.

Agricultural production has an effect on the regional distribution of settlements. Across the ancient Southwest, people in dispersed settlements responded to environmental fluctuations more than did people in aggregated settlements: "prior to about 1000, populations were low enough to have allowed fairly simple behavioral responses to environmental variability" (Dean and others 1994: 85). Environmental models do not as accurately predict changes in settlement location for people in aggregated pueblos (Orcutt 1991), although agent-based environmental models of settlement pattern in the Long House Valley have predicted settlement locations remarkably well (Dean and others 2000). The spatial signature of small-scale agricultural communities is the product of behaviors that organize labor for agricultural production and respond to local environmental changes.

DEFINITION OF THE COMMUNITY

A community is the aggregate of many individual and household decisions and is the most common social institution above the level of the household. Its spatial expression gives residents a shared sense of place (Hine 1980: 21). As an institution, the community is more durable than an individual, household, or single settlement. Community members make decisions guided by those norms that anthropologists study as "structure." Their behavior may or may not follow the norm. Communities range from flexible to stable. The more individuals and households rely on the community to recognize, reproduce, and defend access to economic and social resources, the more community integrity and stability need to be fostered by bureaucracies or ritual (Adler 1996c). Individuals will accept less decision-making power in exchange for having access to community institutions. Hine (1980: 26) noted, at the points where the individuals intersect the group, a community might be seen as a plane where individual needs and desires are resolved in group action and, conversely, where group needs are furthered by individual behavior. Thus the community is an arena of individual-group tensions.

In the archaeological literature, the virtually unquestioned definition of community is that of ethnologist George Murdock (1949: 82–83). He defines the community as a common territory that provides opportunities for social intercourse, cooperative food getting and mutual aid, as well as a place of internal tensions and social control. The community is the focus of associative life. Adler (1996b: 5) adds that "communities serve an important role in defining, maintaining, and defending social access to important resources on the local and regional levels." Minimally, communities are single individuals, families, and settlements held together by overlapping social roles created by kinship, co-residence, economic, and ritual relationships (Lipe and Ortman 2000: 95).

Three approaches have been used to define a community archaeologically: (1) as an area of regular face-to-face interaction (spatial proximity); (2) by the functional complementarity of its institutions; and (3) by its territorial boundaries. The last, control of movement in and out and the establishment of boundaries, is not an important aspect of frontier communities.

To examine Mogollon Rim settlement distribution, I used the database compiled by Joanne Newcomb (1999) to estimate population in the Silver Creek drainage. This database contained 1,024 sites dating between A.D. 400 and 1450. Eliminating early pit houses, the sample initially selected for this study of communities included sites with or without architecture and with any portion of their occupation dating between A.D. 900 and 1150. This time range was broad enough to accommodate the discrepancies caused by various interpretations of ceramic production dates, Haury's phases (1985b), and new dates for the early Carrizo phase (Mills and Herr 1999). Reexamination of dating discrepancies revealed that the sites in this database actually dated between A.D. 1050 and 1150, at the end of the Dry Valley phase and beginning of the early Carrizo phase (1080–1150).

In all, 823 sites met the criteria for inclusion in the database (Table 4.1). The surveys provided 100 percent coverage of 116 square miles, or approximately 13 percent of the 883 square miles of the watershed drained by Silver Creek (Fig. 4.1). To reconstruct communities,

it is best to have survey data from large areal blocks. Although survey coverage was good in the Silver Creek drainage, survey areas were often not continuous. The surveys were biased toward ponderosa pine zones (timber sale surveys) and areas of potential development near cities, lakes, and highways (FLEX projects). Many of the small sites in the Mogollon Rim region have been affected by curation of decorated ceramics from site surfaces, pot hunting, and improvised roads, but usually this damage was not substantial enough to alter broad interpretations of settlement pattern. Rarely has surface collection been so thorough that it renders the site undatable. The great kivas were the most substantially disturbed sites, but despite significant pot hunting their archaeological deposits retained a great deal of integrity.

The excavation of small sites in the area by cultural resource management projects (Fig. 4.2) provided valuable information about the behaviors that occurred at limited activity sites and small habitations in the community. The National Park Service conducted the Corduroy Creek project in the Forestdale Valley (Stafford and Rice 1980); it recorded but did not excavate a masonry great kiva at site AZ Q:13:1 (ASU). The Museum of Northern Arizona excavated seven federal land exchange sites south of Show Low, Arizona (Hartman 1990). The Schoens Dam Flood Control Project (Stebbins and Hartman 1988) was south of Taylor, Arizona, and, nearby, Neily (1984, 1988) surveyed and conducted test excavations at the north end of the Silver Creek drainage, between Snowflake and Mesa Redondo. Two federal land exchange (FLEX) projects, Goodwin and Show Low II, were carried out in the Fools Hollow drainage (S. Dosh 1988) just west of Show Low and approximately 9 km (5.6 miles) north of the Mogollon Rim. A third FLEX project took place in and around Show Low. These excavations of small sites provided essential data that augmented interpretations of life outside the great kiva settlements.

Spatial Proximity of Sites

Murdock's definition of social interaction among community members can be interpreted spatially. If the community is the area where regular face-to-face communication occurs, individuals must live in the vicinity. Spatial proximity often serves as a measure of the level of social interaction (Douglas and Kramer 1992). The intuitive model is one of distance-decay, in which interaction is expected to correlate inversely with distance. Often this is a fair assumption, but because communities can take a wide range of spatial configurations (Adler

Table 4.1. Surveys in the Silver Creek Drainage

Map number, Figure 4.1	Project	No. of sites: project total	No. of sites: Carrizo phase	Reference
1	Aztec	61	44	Green 1984
2	Bagnal	59	56	Neily 1991
3	Bailey	61	30	Hammack 1984
4	Burton	14	12	Gregory 1992a
5	Colbath I	69	65	Greenwald and others 1990
6	Colbath II	16	16	Nightengale and Peterson 1991a
7	Clay Springs	11	9	Nightengale and Peterson 1990a
8	Construction Site	1	0	Logan 1993
9	Dodson	44	42	Peterson and Nightengale 1991
10	East Side Pigs	3	3	Rozen 1988
11	East Side Pigs I	0	0	Newcomb and Weaver 1992
12	East Side Pigs II	0	0	Spalding and Michelson 1993
13	Fence	143	134	Dosh and Maloney 1991
14	Fools Hollow	9	0	Nightengale and Peterson 1991b
15	Heber Habitat – Sundown	4	3	Seymour 1989
16	Lons	86	76	Oliver and Dosh 1992
17	Materials Pit	0	0	Weaver 1989
18	McNeil	23	18	Hohmann and Johnson 1989
19	Heber Habitat – Sackett	13	11	Nightengale and Peterson 1990b
20	Schoens Dam	34	21	Stebbins and Hartman 1988
21	Snowflake	102	48	Lightfoot 1984
22	Snowflake–Mesa Redondo	52	38	Neily 1984
23	Stott	61	54	Ciolek-Torrello 1981
24	Wolf–Mullen	1	0	Gregory 1989a
25	Wolf II	8	2	Gregory 1989b
26	Lewis Canyon	108	88	Dosh and Neff 1996a
27	Sundown South	64	52	Dosh and Neff 1996b
	Cothrun's Kiva	1	1	Herr and others 1999
Total		1048	823	

NOTE: After Newcomb 1999, Table 3.1.

1996a: 5; Stone 1996), it should be tested. Documenting frequent exchanges of information and household material culture is one way to identify habitual interaction and test models of spatial configuration. In the Southwest, the local exchange of sand-tempered plain ceramic cooking or storage vessels provides a useful proxy measure of recurring interaction, but these exchanges are only visible in areas with a great deal of geologic heterogeneity (Abbott and Walsh-Anduze 1995; Duff 1994; Heidke 1998). For Mogollon Rim communities, identification of local exchange of materials and information was not possible because potters used regionally homogenous materials for the manufacture of their utilitarian wares and few whole decorated vessels were recovered from sites in the Silver Creek drainage.

In theory, spatial proximity also measures the exchange of information. Microstylistic analyses have the potential to identify individual artists and groups of crafts people that work together. The assumption is that within a given unit of measurement, in this case the community, there should be greater information flow, and thus greater stylistic homogeneity, within than between communities (Longacre 1970). This proposition is difficult to test because it relies on the archaeologist's ability to differentiate learning frameworks and the medium and context of information display (Van Keuren 2000). Age, sex, and status variably affect the flow of information depending on the complexity of social distinctions made within the community.

Two exploratory data analysis methods were used to identify the spatial clustering of sites within communities: scatter plots and cluster analysis. For the cluster analysis (Wilkinson 1997) in Figure 4.3, I used the Euclidean distance measure and the single linkage method. Because the cluster analysis is interpreting actual

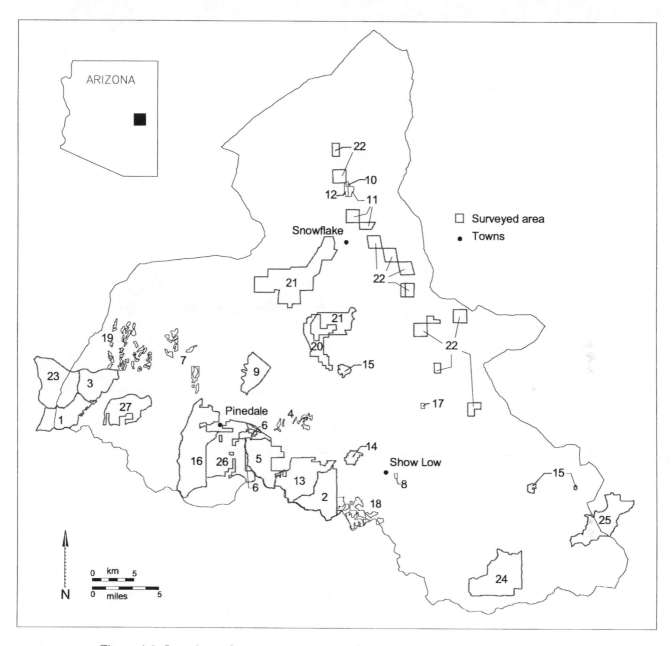

Figure 4.1. Locations of areas surveyed in the Silver Creek drainage; see Table 4.1 for number identifications. (Adapted from Newcomb 1999, Fig. 3.1; graphic by Susan Hall.)

distances between sites, the Euclidean distance (the root mean squared distance) is appropriate. Changing linkage methods (single, median, Ward) did not substantially change the clusters. In only a few instances did isolated sites on the edges of the scatterplot change affiliation. A comparison of linkage methods demonstrates that the clusters are robust. Both scatterplots and cluster analysis are exploratory data techniques, and, in this analysis, the results support the inference of communities on the landscape (Herr 1999).

Functional Classification of Sites

The remaining approach, functional complementarity, is an old anthropological concept, conveying the idea that the whole is greater than the sum of its parts. Complementarity in archaeological communities can be discerned by identifying the context (in public or private space) and type (economic, social, and ritual) of activities performed by residents of the communities.

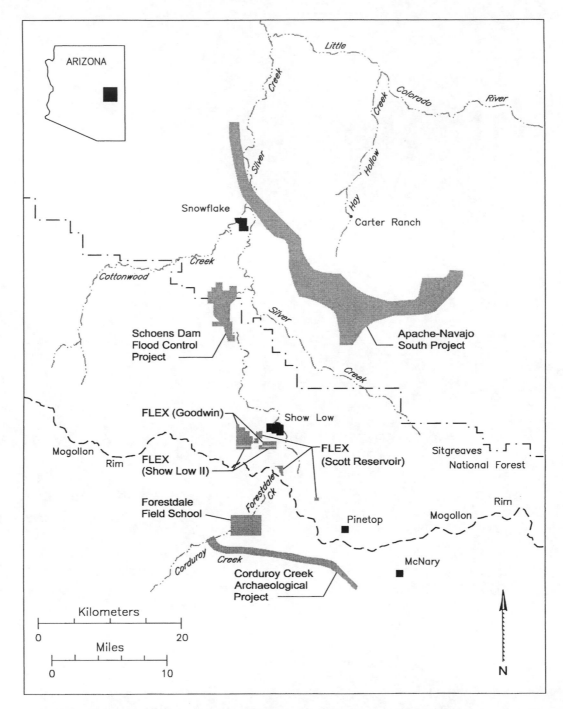

Figure 4.2. The Mogollon Rim region showing the approximate boundaries
of previous survey and archaeological projects. (Graphic by Susan Hall.)

Settlements with public architecture served as centers for nearby residences that lacked communal facilities (Johnson 1975: 286–287). Communities were composed of informal public spaces such as plazas, courtyards, and streets, and shared economic zones on the outskirts. Some of the first communities identified in the South-west were in the Chacoan region, where public architecture such as great houses and great kivas was highly visible. Survey and reconnaissance around "centers" in the San Juan Basin defined patterned clusters of habitations around public architecture as "outlier communities" (Marshall and others 1979; Powers and others 1983).

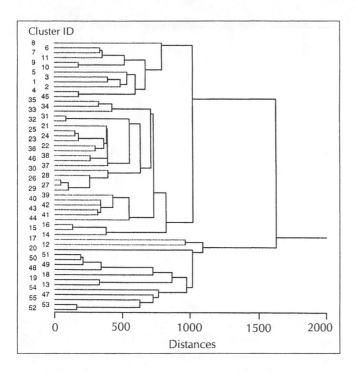

Figure 4.3. Cluster analysis of habitation sites and great kiva sites; see Table 4.3 for cluster identification numbers.

Table 4.2. Survey Site Categories

Site category	No.	Type	Material	No. of rooms
Limited activity*	359			
One-room	123	Room block	Masonry, jacal	1
Small structure	209	Room block	Masonry	2–5
			Jacal	>2
Habitation	98	Room block	Masonry	>5
Great kiva	11	Great kiva	Masonry	
Pit house	23	Pit house	Earthen	

* Includes petroglyphs and water control features.

Even outside the San Juan Basin where great kivas lacked Chacoan formality, these structures served as the focal points of communities (Lightfoot 1984). Platform mounds, ballcourts, and plazas served as public centers in other forms of Southwest communities.

Communities can also be defined through the functional complementarity of different structures in communities. For example, Dean (1996b: 36) distinguished four open (versus cliff) site types: courtyard, plaza, pit house, and ad hoc, as dictated by peculiarities of building locations in the Kayenta area during the Tsegi phase (A.D. 1250–1300). Functional differentiation within communities was not limited to the residential area of the settlement. Not only did the Marana community in the Tucson Basin incorporate functionally distinct architectural types such as platform mounds and residential compounds, it also incorporated distinct productive zones, ranging from irrigated fields on the Santa Cruz floodplain to agave fields and saguaro harvesting areas farther upslope (Fish and Fish 1994: 126). The aggregated fourteenth-century communities of the Rio Grande Valley also integrated diverse productive environments into their communities (Preucel 1988: 83).

Economic, social, and ritual behaviors can be identified with architectural and artifactual information from the surface of late eleventh- and early twelfth-century

sites in the Mogollon Rim region. The distribution of functionally differentiated sites on the landscape, clustered versus unclustered, reveals spatial patterns related to both household and community activities. Definitions of six types of functionally differentiated sites are based on presence or absence of domestic and public architecture, room counts, and wall construction (Table 4.2). Although the site classification takes into account only those structures observable on the surface, the following descriptions are augmented by information from excavations about room size and function. Excavations revealed a variety of ephemeral structures, including ramadas and windbreaks. Extramural hearths indicated that outdoor space was used for food processing and preparation and for various manufacturing activities.

1. Limited activity sites include artifact scatters and petroglyph panels. They vary widely in the size and diversity of their artifact assemblages. Some sites resulted from a single episode of use, such as knapping stations; others like quarries and those with multiple petroglyph panels resulted from repeated short term use. Growths of agave and occasionally the presence of soil and water control features, such as terraces, defined 35 "agave sites." Some artifact scatters may indicate farm plots and the use of trash for fertilizer (Stone 1994; Wilkinson 1982, 1989). The functions of the 359 limited activity sites ranged from procurement to manufacture, subsistence activities, and communication (signified by the petroglyph panels). What these sites have in common is the limited overall duration of their use.

2. Functions of the 123 sites with one room of jacal or masonry cannot be ascertained without excavation, but they may have served as temporary housing during sowing or harvesting, as storage for field implements, or as temporary storage for the harvest. Additionally, these structures may have been land claim markers (Kohler 1992; Sullivan 1994). Of the 23 single-room

structures excavated in the Mogollon Rim region, 15 contained hearths (probably habitation rooms), 2 had mealing bins (perhaps processing rooms), and 4 had no floor features (storage structures). The habitation structures were built of masonry, jacal with or without masonry foundations, or brush. Three of the four storage structures were masonry, the other was jacal. The single brush structure had a hearth and was classified as a habitation. The majority of the structures were insubstantial and, if functioning as residences, were probably not inhabited year-round.

3. The 209 locations with two to five masonry rooms or more than two jacal rooms are grouped together as small-structure sites. Hearths indicate many of these structures were used as habitations. Numerous structures with masonry foundations supported jacal upper walls, as indicated by foundation stones and posthole patterns and by insufficient masonry for full-height walls (Dosh 1988). The large number of small structures on the landscape resulted, in part, from the increased occupancy of the Mogollon Rim region in the late eleventh and early twelfth centuries, but also from the short use life of the structures. Together, one-room and small-structure sites form the majority of early Carrizo phase structures and account for 40 percent of the sites identified by survey.

Ten two-room to five-room structures were excavated by five area projects (Dosh 1988; Neily 1988; Stafford and Rice 1980; Stebbins and Hartman 1988). Seven of the structures were masonry, one was masonry and jacal, and the other two were jacal. Walls were constructed of unshaped stones and were up to 80 cm wide. Four structures were composed solely of habitation rooms, five had both storage and habitation rooms represented, and one structure had rooms of unknown function. Three of the excavated room blocks were breezeway structures (Fig. 4.4), whose enclosed rooms were divided by a centrally placed three-wall room, the breezeway (sites NA 17,271 Component A, NA 18,346 Feature 1, and NA 18,350 Feature 2; Dosh 1988; Stebbins and Hartman 1988). Another structure, site AZ P:16:12 (ASU), had an unusual jagged wall joining the three west rooms to the two east rooms (C. R. Stafford 1980).

4. The 98 habitation sites without great kivas ranged from 6 to 450 rooms; 93 percent of them had 35 or fewer rooms and the remaining 5 had 50, 73, 80, 150, and 450 rooms. The three largest sites were multicomponent, with early dates at A.D. 1100 and abandonment dates in the fourteenth or early fifteenth centuries.

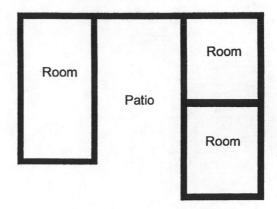

Figure 4.4. Schematic breezeway structure. (Graphic by Susan Hall.)

Two sites with six masonry rooms have been sampled or excavated (Hartman 1990); both had habitation and storage rooms. Walls were constructed of single-width and double-width masonry coursing and post-reinforced jacal with or without masonry foundations. Excavators estimated the full masonry walls rose between 1.4 m and 1.7 m above the structure floor. Unshaped and minimally shaped masonry was wet-laid in mortar. Extramural features included ancillary jacal structures and storage pits. One room at site NA 18,422 may have been used for both habitation and food processing. Excavations concentrated on architecture; the density of trash remains unknown, but duration of occupation was probably not particularly long as none of the rooms showed signs of remodeling.

5. Settlements with great kivas (11 in the survey) were the ritual foci of the dispersed communities of the Mogollon Rim region in the late eleventh and early twelfth centuries. Great kivas were usually associated with large settlements, although one isolated great kiva has been identified. Cothrun's Kiva, with five to six rooms, had the smallest room block of the great kiva settlements; others had between 8 to 65 rooms.

Rooms at four great kiva sites have been excavated: Carter Ranch Pueblo, Cothrun's Kiva, Hough's Great Kiva Site, and Tla Kii Pueblo. The two excavated rooms at Hough's Great Kiva and two of the three excavated rooms at Cothrun's (the third was vandalized) were habitation rooms. Tla Kii Pueblo had 13 identified habitation rooms and 6 storage rooms. Carter Ranch Pueblo, whose occupation extended slightly later than that at the other pueblos, had 15 habitation rooms, 5 storage rooms, 1 habitation and ceremonial room, and 1 ceremonial room.

6. Twenty-three pit house settlements had some portion of their occupations dating to the time between A.D. 900 and 1200: 14 sites had beginning dates before the eleventh century and 8 of the remaining 9 had beginning dates in the eleventh century. Three or four of these sites may legitimately have been late pit house settlements, but the others represent poorly dated multi-component sites. Late pit houses have been excavated in several areas along the Middle Little Colorado drainage (Ambler and Olson 1977; Gumerman 1988; Harrill 1973; Young 1998a). Early pit house settlements there were part of a strategy of residential mobility, in which occupants moved from the Little Colorado River to higher areas toward the Mogollon Rim to use the resources available in diverse elevation and vegetation zones (Young 1996a). It is possible that the Silver Creek pit houses, and some of the other one-room and small structures in the Mogollon Rim region, were part of the mobility strategies of people whose primary habitations were outside the Silver Creek drainage.

MOGOLLON RIM COMMUNITIES

As the only integrative architecture on the Mogollon Rim in the late eleventh and early twelfth centuries, circular great kivas served as the public foci of communities. Accordingly, they are considered appropriate anchors for defining the spatial clusters of settlements. A series of scatterplots shows a comparison of the distribution of limited activity, one-room, small-structure, and habitation sites to the distribution of great kiva sites. The results are restricted by the boundaries of the survey areas. The best results from the community study came from the southern portion of the Silver Creek drainage, the only area with enough survey coverage to identify site clusters.

The cluster analyses and the scatter plots show that limited activity sites, one-room sites, and small structures of jacal or masonry did not cluster around the great kivas. They were distributed evenly across the surveyed area. The masonry structures with more than five rooms did show a tendency to cluster and these clusters of habitations around the great kivas are interpreted as the residential cores of distinct communities. The pattern is not as simple as one great kiva to one cluster of habitations, however. Some communities had more than one great kiva, others had none. Figures 4.5 through 4.9 show the location of the community study and the settlement clusters in the southern portion of the Silver Creek drainage.

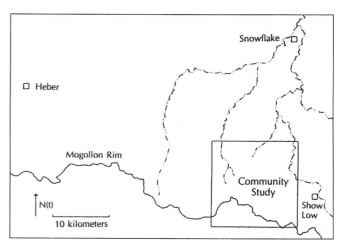

Figure 4.5. Location of the community study.

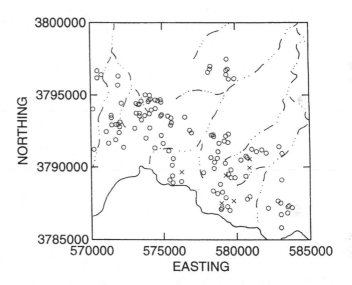

Figure 4.6. Distribution of limited activity sites (o) and great kiva sites (x) in the community study area. Grid indicates meters in the Universal Transverse Mercator Zone 12.

Considering the short occupation span of the excavated great kivas, it is possible that when two great kivas were within community boundaries, they were used sequentially. A similar chronological concern applies to habitation sites. The scatter plots provide clues as to how settlements were patterned on the landscape during the 70- to 100-year period assigned to the early Carrizo phase, but they are static images of what were rapidly shifting settlements. A scenario of relatively stable integrative centers surrounded by small settlements of mobile households has been described for the Mesa Verde region during this period (Adler 1996a) and it is an appropriate model for the Mogollon Rim region.

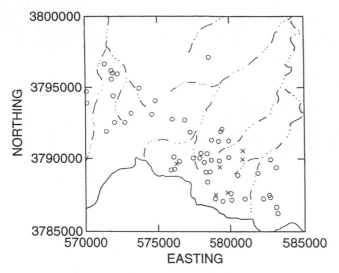

Figure 4.7. Distribution of one-room sites (o) and great kiva sites (x) in the community study area. (For grid, see Fig. 4.6 caption.)

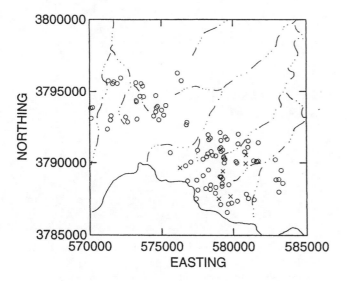

Figure 4.8. Distribution of small-structure sites (o) and great kiva sites (x) in the community study area. (For grid, see Fig. 4.6 caption.)

Three communities have boundaries not affected by the survey limits (Table 4.3). Communities A and D had two great kivas each; Communities B and C had one great kiva each, and Community E had none. Areas around Communities D and E were not completely surveyed. Smaller settlements existed both within and outside the boundaries of these habitation clusters. No sites with architecture were found in the high elevations and rocky slopes of Juniper Ridge, shown by the gap in the schematic community scatter plots.

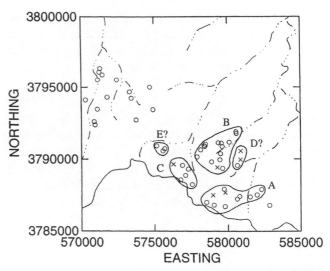

Figure 4.9. Distribution of habitation sites (o) and great kiva sites (x) in the community study area, showing three complete (A, B, C) and two partial (D, E) communities. (For grid, see Fig. 4.6 caption.)

The distribution of habitation settlements was not completely random, and proximity played an important role in the maintenance of economic, social, or ritual relationships of Mogollon Rim migrants. Habitation settlements formed clusters around the great kivas, and there was a value attributed to proximity to other habitations and to the ritual structure. The locations of small-structure and limited activity sites show less patterning on the landscape and reflect choices about agricultural potential and wild plant and animal procurement. Their short occupation spans provide evidence of patterns of extensive exploitation of land and its resources.

Community Centers

The dispersed community pattern and short duration of settlements indicate a mobile population during the late eleventh and early twelfth centuries. Circular great kivas provided a stable focal point for these dispersed habitations, farmsteads, and limited activity sites. The room blocks at great kiva settlements were generally the largest habitations on the landscape at this time and had the longest occupation. But even these settlements were probably not occupied for more than two or three generations. In communities with more than one great kiva, the great kivas may have been used consecutively.

Excavations have been conducted at five great kiva sites in the Mogollon Rim region. Much of our understanding of the late eleventh and early twelfth centuries

Table 4.3. Description of South Silver Creek Communities

Cluster	Community size (km)	Great Kiva site (ASM AZ)	Cluster ID	Habitation site (ASM AZ)	Cluster ID	No. of rooms at habitation sites
A	4.7 x 1.9	P:16:160	4	P:16:96	1	133
		P:16:153	2	P:16:128	45	
				P:16:154	3	
				P:16:166	5	
				P:16:176	6	
				P:16:177	7	
				P:16:197	9	
				P:16:199	10	
				P:16:200	11	
B	3.8 x 2.5	P:16:99	38	P:12:47	21	155
				P:12:53	22	
				P:12:57	23	
				P:12:65	24	
				P:12:71	25	
				P:12:79	26	
				P:12:83	27	
				P:12:85	28	
				P:12:97	29	
				P:12:99	30	
				P:12:113	31	
				P:12:114	32	
				P:16:95	36	
				P:16:97	37	
				P:16:137	46	
C	2.5 x 1.6	P:16:112	39	P:16:119	40	63
				P:16:122	41	
				P:16:123	42	
				P:16:124	43	
				P:16:126	44	
D?	Incomplete	P:12:128	33	P:16:91	35	11
		P:16:90	34			
E?	Incomplete	None		P:12:248	14	31
				P:12:258	15	
				P:12:259	16	

NOTE: Missing sites (Cluster ID 8, 12, 13, 17–20, 45, 47–55) could not be assigned to communities.

comes from the artifact assemblages of these sites. Tla Kii Pueblo was excavated by Emil Haury (1985d), the University of Arizona Archaeological Field School, and Apache laborers in the summers of 1940 and 1941. Carter Ranch was excavated by Paul Martin and his staff and students in the summers of 1961 and 1962 (Martin and others 1964). Three circular great kiva sites were excavated by the Silver Creek Archaeological Research Project (SCARP) during summers in 1995, 1996, and 1997 (Herr and others 1999). These last three, Hough's Great Kiva (AZ P:16:112 ASM), AZ P:16:160 (ASM), and Cothrun's Kiva (AZ P:12:277 ASM) provide the updated methods and comparative information needed to

integrate the previously excavated sites into reconstructions of regional sociopolitical organization. Published and unpublished data from these pueblos are reviewed in order to understand site construction, occupation, and abandonment histories.

Together, these five excavated great kiva sites are positioned along a north-south swath through the study region. Tla Kii Pueblo, in the Forestdale Valley, is 13 km (8 miles) south of the Mogollon Rim at an elevation of approximately 1,846 m (6,000 feet) above sea level in a narrow valley about 6.5 km (4 miles) long. The environment today is one of hills enclosing a series of terraces suitable for agriculture. Tla Kii Pueblo is on the two oldest terraces above the creek and below a bluff. Ponderosa pine and manzanita grow on the hills above the site, and the early settlers of the valley recall seeing willow along the creek (Haury 1985d: 19).

Moving north, Hough's Great Kiva and site AZ P:16:160 (ASM) are approximately 3.4 km (2 miles) apart and within 1.5 km (about a mile) of the Mogollon Rim among ponderosa pine, Utah and alligator-bark juniper, and Gambel oak at elevations of 1,996 m (6,085 feet) and 1,993 m (6,075 feet), respectively. Walter Hough photographed the site of Hough's Great Kiva in 1901. The photo, taken before lumbering activities in the 1920s, shows a shrubby oak woodland rather than the dense ponderosa pine forest that now characterizes the area (Hough 1903, Plate 17). Cothrun's Kiva is approximately 11 km (6.8 miles) north-north-west of Hough's Great Kiva and site AZ P:16:160, at 1,908 m (5,815 feet) above sea level. Clusters of pinyon and juniper and grassy open areas characterize these lower elevations. Hough's Great Kiva and AZ P:16:160 are located in environments with small ridges and ephemeral washes. Cothrun's Kiva is on a broad mesa top.

Carter Ranch Pueblo, about 16 km (10 miles) south of the Little Colorado River, is on a mesa ranging between 1,768 m and 1,951 m (5,800 to 6,400 feet) in elevation. Vegetation includes juniper trees, grama grass, prickly pear, and rabbit brush (Rinaldo 1964a: 15). Cattail pollen and algae in archaeological samples from the nearby Schoens Dam Flood Control Project area indicate that Show Low Creek may once have had areas of standing brackish water (Hartman and others 1988: 223).

Chronology

The great kiva pueblos date to the period of the first large-scale occupation of the Mogollon Rim region, between A.D. 1050–1080 and 1150. The ceramic assemblages from most of them contain Red Mesa Black-on-white (including Black Mesa style), Reserve Black-on-white, and Snowflake Black-on-white pottery, indicative of the early Carrizo phase (Mills and Herr 1999). Seven tree-ring dates from Hough's Great Kiva include one cutting date of 1123–1124 from a beam in Room 1. According to Jeffrey Dean, the other six 'vv' dates cluster between 1119 and 1123. These dates accord well with those from Tla Kii Pueblo (Haury 1985d) and other sites in the area (Dosh 1988; Doyel 1980; Neily 1988). Six samples comprising 12 corn kernels from roof fall in Rooms 1 and 4 at Cothrun's Kiva were

dated by the AMS radiocarbon lab at the University of Arizona (AA28738–AA28743; Herr 1999). At a 2σ range, approximately 90 percent of the calibrated curve falls between A.D. 880 and 1050 (Ramsey 1995; Stuiver and Kra 1986). The remaining 10 percent of the curve falls between 1080 and 1160. Ceramic cross-dating of contexts across the site indicates that dates before 1000 are unlikely.

The three great kiva sites in the Silver Creek drainage, Hough's Great Kiva, Cothrun's Kiva, and site AZ P:16:160 (ASM), were inhabited for little more than a single generation. Mogollon Rim region community centers with agglomerated room blocks were occupied longer, as exemplified by Tla Kii Pueblo. At Carter Ranch, the architectural, ceramic, and tree-ring evidence indicates that it was inhabited for well over a hundred years, from the late eleventh century into the thirteenth century. Cothrun's Kiva and Tla Kii Pueblo had been previously occupied, but their late eleventh- and early twelfth-century settlements were the most substantial and the latest.

HOUGH'S GREAT KIVA SITE

Hough's Great Kiva has long been known in the literature of the Mogollon Rim (Hough 1903). In 1901 Hough visited the site at least long enough to make a sketch map and to take a photograph from the center of the great kiva out toward the room block. He did not mention excavating the site. Back at the Smithsonian Institution his sketch map was redrafted into a depiction of a massive rectangular room block and a structure with a wheellike plan of two concentric walls with spokes between, a site structure that might be easily mistaken as Chacoan (Herr and others 1999). His description mislocated this "small site near Linden" (Hough 1903: 298), situating it two miles west, rather than two miles south, of Linden (Pottery Hill). The site was also mentioned by Spier (1918: 361) as Site 220 and by Reagan (1930: 113) as Site 126. Both perpetuated the error in position. Site 126 is Linden Pueblo, but Hough's Great Kiva is often included in these old references as "the small site near Linden."

The entryway to the circular great kiva was oriented to the southeast and the structure was downslope from the ⊓-shaped room block, which had a remarkably formalized plan (Fig. 4.10). The room block also faced southeast. An ashy midden was less than 20 m east of the two structures.

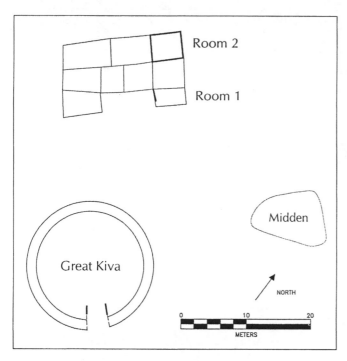

Figure 4.10. Plan of Hough's Great Kiva Site. (Graphic by Doug Gann.)

Room Block

The room block was atop a small ridge overlooking the great kiva. The rubble of the 9-room structure measures 28.2 m by 17.3 m. Walls were double-coursed and nearly 0.5 m wide. Evidence from the excavation shows that the back (northwest) and northeast walls of the room block were constructed in one building episode. The dated tree-ring specimen from Room 2 is contemporaneous with the tree-ring dates from Room 1.

Rooms in the Mogollon Rim region were large compared with contemporaneous rooms in pueblos to the east and north. Those at Hough's Great Kiva Site were among the largest, and habitation, storage, and manufacturing activities were *all* performed in these general purpose rooms. Two rooms on the northeast side of the room block were excavated by SCARP. Room 1 contained a circular clay-lined hearth, a large corrugated storage or cooking jar, ground stone artifacts, burned seeds, and a *puki* (turntable for forming ceramic vessels) on the floor, providing evidence of multiple activities. The internal abutting wall on the west side of Room 2 created a space one meter wide that was probably used for storage. The remainder of Room 2, with its large, rectangular, slab-lined hearth, was used for habitation.

Great Kiva

The circular great kiva was an impressive structure, measuring about 24 m from wall to wall and 20 m across the floor. Unlike earlier earthen great kivas in the region (like Bluff Site and Bear Ruin), this semisubterranean structure was built of both earth and masonry. Above grade, the walls were about 1 m high, of compound construction, and built with massive stones; below grade, the walls were earth and plaster. A double bench encircled the inner circumference of the great kiva, stopping only at the ramped entry to the southeast. No floor features appeared in the 8 square meters of excavation in the floor. The great kiva had full standing walls and bench architecture, which suggest that the structure was built to support a roof. Although evidence is controversial, I suggest that it had some sort of wooden superstructure (Chapter 5). Artifacts on the floor, including a large San Pedro point, indicate that the structure was completed and used. Portions of the roofing material may have been scavenged before the structure was burned, which might explain why there was not more substantial evidence of roofing even though small pieces of charcoal and daub were ubiquitous in the great kiva fill.

The great kiva was entered from the southeast via a long ramp. A one-course wide wall marked the edge of the bench on each side of the 3–m wide entry. Construction fill was piled against these small walls. The center of the ramp was flat, but the overall cross-section was U-shaped.

Midden

Today the midden is 70 cm deep and 23 m by 21 m across. The density of ceramics in the midden is approximately 1,060 sherds per cubic meter. No stratigraphy was visible and the bottom of the midden was mixed into native soil. A cluster of turkey bones appeared to be an individual dumping event.

Comments

The duration of occupation at the Hough's Great Kiva settlement was probably short, but year round. No rooms were added to the original construction of the room block, nor were satellite structures built in the immediate vicinity. The dividing wall in the west half of Room 2 may indicate an episode of remodeling, but neither Rooms 1 or 2 had more than a single floor surface and wall plastering was not preserved.

Based on tree-ring dates and ceramic cross-dating, the settlement probably was occupied for 20 to 30 years. Year-round occupation longer than a few years is indicated by the density of trash fill in the approximately 179 cubic meters of midden and the presence of burials in the midden.

The lack of trash fill in either excavated room and the fact that only a few artifacts remained on the floor denote rapid abandonment. Charred roof beams on the floor of Room 1 showed that burning closely followed the last occupation of the room, and Room 2 also appeared to have been burned. Apparently the abandonment of the pueblo involved the intentional burning of room structures and perhaps even the great kiva itself (Herr 1995: 21).

SITE AZ P:16:160 (ASM)

Site AZ P:16:160, first recorded by Neily (1991), had a settlement structure like and was contemporaneous with Hough's Great Kiva. The 56–m by 54–m settlement contained three major features: a circular great kiva, a room block, and a midden (Fig. 4.11). Neily (1991) recorded a depression near the great kiva as possibly a pit house. An extensive but shallow midden was about 20 m north of these structures. Sampling of the midden and great kiva provided evidence for comparison with other SCARP sites, but no excavation was conducted in the room block.

Room Block

The large room block measured more than 23 m by 17 m, but the layout and orientation of the room block are uncertain because a logging road over the top of the pueblo destroyed wall alignments and trees obscured other portions of the structure. It had an estimated 10 to 15 rooms; visible walls are shown in Figure 4.11.

Great Kiva

One of the more remarkable features of the circular great kiva is the visible architecture: four courses of masonry still standing above grade on the north side. The great kiva had a diameter of 15.5 m, smaller than that of Hough's Great Kiva, but the wall construction was similar. The double wall was formed of minimally shaped sandstone blocks wet-laid around an earthen core. A low clay bench encircled the interior. The top of the bench was not faced, but the vertical face may have been supported by medium sized blocks. Most of

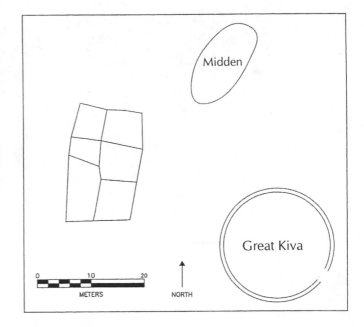

Figure 4.11. Plan of site AZ P:16:160 (ASM). (Graphic by Doug Gann.)

a Reserve Black-on-white bowl was found in the bench construction material; the vessel may have been a ritual offering during the building of the great kiva. The communal structure was originally thought to have had two entrances (Neily 1991; see also Doyel and Lekson 1992, Fig. 2-4 *top*), but after more intensive study, it now appears that the structure had only one entrance, to the southeast. Ramp construction was similar to that at Hough's Great Kiva. The boundary between the bench and entryway was defined by a single-course wall on each side. Construction fill was placed against these thin walls, creating a ramp with a wide U-shaped cross section.

The great kiva was not burned. No charcoal fragments or impressed daub pieces were in the fill. The walls were massive and high enough to suggest that they may have been intended to support a roof, but floor preparation was minimal. The structure may have been unroofed or incomplete, because no floor was visible in the center of the kiva.

Midden

The present midden area is extensive, measuring 8 m by 17 m, but it is less than 20 cm deep and not well developed. The midden has a low to medium density of artifacts, with approximately 510 sherds per cubic meter.

Comments

Because of limited excavation, knowledge of the occupation at site AZ P:16:160 is not as comprehensive as that for occupation at Hough's Great Kiva Site. The settlement may have existed for a shorter time than originally intended by its inhabitants. The established midden area was shallow and not well developed, artifact density was low throughout, the great kiva was unroofed or not completed, and the kiva was certainly not ceremonially burned when abandoned. The walls were lower than those at both Hough's Great Kiva and Cothrun's Kiva sites, and the floor was ephemeral and only discernible close to the structure wall. It is interesting that this seemingly short-lived settlement was in the same community cluster as site AZ P:16:153 (ASM), perhaps indicating that the latter was a more substantial community center before or after the occupation of site AZ P:16:160.

COTHRUN'S KIVA SITE

Cothrun's Kiva (AZ P:12:277 ASM) conforms only partially to the picture of great kiva structure exemplified by Hough's Great Kiva and AZ P:16:160. The site covers an area approximately 220 m by 240 m on the high point of a mesa above a tributary of Bull Hollow Draw and bounds an extensive and, in places, dense scatter of surface artifacts. A circular great kiva, a room block, a small ill-defined room block, and a midden form the core of the site (Fig. 4.12). No small structures have been located in the immediate vicinity.

Radiocarbon dates intimate that Cothrun's may be one of the earliest great kivas in the region. Factors supporting the possibility of a component predating the Carrizo phase occupation include: (1) a slab-lined baking pit that precedes the accumulation of midden materials; (2) numerous metates within the wall fall; (3) a basin metate in the midden; and (4) pit features below Rooms 1 and 4. Less conclusive perhaps are Kana'a Black-on-white ceramics (with production dates of A.D. 825–1000) identified in an artifact scatter near the room block. Finally, the dense clusters of artifacts in the scatter that now forms a large portion of the site may indicate subsurface features such as pit houses. The satellite building southeast of the room block represents another construction event, but its temporal relationship to other structures has not been established. Until these features are excavated, it is impossible to tell if occupation was continuous. The SCARP investigations of the great kiva and room block concentrated on the latest period of occupation.

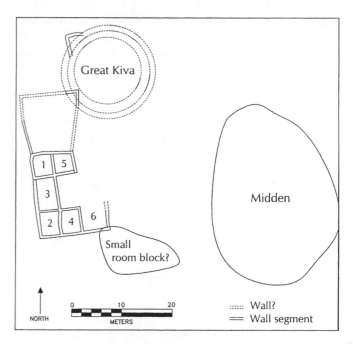

Figure 4.12. Plan of Cothrun's Kiva Site. (Graphic by Doug Gann.)

Room Blocks

The main room block is a ⊏ -shaped structure, oriented to the east, with five extant rooms. The foundation level and the first course of a sixth room may be the remains of unfinished construction, a room that was stone robbed for the nearby outlying structure, or perhaps a wall enclosing an exterior space. The outlying room block, less than two meters southeast of Room 6, was once a two- to three-room structure but now is rubble severely disturbed by pot hunting. Wall alignments are unclear and no excavations were conducted in this area. The proximity of the smaller structure to the larger room block and the lack of stone robbing on the smaller structure may indicate it was built by people moving to the settlement after the larger room block was occupied.

As at Hough's Great Kiva, rooms in the main pueblo were large. Rooms 1 and 2 were back rooms on the west side of the pueblo, Room 4 was a front room on the east side. An east doorway between Rooms 1 and 5 had been closed prior to the abandonment of the room, but an open doorway to Room 3 was in the south wall of Room 1. An open doorway in Room 4 led to the space called Room 6.

Floor assemblages were of minimal use for determining activities in the rooms. Artifacts on the floor were mainly waste materials, including sherds, lithic debitage, and manos without metates (Room 4). Architecture and floor features gave a better picture of room function, particularly the floors and hearths of Rooms 1 and 4 that showed these spaces were used for habitation. Use of Room 2 remains uncertain; although care was taken plastering the walls of Room 2, the floor was not well prepared and had been destroyed by vandals.

All rooms appear to have been one story and activities occurred on roof surfaces. In Room 1, large pieces of the roof packing and plaster still carried remains of the roof surface. Associated trash indicated vessel storage and the processing, drying, or storage of corn took place on the roof. Carbonized corn and corncobs were in the roof fall of Room 4. The main room block was abandoned quickly, perhaps even all at once. Rooms 1 and 4 were burned after abandonment and no trash was tossed into the empty rooms.

Great Kiva

The wall-to-wall diameter of the great kiva is 17.5 m and the bench-to-bench diameter is about 14.5 m. Unlike other local great kivas, this structure had a northwest orientation. The subterranean portion was circular, but above ground the compound masonry walls (1.0–1.4 m high) formed a modified keyhole shape. The structure was excavated 1.02 m below grade, and 14 square meters of trenches extended over the central portion of the southeast quadrant. The only floor feature located was a small pit, not big enough to hold a large roof support.

Midden

The large midden southeast of the two room blocks measures 24 m by 25 m and is approximately 50 cm deep at its highest point. The density of ceramics is high, with 2,123 sherds per cubic meter. During excavation a slab-lined pit, possibly a cooking pit, was discovered below the midden, suggesting previous activities had occurred in this exterior space. Similar pits were found at Tla Kii Pueblo (Haury 1985d: 57) and at site NA 18,343 (Feature 13; Dosh 1988: 63–64).

Courtyard

An unusual architectural feature at Cothrun's was the attachment of the great kiva to the room block by a series of walls enclosing what we have called an outdoor "courtyard." The only opening into this space was in the southeast wall. Occupants of the room block would have had to go around the back of the room

block-courtyard complex to enter the great kiva from the northwest. Correspondingly, visitors to the great kiva would not have had access to the courtyard or room block without going around the great kiva. The limited access to the courtyard seemingly indicates that this space was used by residents of the pueblo and that it was not part of the ritual space of the great kiva.

Comments

The established midden, similar in size to that at Hough's Great Kiva Site, signified year-round occupation at Cothrun's Kiva settlement. Remodeling occurred in all rooms but was not substantial. In Room 1 the poles around the east doorway and the capped posthole of Feature 4 may have been added after initial construction to support the roof. The east doorway was sealed, indicating a change in relationship between the inhabitants of Rooms 1 and 5 or a change in room function. Three layers of wall plaster in Room 2 reflect at least two episodes of replastering. The west wall of Room 4 was replastered at least once.

The process of abandonment and room collapse was different in each excavated room, although in each case the abandonment was quick and intentional. Artifacts near the floor were associated with collapsed roofs. Although several whole vessels were in the rafters or on the roof at abandonment, the limited number of artifacts on the floor indicates that the rooms were cleaned out when abandoned. None of the excavated rooms had been filled with trash and Rooms 1 and 4 were burned at, or shortly after, residential abandonment. Room 2 did not appear to have been burned and perhaps its roof had been removed before the burning of the pueblo after abandonment.

TLA KII PUEBLO

At Tla Kii Pueblo, excavated in 1940 and 1941, Haury (1985b) defined three chronological phases: Corduroy, Dry Valley, and Carrizo, with dates between A.D. 800 and 1150. The major occupation occurred during the Carrizo phase and included the pueblo, the great kiva, one storage structure, and possibly an unfinished kiva. Trash had been deposited in a midden northeast of the room block and in rooms and storage pits. Haury (1985d: 46) felt that the midden was too small for the scale of occupation indicated by the architecture and suggested that pueblo occupants may have tossed their trash into Forestdale Creek. Evidence of earlier occupation was abundant. Three early pit houses were discov-

Table 4.7. Tla Kii Pueblo Chronology

Provenience	Specimen number	Tree-ring date	Construction phase*	Provenience	Specimen number	Tree-ring date	Construction phase*
Room 1	FST-52	1103vv	3	Room 20	FST-175	1100vv	
Room 2	FST-93	1089vv	3		FST-174	1102vv	
	FST-92	1093vv			FST-314	1103vv	
	FST-94	1093vv			FST-172	1104vv	
Room 3			3	Room 21	FST-312	1102vv	6
Room 4			3	Kiva 1	FST-60	1008vv	N/A
Room 5			4		FST-70	1069+vv	
Room 6			5		FST-62	1070vv	
Room 7	FST-54	1095vv	5		FST-55b	1082vv	
Room 7a	FST-61	1107vv			FST-56	1088vv	
Room 8			5		FST-55a	1102vv	
Room 9			5		FST-58	1105vv	
Room 10			5		FST-57	1114vv	
Room 11			5		FST-59	1115vv	
Room 12			5	Kiva 2	FST-66b	1035vv	N/A
Room 13			2	Storage Pit 2	FST-87	1096vv	N/A
Room 14			2		FST-90	1106r	
Room 15			2		FST-85	1107vv	
Room 16	FST-107	1066vv	1		FST-86	1107vv	
	FST-185	1088vv			FST-88	1110vv	
	FST-316	1110vv			FST-91	1110vv	
Room 17			1	Storage Pit 3	FST-98	1087vv	N/A
Room 18	FST-305	1099vv	1		FST-97	1093v	
	FST-77	1104v		SW Broadside	FST-197	1052vv	N/A
Room 19	FST-315	1082vv	1		FST-183	1080vv	
	FST-74	1104vv			FST-177	1084vv	
	FST-308	1106vv			FST-179	1084vv	
Room 20	FST-171	1087vv	6		FST-178	1096vv	
	FST-176	1096vv			FST-120	1100vv	
	FST-111	1100v			FST-121	1102vv	

* Based on Vickery 1941

NOTE: Storage Pit 3 was underneath the pueblo, but Haury (1985d: 59) questioned the context of the cutting date sample.

ered outside the pueblo walls. Five storage pits and a hearth were associated with an early occupation. Bear Ruin (AZ P:16:1 ASM), which dates between A.D. 600 and 800, is less than 500 m north of Tla Kii. Old footing walls under Rooms 13 and 15 revealed remodeling within the pueblo. Haury (1985d: 46) observed that these walls were built directly on sterile soil, whereas many other pueblo walls, such as those of Rooms 20 and 21, were built on a layer of trash.

Tree-ring dates from the room block provide the two cutting dates of A.D. 1100 and 1104 (Table 4.7, Fig. 4.13). The mode of the distribution of the other tree-ring dates indicates that much of the pueblo was constructed in the first decade of the twelfth century.

Room block		Kiva 1	
111	0	111	45
110	00223344467	110	25
109	33569		
108	2789	108	28
		107	0
106	6	106	9
		100	8

Figure 4.13. Stem and leaf diagrams of cutting dates (underlined) and noncutting dates from A.D. 1008 to 1115 from the room block and Kiva 1 at Tla Kii Pueblo. "Stems" represent decades and "leaves" indicate specific years.

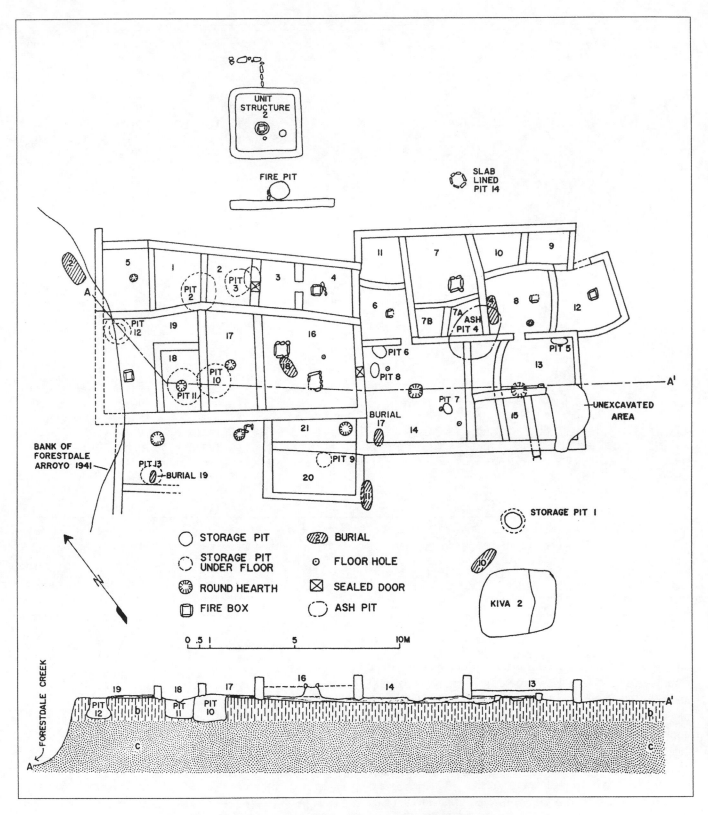

Figure 4.14. Plan and section of Tla Kii Pueblo, "showing some construction details and relationships to subfloor features: *a*, silt and refuse; *b*, black clay; *c*, yellow sandy silt." (Haury 1985d: 35, Fig. 14; copyright The Arizona Board of Regents, reprinted by permission of the University of Arizona Press.)

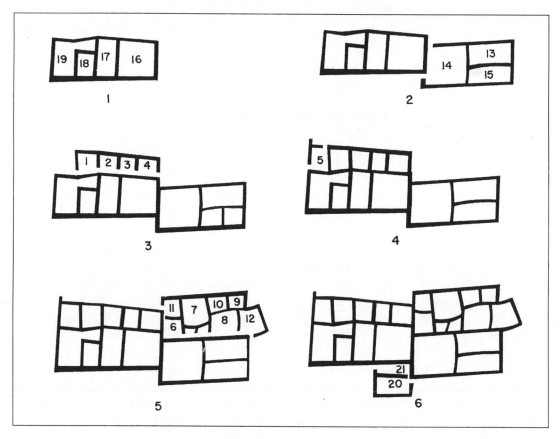

Figure 4.15. Tla Kii Pueblo building episodes. (Haury 1985d, Fig. 15; copyright The Arizona Board of Regents, reprinted by permission of the University of Arizona Press.)

Room Block

The pueblo was an agglomeration of at least 21 rooms (Fig. 4.14). All of them were excavated completely except Room 15, where a small cluster of trees hampered access. Field school assistant Parke Vickery (1941) deciphered the construction sequence of the pueblo (Table 4.7; Fig. 4.15). Bond-and-abutment patterns and distinctive masonry styles across the pueblo revealed six building episodes. Construction started in the northwest portion of the pueblo, and one to seven rooms were added in each subsequent enlargement. The internal subdivisions of these rooms may not have occurred with the initial building of the rooms. For example, Haury described Room 18 as an afterthought to Room 19. Room 13 was subdivided after at least one episode of floor remodeling to create Room 15. Tree-ring dates indicate that only short intervals elapsed between building episodes (Haury 1985d: 37).

Rooms at Tla Kii Pueblo showed slightly more functional variability than those of the SCARP great kiva

sites, and the pueblo apparently had a longer occupation, indicated in part by more evidence of remodeling. Most of the rooms at Tla Kii Pueblo were used for habitation. At some point during the pueblo occupation, all of the large west-southwest "front" rooms had hearths (Rooms 13, 14, 16, 17, and 19). Some of the subdivided areas within the rooms were assigned room numbers by the excavators but not all of these areas had hearths (Rooms 7a, 7b, 15 and 18) and probably represent storage or processing areas within larger rooms. Back rooms were smaller; the plan is reminiscent of pueblos in the Four Corners area where household units had one large room paired with two smaller back rooms. However, at Tla Kii Pueblo six of these back rooms had hearths (Rooms 4, 5, 6, 8, and 12), suggesting that they, too, functioned as habitation rooms. Back rooms 1, 3, 9, 10, and 11 and front Room 20 lacked floor features and perhaps were storage rooms.

Haury's identification of a small masonry structure northeast of the room block, constructed on top of early Pit House 3, as a possible menstrual hut is difficult to prove. Because this small structure (1.65 m by 2.25 m) had few sherds, had no hearth or other floor features, and was near the room block, it may have been auxiliary storage space. As a one-room structure it is, however, subject to all the same questions of function as posed by field houses.

The best evidence of the generalized activities that took place in the pueblo came from three rooms on the southeast side. Rooms 13, 14, and 15 each had a hearth and was used for habitation. Other activities in these rooms included storage, manufacturing, and processing. Three storage pits in Room 14 (Pits 6, 7, and 8) and one in the east corner of Room 13 (Pit 5) were contemporaneous with the occupation of the rooms. A trough metate with one open end was in Room 14 and a trough metate with two open ends was in Room 13; four manos came from these rooms.

Before the wall creating Room 15 was built in Room 13, an internal wall was dismantled and a new floor (Floor 1) was built, sealing over a potter's work area on Floor 2 (Chapter 5). Lithic manufacturing was represented by a hammerstone and two point blanks. Debitage was not collected in these excavations, which were conducted during the 1940s, but unworked red stone and two red stone beads from Room 15 indicated that ornaments were manufactured in this room. Ochre and red paint were in Room 13. Worked bone indicated bone ring manufacture. The purpose of a shaped slab painted with red pigment is uncertain.

The floors used just before the abandonment of the pueblo lacked this type of well-preserved assemblage. Like the rooms at Hough's Great Kiva and Cothrun's Kiva sites, they were cleaned of most of the useful artifacts before the occupants left the room block. The three rooms at the southeast end of Tla Kii Pueblo provided the best glimpse of daily life in the late eleventh and early twelfth centuries in the Mogollon Rim region.

Great Kiva

The great kiva, approximately 18.2 m in diameter from wall to wall and 15.8 m in diameter from bench face to bench face (Fig. 4.16), was located southwest of the room block. It was discovered in the profile of a small gully. Approximately two-thirds of the structure had been cut away and then tons of floodplain silt had been deposited on top of it by Forestdale Creek. What remained of the structure was excavated entirely in 1941. In 1998 the body of the great kiva was almost entirely gone and only the ramp remained intact. From

the 1941 excavations it is clear that this was the most formalized of the Mogollon Rim region great kivas excavated so far. The walls are preserved only a few courses above surface grade. On the south side of the structure, the double walls are nearly 1 m thick. On the north, the walls are only a single course wide and approximately 0.5 m thick.

Entrance to the structure was through a long ramp to the southeast. The ramp descended by low steps marked by log risers. Inside the great kiva, a bench 1.5 m wide was built around the entire circumference of the structure, interrupted only for the ramp entry. The bench was faced vertically with small stones. The floor was made of an even, hard-packed clay. Floor features included a hearth and three postholes in a pattern from which a fourth can be extrapolated. Smaller postholes were in the bench near the entryway. Burned material in the fill indicated the presence of a roof over at least the body of the structure if not the ramp (Haury 1985d: 47–52). Two "alcove" rooms were not excavated on the south side of the great kiva. Such spaces are traditionally interpreted as storage for food or ritual paraphernalia but, according to Mike Jacobs in 1998, the small size and irregular shape of these rooms may mean that they functioned to buttress the walls and superstructure of the great kiva.

Comments

The room block and great kiva were used during the most substantial occupation of Tla Kii Pueblo. Remains of pits and pit houses from below rooms and outside the room block denote some habitation during the earlier Corduroy and Dry Valley phases, but that occupation and the later one apparently were discontinuous. The use history of the room block itself is longer than that of Hough's Great Kiva, AZ P:16:160, and Cothrun's Kiva, as demonstrated by the agglomerative, if quickly built, pueblo, and the remodeling indicated by walls under the latest iteration of the room block. Many of the tree-ring dates span three decades, and Tla Kii Pueblo was probably occupied a decade or two longer than the SCARP sites.

The final abandonment of the room block was quick and intentional. Floors were cleared of useful artifacts and the rooms were not filled with trash after their occupants left. At least five of the rooms and the great kiva were burned. The pueblo was not reused, although the large sites of Forestdale and Tundastusa indicate that people continued to live in the valley in aggregated pueblos.

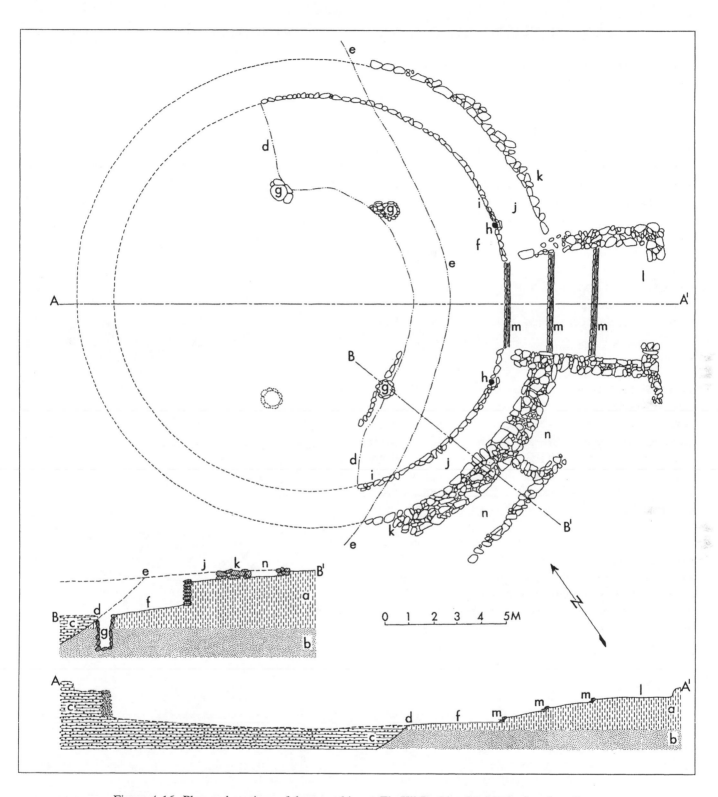

Figure 4.16. Plan and sections of the great kiva at Tla Kii Pueblo: "*a*, black clay; *b*, yellow sandy silt; *c*, sandy silt of third terrace; *d*, approximate edge of old arroyo at floor level; *e*, approximate edge of old arroyo at present surface level; *f*, floor; *g*, primary postholes; *h*, secondary posts in wall; *i*, bench face; *j*, bench surface; *k*, outer wall; *l*, entrance; *m*, stone and log risers; *n*; annexed rooms." (Haury 1985d: 48, Fig. 20; copyright The Arizona Board of Regents; reprinted by permission of the University of Arizona Press.)

CARTER RANCH PUEBLO

Of the excavated Mogollon Rim region great kiva sites, Carter Ranch Pueblo has the most complex structure and life history. Features included a large room block of approximately 38 rooms, a great kiva, and a plaza. The plaza contained a small D-shaped kiva, a small platform kiva, and a jug-shaped granary pit. None of the ritual structures were attached to the room block. The great kiva was located approximately 16 meters northwest of the room block and the two smaller kivas were within an enclosing plaza wall (Nash 2001). A large midden was southeast of the room block. Tree-ring cutting dates approximately eight decades apart indicate that Carter Ranch Pueblo had the longest span of construction and occupation of the five sites considered here. The contemporaneity of features, particularly those outside the room block, remains to be resolved.

Chronology

There are 19 tree-ring dates from Carter Ranch Pueblo (Table 4.8; Fig. 4.17). In the fall of 1997, 12 new tree-ring dates were added to the 7 previously published (Bannister and others 1966: 58; Longacre 1970: 26; Nash 2001). The 8 cutting dates range from A.D. 1112v to 1194c. Most of the noncutting 'vv' dates are close to this range, except a 1062+vv date from a specimen in the fill of Room 7. Two early 'vv' dates were also added to the site chronology in 1997: A.D. 978++vv from Plaza Trench H, Square I is from deadwood in a midden context; 965+vv is from a bell-shaped storage pit in Room 21. Room 21 was used as a dump after its abandonment and Jeffrey Dean indicated that this date may relate to the weathering or burning of exterior rings or the secondary deposition of trash.

These tree-ring dates and the relative ceramic dates signify that although the early occupation was contemporaneous with the SCARP sites and Tla Kii Pueblo, residence continued much later and certainly overlapped the late twelfth-century occupation of Roundy Canyon (A.D. 1170–1180) and possibly even Pottery Hill, whose main occupation occurred between A.D. 1200 and 1280. Based on proposed dates, Carter Ranch Pueblo was inhabited between 1050 and 1250, and the seriation of ceramic assemblages from the great kiva sites supports this dating (Mills and Herr 1999). Architectural analogies suggest that the Carter Ranch great kiva was built earlier than the two smaller kivas. Typically, suprahousehold kivas were associated with thirteenth- and fourteenth-century settlements. Stratification

of the midden also provided evidence of a long occupation (Rinaldo 1964a: 19).

Table 4.8. Carter Ranch Pueblo Chronology

Provenience	Specimen no.	Tree-ring date	Construction phase	Comments
Room 1			5	
Room 2			4	
Room 3			1	
Room 4	CAR-2	1112v	5	
Room 5			1	
Room 6	CAR-3	1118r	5	West wall
Room 7	CAR-26	1120+vv	4	
	CAR-29	1062+vv		Fill
Room 8			4	
Room 9			4	
Room 10	CAR-7	1194c	1	Roof over burial
Room 11			2?	
Room 12			1	
Room 13			1	
Room 14			3	
Room 15	CAR-19	1130r	2	Floor II
	CAR-10	1116c		Floor II
	CAR-11	1130v		Floor II
Room 16			1	
Room 17			4	
Room 18*	CAR-13	1136+vv	2	Lower clay
	CAR-17	1169+vv		Ash fill
Room 19			1	
Room 20			3	
Room 21	CAR-23	965+vv	4	Storage Pit
Room 22			4	
Room 23			3	

*Tree-ring from lower clay, just above floor.

119 2<u>47</u>	107
118	106 2
117	105
116 9	104
115 1<u>66</u>	103
114 <u>24</u>	102
113 <u>006</u>	101
112 0	100
111 <u>268</u>	99
110	98
109	97 8
108	96 5

Figure 4.17. Stem and leaf diagram of cutting dates (underlined) and noncutting dates from A.D. 965 to 1197 from Carter Ranch Pueblo. "Stems" represent decades and "leaves" indicate specific years.

Room Block

Of the estimated 39 pueblo rooms, 22 were excavated (Fig. 4.18). The room block was built in at least six construction events (Fig. 4.19). The 10 rooms on the northwest side of the pueblo were among the earliest (including excavated Rooms 3, 5, 10, 12, and 16), although the only tree-ring date from this portion of the room block is one of the latest dates from the pueblo (A.D. 1194c). The four to five rooms near the southwest corner of the pueblo (including excavated Rooms 13 and 17) were built separately. Because they were not contiguous with the other rooms and because they contained no tree-ring specimens, they cannot be related chronologically to the northwest rooms; they might have been earlier, contemporaneous, or slightly later in construction. A third construction event, during which Rooms 15, 18, and 21 were built, joined the two earlier sets of rooms and created a single room block at the pueblo. Two cutting dates and one 'v' date (A.D. 1116c, 1130r, 1130v) are available from Room 15, and Room 18 has two 'vv' dates, A.D. 1136 and 1169. The storage pit in Room 21 has a 965+vv date. To this core, a set of five to six rooms (including Rooms 20, 23, and possibly 22) was added on the plaza side of the room block to the east, and later Room 9 was added still farther east. Two to three rooms (including Rooms 2, 8, and possibly 7) were added to the south, and to this southern set Rooms 1, 4, and 6 were added to the east. Tree-ring dates from Room 7 are A.D. 1062+vv and 1120+vv; Room 4 has an 1112v date and Room 6 has a 1118r date. Room 11 was at the northeast side of the pueblo, connected only by a wing wall; it had no tree-ring specimens. Unfortunately, no room had enough specimens to examine clusters of dates for indications of construction and remodeling events, but the dates available do suggest that the construction events occurred in quick succession. Dates for the south side of the pueblo are as early as those from central rooms, but the south rooms were built on trash.

The functional diversity of Carter Ranch Pueblo rooms exceeded that at the other great kiva settlements and included 15 habitation rooms, 5 storage rooms, 1 combined habitation and ceremonial room, and 1 ceremonial room. Room 17 was identified as both a habitation and a ceremonial room based on hearth-related features, Room 6 as a storage and grinding room because of a smooth slab with adjacent ceramic and basketry flour receptacles, and Room 19 as a habitation and manufacturing room because a flesher and several projectile points were on the floor. The functional diversity of rooms, which was characteristic of late pueblos, is another reason Carter Ranch is interpreted as having a longer occupation than the other great kiva settlements discussed here.

Ritual Architecture

One D-shaped kiva (Kiva 1), one rectangular kiva, and one circular great kiva comprised the ritual architecture at Carter Ranch. The chronological relationship of these structures is difficult to assess architecturally or through tree-ring dates. Temporal suppositions are based on analogies with other sites with kivas in the region.

The great kiva construction was less elaborate than that of the smaller ritual structures. Like the great kivas excavated by SCARP, the great kiva at Carter Ranch Pueblo was a semisubterranean structure of masonry and earth construction (Fig. 4.20). The diameters of the structure are north to south from wall to wall 17.3 m, and from bench face to bench face 14.8 m. The subterranean walls were faced with unshaped stones and the bench was faced with unshaped sandstone slabs. No plaster was found on the pit wall or on the bench. Above ground, sandstone and igneous rocks were used to build massive semicoursed walls, with the largest stone measuring 120 cm by 18 cm by 15 cm. The surface walls were preserved only 53 cm above modern grade but the excavators estimated that the large amount of wall fall inside and outside the structure accounted for one to two meters of wall height.

The depth of the subterranean portion of the structure was 163 cm. The floor was unprepared and simply cut into the native clay. The hearth area was similarly informal, and no stones or clay lining bound the burned area of charcoal and ash that, at its widest extent, measured 2.7 m and was only about 5 cm deep. Floor features included three small, rectangular, stone-lined pits (one adjacent to a pillar); the few sherds found within gave no hint of the pits' function. There is good evidence that the structure was roofed. Four masonry pillars (similar to those in Great Kiva I at Village of the Great Kivas, Roberts 1932: 88) were placed in a quadrilateral symmetrical pattern. A fifth masonry pilaster on the west also helped support the roof.

The ramped entry to the structure was oriented to the southeast. Despite similarities in orientation, the construction of ramped entries varied at the great kiva sites. The unusual entry to the Carter Ranch Pueblo great kiva was 3 m wide and 5 m long, but it was divided into two paths. The southern one-third was several

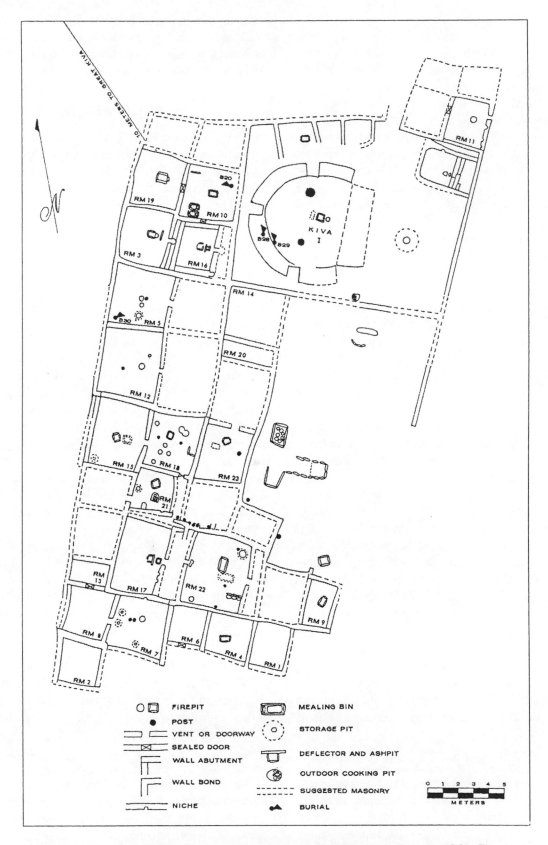

Figure 4.18. Plan of Carter Ranch Pueblo. (Adapted from Martin and others 1964, Fig. 1; reprinted by permission of the Field Museum of Natural History, Chicago; graphic by Ellen Herr.)

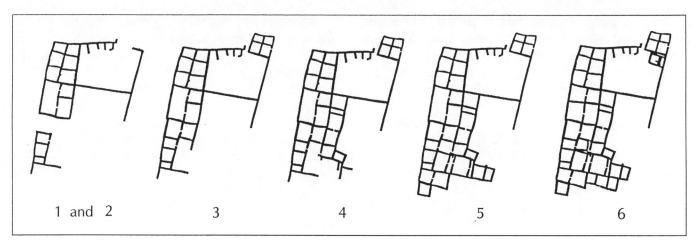

Figure 4.19. Building episodes at Carter Ranch
Pueblo. (Graphic by Ellen Herr.)

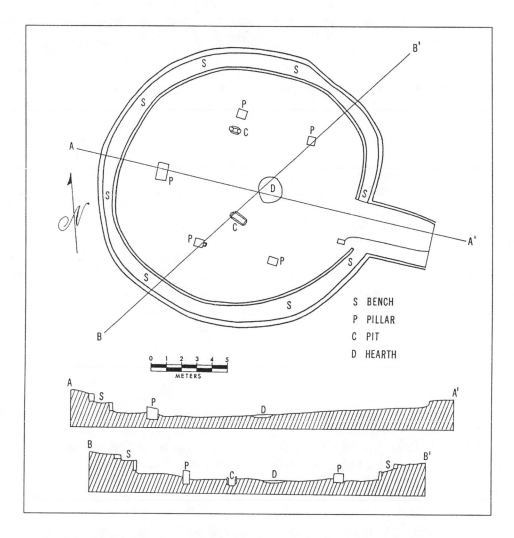

Figure 4.20. Plan and sections of the great kiva at Carter Ranch
Pueblo. (From Martin and others 1964, Fig. 1; reprinted by
permission of the Field Museum of Natural History, Chicago.)

centimeters higher than the rest of the path. The higher section, the only portion of the floor with plastering, turned slightly to the south on entering the body of the structure and ended near the bench at a small sixth pillar (Martin and others 1964: 40–47).

The small kivas were constructed more formally than the large communal structure. The D-shaped kiva had a north to south wall-to-wall diameter of 8.1 m. The walls were faced with a sandstone veneer that was then covered with plaster and a gray finishing coat. The floor was prepared with hard-packed adobe plaster. The hearth complex included a rectangular slab-lined hearth, a round ash pit adjacent to the hearth, and a deflector east of the fire pit. A small, ash-filled trench was situated west of the firepit. A platform was built on the east side of the room and a bench followed the circumference on all but the east side of the kiva. The vertical face of the bench had a veneer of small stones and the top of the bench was plastered. Three pilasters supported the structure's roof (Martin and others 1964: 35–36).

The rectangular kiva was 2.4 m long by 2.0 m wide. Like the D-shaped kiva, it had a wall with a veneer of small stones, a coating of plaster, and a floor of hard-packed adobe plaster. The hearth complex had a clay-lined hearth (roughly D–shaped), a square slab-lined ash pit, and a deflector. At the east end of the kiva a ventilator was located below a platform that measured 1.2 m deep and rose 46 cm above the floor; the vertical edge was faced with a veneer of small stones, and the top was covered with gray adobe plaster. Another pilaster recessed into the north wall may have provided a roof support, although the small size of the kiva indicates that elaborate methods of roofing were unnecessary (Martin and others 1964: 37–39). No mention was made of entries into these structures, nor were any noted on the map; roof entry is assumed.

Comments

After the sequential construction of the room block, which, according to tree-ring dates, happened fairly rapidly, the rooms were unevenly used and abandoned. Eighteen of the excavated rooms were remodeled, ranging from replastering the walls (N = 12) to sealing doorways (N = 2) and reconstructing floors (N = 9) and hearths (N = 1). A bench was added to Room 16, a ceremonial room. Occupation appears to have been longer than in the other described Mogollon Rim region sites. The similarity of the Carter Ranch ceramic assemblage to that at Pottery Hill may mean that occupation at Carter Ranch continued into the early A.D. 1200s.

Abandonment of the room block was not abrupt. Some of the earliest rooms apparently were some of the longest occupied. Room 10, with the latest cutting date and multiple floors, was probably one of the earliest constructed rooms. Nearby Rooms 3, 5, and 14 were abandoned earlier, as indicated by trash in their fill. Rooms 18, 21, and 23 were also filled with trash. Rooms 7 and 8, built on trash, were later filled with trash, indicating relatively late construction and early abandonment. The great kiva was abandoned and burned and was not used as a trash dump. The relationship of its abandonment to the chronology of the rest of the settlement is uncertain.

COMMUNITY FORMATION

When farmers from the Ancestral Pueblo regions to the north and east settled in the Mogollon Rim region, they moved into an area where land was abundant and populations were small. On the frontier, families were land-rich and labor-poor. They moved widely to acquire resources rather than improve those closer at hand. At the same time, some degree of residential stability and interaction with other families was both necessary and desirable. These economic pushes and social pulls are apparent in the spatial expression of late eleventh- and early twelfth-century Mogollon Rim region communities. Patterns of settlements varying in size, duration, situation, and function reflect the compromises made by the early residents.

Numerous small, one-room structures with light trash scatters were dispersed across the landscape and were associated with an extensive subsistence strategy that included farming and gathering of wild resources. They may have provided short term habitation and storage space close to fields. Only two habitation sites without public architecture have been excavated, but they reveal a more substantial investment in construction compared with the small structures. The few excavated rooms show little evidence of extended use. Community centers, defined by the presence of at least one great kiva, were among the largest and longest occupied settlements, and habitation settlements clustered loosely around them. Considered together, these architectural features define a pattern of families or small groups who used much of the productive landscape in a flexible pattern of short term occupation and mobility.

Farmers' perceptions of agricultural productivity, risk, stability, and acceptable work load guide their choices. Where land is widely available and boundaries few or nonexistent, fields can be quickly used and left to fallow by mobile pioneers. This reconstruction of frontier behaviors associated with low population densities and extensive agricultural practices explains the distribution of many of the eleventh- and twelfth-century settlements in the Mogollon Rim region.

Subsistence pursuits were only one criteria guiding settlement choices. Ritual, and other integrative activities associated with the great kiva attracted settlers to Mogollon Rim region communities. As shown by ethnographically and historically documented frontier families, access to other households is important. People in the habitations that were clustered around the circular great kivas probably participated in cooperative enterprises. Households would have been called on for decision making and choices that affected the community, including the sanctioning of marriages, the scheduling of agricultural and other economic tasks, and the distribution of available resources. On the frontier, the compromise between household independence and community stability was a delicate one.

CHAPTER FIVE

Integration of Households and Communities

The variability of material patterning on frontiers is representative of the variety of economic, social, political, and ritual behaviors that characterize liminal areas. Expectations about the frontier as place and process are compared to the remains of daily life on the late eleventh-century and early twelfth-century Mogollon Rim frontier in order to draw inferences about the size and structure of families, the means by which the family sustains and reproduces itself, the isolating or cooperating behaviors of pioneer households, and the restructuring of homeland values on the frontier. In Chapter 6, larger questions are considered, such as the formation of frontier social institutions, leadership, the durability of the frontier political structure, and the relative place of the Mogollon Rim frontier on the social and political landscape of the late eleventh and early twelfth centuries.

That a migration brought populations to the Mogollon Rim region in the tenth and eleventh centuries has been established (Chapter 3). To examine how migrants organized households into communities in their first 75 to 100 years of settlement in the region, five activities (production, distribution, transmission, reproduction, and co-residence) that define an ethnographic household (Wilk and Netting 1984) provide an ideal model for archaeologists. These activities cannot always be addressed directly from material remains, but examination of a number of artifact classes provides layers of information that show, from many angles, trends in the economic and social behavior of frontier households and communities. An eclectic array of data and methods of interpretation are drawn together in an attempt to create a rich picture of eleventh- and twelfth-century household and community life in the Mogollon Rim region.

The activities of a single household may involve members of other households but are distinguished from community activities in that the interest served is ultimately that of the household. Expectations for the material expressions of production, distribution, transmission, reproduction, and co-residence, and the means

by which they are discerned, are summarized in Table 5.1 Although ethnographic analogy supports many of the assumptions and discussions of the following analyses, it is referenced explicitly when archaeological evidence is weak and ethnographic analogs for the behavior in question are particularly strong.

HOUSEHOLD PRODUCTION

The frontier model posits extensive production. On the frontier, the initial value of land is low, but the cost of labor is high. Pioneers are expected to take an exploitative rather than a resource management approach to the use of wild resources and land. To examine questions of agricultural production, wild resource procurement, and processing, the relative contributions of cultivated and wild resources to the diet are assessed. In the model, craft production is expected to be extensive and to focus on the manufacture of utilitarian rather than prestige items.

In the Mogollon Rim region, the distribution of prehistoric limited activity sites and limited use structures shows patterns of land use that were not guided by residential considerations. Archaeobotanical samples and faunal remains divulge what the migrants extracted from the land around them. Ceramic production in households has been documented by a number of different parameters and work on hides may have been common. Evidence for the production of textiles, ornaments, or any type of prestige item is sparse. These activities meet the expectations of the frontier model.

Food Acquisition

In the late eleventh and early twelfth centuries, land in the Mogollon Rim region was plentiful and food acquisition methods were extensive. Architectural and artifactual data indicate that small structures with light trash scatters were used seasonally for a limited number of activities. Settlements with more substantial architecture, more artifactual and botanical diversity (Ruppé

Table 5.1. Methods for the Analysis of Frontier Organization for Households and Communities

Activity	Expected Behavior	Variable	Method of Analysis
Households			
Production	Extensive agriculture and residential mobility	Land use patterns Location of fields Horticultural priorities Use of wild resources	Settlement pattern Pollen ubiquity Macrobotanical ubiquity
	Low labor investment in food procurement Low intensity food processing Craft production for household use	Organization of hunting Intensity of grinding Context of lithic manufacture Context of ceramic manufacture Other craft manufacture	Faunal frequency and diversity Intrasite ground stone distribution and use wear Intrasite flaked stone distribution Intrasite ceramic distribution Ceramic composition Worked sherd distribution Presence, absence of other craft-related tools
Distribution	Households with widespread social networks	Availability of storage Household participation in exchange relations	Size and location of storage rooms in settlement Size and location of storage within rooms Ceramic evidence for intraregional exchange Ceramic evidence for extraregional exchange Evidence from other material for extraregional exchange
Transmission	Little evidence of ownership	Markers of land ownership vs. usufruct rights Markers of personal property	Presence, absence, and location of field houses, shrines Ethnographic analogy Presence of grave goods in burials
Reproduction	Physical reproduction, large household size Socialization	Household size and structure Division of labor	Remodeling episodes Spatial organization of households
Co-residence	Single family households	Size of household	Room size; Vessel size
Communities			
Production	Few labor intensive constructions Importance of work groups and organizations Communal production	Organization of communal labor Organization of agricultural labor Communal food processing Acquisition of ritual materials	Great kiva construction techniques Ethnographic analogy Use wear and context of ground stone Identification of ritual fauna
Distribution	Redistribution and communal ceremonies	Context of storage Evidence for feasting	Identification of storage structures outside household Trash disposal; Vessel size calculation; Vessel function
Transmission	Unmarked community boundaries	Boundary markers	Identification of defensive sites, shrines
Reproduction	Duration of community centers Shared community institutions Few formalized organizations	Duration of occupation Communal ritual Suprahousehold organizations	Large trash concentrations Absolute and relative dates Communal level architecture Suprahousehold architecture below community level
Co-residence	Low density of habitation structures in dispersed communities	Spatial organization of communities	Population estimate Settlement pattern

1988: 316), and dense trash concentrations were the locations of habitations and year-round occupation. Lowland areas, particularly near ephemeral washes, were used regularly; use of upland areas was more limited (Neily 1988: 292). Nonhabitation sites tended to be situated away from high elevations, steep slopes, and rocky soils (Newcomb 1997: 109) and were dispersed across the landscape. Steven Dosh (1988: 334) noted that there was a slight tendency for sites to be located on natural prominences such as knolls and ridge tops, overlooking arable land.

Migrants to the Mogollon Rim region were small-scale farmers, and corn formed a significant portion of their diet. Corn is ubiquitous at both the small structures used seasonally and at year-round habitations. Squash and beans were also cultivated, but their remains do not preserve well and are less prevalent in archaeological samples. Pollen samples from large and small sites in the FLEX Goodwin and Show Low II project areas and from Schoens Dam contain an abundance of *cheno-ams,* plants associated with ground disturbance, in this case caused by farming (Hartman and others 1988: 224), but the

> record contains no evidence to suggest that massive forest clearing took place during the occupation of these sites . . . .Instead, it appears that smaller parcels of arable land were exploited for the cultivation of at least maize and squash at most of these sites. In the absence of evidence that a significant portion of the landscape was modified to accommodate horticulture, it seems probable that certain sites may have been situated expressly for convenience to arable land (Cummings 1988: 296–297).

Similarly, in the Silver Creek drainage there is no evidence for the use of nonlocal wood, such as species growing at higher or lower elevations, as might be indicated if people were over-exploiting local areas (Huckell 1999: 502–503). People put minimal labor into forest clearing and probably relocated gardens frequently across the available expanse of land. Runoff was used for watering crops (Neily 1991: 22, 28), but farmers did not invest in water or soil control features.

Wild plants consistently supplemented corn in the prehispanic diet. In one hearth complex in Room 1 at Cothrun's Kiva, the 19 genera and species identified were: carbonized *chenopodium, chenoam,* maize (cupules and kernels), winged pigweed, pitseed goosefoot, sage, sunflower, tansy mustard, and other grasses. The ash dump contained maize cupules and kernels, squash

rind, juniper seeds and fruit, walnut shells, *chenopod* seeds, amaranth, *chenoams*, bug seed, winged pigweed, prickly pear, purslane, probably sage, stick leaf, ground cherry or nightshade, sunflower tribe, grasses, dropseed, probably a pinyon nut shell (Huckell 1999: 489), aggregates of corn, and more than 247 fused winged pigweed seeds.

This suite of wild plants, although containing more diversity than appears in most other single assemblages, accords well with the flora that has been documented in the region (Cutler 1964: 234; Hartman and others 1988; Neily 1988: 280; Ruppé 1990: 185). Manzanita was an important resource at Hough's Great Kiva and at site NA 18,346 (Cummings 1988: 299) closer to the Mogollon Rim. South of Show Low and in the Snowflake–Mesa Redondo area, cacti and wild grasses supplemented the corn diet (Cutler 1964; Hartman and others 1988: 213; Ruppé 1990: 185). Pollen from storage pits and seeds from features like those at Cothrun's Kiva indicate that native plants were gathered, processed, and stored (Cummings 1988: 298). Residents "enjoyed a diverse and nutritious diet" (Huckell 1999: 495). No evidence has been found for specialization in plant procurement (Cummings 1988: 299).

Wood was the most common wild resource used for nonsubsistence pursuits such as construction, cooking, heating, and craft production. The use of wood in hearths reflects what was locally available; occupants of the settlement at Cothrun's Kiva made frequent use of juniper, whereas those at Hough's Great Kiva preferred ponderosa pine (Huckell 1999). Ponderosa pine was the preferred roofing material at both settlements.

In both horticultural pursuits and the gathering of native plants, residents of the Mogollon Rim region took advantage of the abundance of land. The small size of field structures and habitation settlements indicates that single households were the typical unit of production. Residents changed fields often and invested little labor in the exploitation of resources. Residential mobility, rather than agricultural intensification, was the regular response to changes in resource availability.

Although consistent across the region, the archaeological faunal assemblage lacked the richness and abundance of the botanical assemblage (Tables 5.2, 5.3). Cottontails and jackrabbits were the most common animals processed and consumed. The dominant genus varied by settlement, perhaps in relation to the ground cover across the region (Szuter and Gillespie 1994: 70). At Cothrun's Kiva Site, jackrabbits dominated the assemblage in all contexts. Antelope bones were the only large animal remains recovered; otherwise, rodents

Table 5.2. Identified Faunal Remains from Cothrun's Kiva Site by Context

	Room 1		Room 2		Room 4		Room 6		Great Kiva		Midden	
	NISP	MNI	NISP	MNI	NISP	MNI	NISP	MNI	NISP	MNI	NISP	MNI
Antelope	1	*1*	7	*2*								
Mule Deer					1	*1*						
Rock Squirrel	1	*1*	2	*2*								
Abert's Squirrel	1	*1*									1	*1*
Prairie Dog	1	*1*										
Pocket Gopher	2	*1*										
Jackrabbit sp.	111	*7*	23	*3*	30	*5*	3	*2*	1	*1*	60	*6*
Cottontail sp.	63	*6*	9	*2*	25	*3*					41	*6*
Woodrat	49	*2*									4	*1*
Kestrel											1	*1*

NOTE: Data are from Horner 1999.

Table 5.3. Identified Faunal Remains from Hough's Great Kiva Site by Context

	Room 1		Room 2		Midden	
	NISP	MNI	NISP	MNI	NISP	MNI
Bighorn sheep	1	*1*				
Jackrabbit sp.	7	*2*	1	*1*	66	*3*
Cottontail sp.	2	*1*	1	*1*	8	*2*
Turkey					73	*4*
Red Fox					4	*1*

NOTE: Data are from Horner 1999.

and small mammals completed the faunal subsistence assemblage. In the unusual assemblage from Hough's Great Kiva Site, jackrabbits were followed by cottontails and turkeys in abundance (Table 5.3 total *MNI*; Horner 1999). The faunal percentages are skewed by one dumping episode of turkey bones in the midden. The elements recovered indicate that turkeys were used for food, although ritual uses cannot be entirely discounted (Horner 1999). The only evidence to suggest that turkeys at Hough's Great Kiva may have been domesticated is that all birds were immature (Haury 1985d: 69; Horner 1999; Senior and Pierce 1989). In all, small mammals constitute more than 98 percent of the Cothrun's Kiva Site assemblage and 95 percent of the Hough's Great Kiva Site assemblage (Horner 1999: 434).

The hunting practices implied by a faunal assemblage dominated by small mammals and large birds are more meaningful when compared to assemblages from late sites. Large mammal remains increased from less than five percent of the great kiva assemblages to more than 35 percent of the Bailey Ruin assemblage. Changes in faunal assemblages reflect the interrelationship of hunt-

ing patterns, village permanence, and the degree of dependence on starchy crops (Speth and Scott 1989: 72–74). The large animals eaten at the Bailey Ruin settlement fulfilled a need for an efficient source of protein that was not expressed at the great kiva settlements (Horner 1999).

The ready availability of labor at late aggregated pueblos affected the composition of hunting groups and the potential volume of their returns. In contrast, the hunting and snaring of small animals, such as recovered at the great kiva settlements, may have been conducted by single men, women, or children, rather than by groups. Small animals may have been acquired during other subsistence activities such as gathering and tending fields (Szuter 2000). "Garden hunting" eliminates scheduling conflicts because people hunt the animals near their fields (Hodgetts 1996: 154; Linares 1976).

Food Processing

Examining the processing of food provides a way to look at the context of production in domestic space. In the Mogollon Rim region, corn and wild plants were stored in pueblo rooms rather than in outside pits and storage structures (Hartman and Keller 1990: 101; Ruppé 1988: 323). When ready for use, domesticated and wild cereals were probably parched and ground into dry flour on trough and slab metates for baking into flat breads and for thickening stews, beverages, dumplings, and puddings (Adams 1999).

Design characteristics and evidence of wear management on manos indicate the intensity of food processing (Adams 1994: 81; 1999). Use wear on two adjacent sides (creating a beveled or wedge-shaped cross-section), rather than on one side or two opposite sides, re-

Table 5.4. Metate Shape by Site and Site Type

Site	Basin	Slab	Trough	3/4 Trough	Open Trough	Bin	Reference
Great Kiva Sites							
Tla Kii				1	1		Haury 1985d
Carter Ranch	1	Present		Present	12	2	Martin and others 1964
	5%	47.5%	47.5%				Plog 1974
Hough's Great Kiva					2		Valado 1999
Cothrun's Kiva		1	1		1		Valado 1999
Habitation Sites							
AZ Q:13:9 (ASU)		6	13				B. Stafford 1980
AZ Q:13:16 (ASU)		1	1				B. Stafford 1980
AZ P:16:10 (ASU)		2					B. Stafford 1980
AZ P:16:44, 45 (ASU)			2				B. Stafford 1980
NA 17,271			5				Stebbins 1988
NA 17,282		2	2				Stebbins 1988
NA 18,126		2	2				Hartman 1990
NA 18,343			6				Greenwald 1988
NA 18,346			4				Greenwald 1988
NA 18,350		2	12				Greenwald 1988
NA 19,330		2	3				Greenwald 1988
NA 19,331		2	4				Greenwald 1988
AZ Q:9:5					1		Neily 1988
AZ Q:9:26		1			13		Neily 1988
Small-structure Sites							
AZ P:16:12 (ASU)		9	16				B. Stafford 1980
NA 17,285	1						Stebbins 1988
NA 18,175		3	1				Hartman 1990
NA 18,176		3					Greenwald 1988
NA 18,345		1	1				Greenwald 1988
NA 19,332	1	3	1				Greenwald 1988
NA 19,334		2					Greenwald 1988
Limited Activity Sites							
AZ Q:13:4 (ASU)			1				B. Stafford 1980
AZ P:16:5 (ASU)		4	4				B. Stafford 1980
AZ P:16:13 (ASU)		9	2				B. Stafford 1980
NA 17,284	1		1				Stebbins 1988
NA 18,348	1		1				Greenwald 1988
AZ Q:9:30		1			1		Neily 1988

NOTE: AZ is Arizona State Museum site number (except as noted); NA is Museum of Northern Arizona site number.

veals that the grinder was trying to get the greatest possible use out of a favorite mano and provides a measure of increasing grinding intensity (Adams 1994: 83). Slab metates did not generally restrict motion and were designed for more intensive grinding than trough metates. If grinding was simply for household purposes, evidence of intensification would be minimal, but if grinding was for food consumption by large groups, the number of grinding surfaces on manos would be greater and tools would show more indications of tool design, maintenance, and wear management. Multiple grinding stations would indicate substantial time investment in food preparation for groups larger than the household, whereas portable metates or ground stone dispersed throughout the room block might signal production solely for the household (Adams 1994: 220–224).

Ground stone artifacts from Mogollon Rim sites have been reported in myriad ways. Ground stone from Carter Ranch was recorded by Rinaldo (1964b) and by Plog (1974: 141), whose reports are not in accordance. Because no metates from Carter Ranch were curated, the differences cannot be reconciled. The diversity of reporting is reflected in Tables 5.4 and 5.5, and comparisons can only be qualitative. Counts in these tables represent partial and complete manos and metates from floors, extramural surfaces, and fill.

Table 5.5. Mano Wear Management Strategies by Site and Site Type
(Percents are by row)

Site type Site	Wear on one surface (%)	Wear on a second surface (%) Opposite	Adjacent	Unknown	Total	Reference
Great Kiva Sites						
Hough's Great Kiva	8 (88.9)		1 (11.1)		9	Valado 1999
Cothrun's Kiva	9 (75.0)	2 (16.7)	1 (8.3)		12	Valado 1999
Tla Kii	21 (70.0)	9 (30.0)			30	Haury 1985d
Carter Ranch	Most	Least	Moderate		326	Martin and others 1964
Habitation Sites						
AZ Q:13:9 (ASU)	Most			Least	?	B. Stafford 1980
AZ Q:9:5	1 (16.7)			5 (83.3)	6	Neily 1988
AZ Q:9:26	24 (80.0)			6 (20.0)	30	Neily 1988
NA 17,271	10 (56.0)	8 (44.0)			18	Stebbins 1988
NA 17,282*	4 (50.0)	4 (50.0)			8	Stebbins 1988
Small-structure Sites						
AZ P:16:12 (ASU)	Most			Least	?	B. Stafford 1980
NA 17,266	1 (50.0)	1 (50.0)			2	Stebbins 1988
NA 17,273	1 (100.0)				1	Stebbins 1988
NA 17,285	1 (100.0)				1	Stebbins 1988
Limited Activity Sites						
AZ P:16:5 (ASU)	Least			Most	?	B. Stafford 1980
NA 17,284	4 (100.0)				4	Stebbins 1988
NA 17,286	3 (100.0)				3	Stebbins 1988
NA 17,286A	1 (50.0)			1 (50.0)	2	Stebbins 1988

NOTE: AZ is Arizona State Museum site number (except as noted); NA is Museum of Northern Arizona site number.
* One mano had wear on four sides.

Type of metate correlates with type of site, indicating a different intensity of grinding between small and large settlements. Trough metates were the most common food processing tool at large habitation settlements, with or without communal architecture. Proportionally, slab metates were more common at small-structure settlements and metate types were more diverse than at larger habitations, even though sample sizes were smaller. There was no other evidence of intensive food processing at the small sites; perhaps the reason for the greater proportion of slab metates is because less labor was invested in their construction or they were more versatile tools.

Where wear management was recorded, manos used on one side predominated, followed by those used on two opposite surfaces, and then by beveled surfaces. At Cothrun's Kiva and Hough's Great Kiva sites, 75 and 89 percent of the manos, respectively, were unifacially used, and no more than two sides were used. Wear was usually heavy on the manos at Hough's Great Kiva and Carter Ranch, and moderate to heavy on ground stone from Snowflake-Mesa Redondo area sites (Neily 1988: 263). Moderate to heavy wear indicates that manos were used for a long time, probably extensively.

The dispersion or aggregation of grinding facilities was used to assess whether grinding occurred at the household level or in groups for suprahousehold or communal consumption. Two metates were associated with roof surfaces: one at Carter Ranch (Rinaldo 1964b: 65) and the other in Room 1 of Hough's Great Kiva Site. Mealing bins were constructed at Carter Ranch and at sites NA 18,343, NA 18,350, NA 18,176, and NA 19,334, and a mealing pit was constructed at AZ Q:9:26 (ASM). Single metates, in mealing pits, mealing bins, or on the floor, were in 17 rooms in the Mogollon Rim region; no other excavated rooms had metates in situ. Metates were also used on extramural surfaces and in ramadas. The three latest sites in the sample had double mealing bins: Carter Ranch and sites NA 18,343 and NA 18,350 (Dosh 1988: 173, 192).

Grinding areas were dispersed throughout room blocks and communities. Six excavated rooms have been identified exclusively as processing rooms. All other grinding facilities were in rooms that were also used for other activities. Low intensity flour processing in the late eleventh and early twelfth centuries occurred in households throughout the settlements. There is little evidence for high intensity use or grinding for large groups.

Lithic Production

Exposures of gravels, washes, and outcrops of sandstone, limestone, and basalt in the Mogollon Rim region provided abundant materials (chert, quartzite, petrified wood, chalcedony, diabase, and other igneous materials) for the manufacture of cutting tools. Materials closest to home were used most often, with little extra effort expended for higher quality materials. When available, chert was preferred (Greenwald 1988; Kaldahl 1999; Neily 1988; B. Stafford 1980: 279). Petrified wood occurs unevenly throughout the area and its use varied widely. Two partially buried petrified wood logs near site NA 18,216 were quarried for raw material by prehistoric residents (Hartman and Keller 1990: 91).

Because of abundant raw materials and a generally sedentary life, bifacial tools were uncommon, and there is no evidence of extended curation of tools (Kaldahl 1995; Young 1994). A combination of hard and soft hammer techniques was used to make expedient tool kits (B. Stafford 1980) of projectile points, drills, saws, gravers, flake knives, scrapers, choppers, notched flakes, and scraper planes. Activities represented by flaked lithics include the procurement and processing of food and perishable materials like wood, bone, and hide.

Technological and functional variables demonstrate the range of behaviors that occurred at different types of sites (Greenwald 1988: 254; Most 1987). Diversity indices applied to lithic assemblages show that a narrow set of activities occurred at small-structure and limited activity sites. Site AZ Q:9:30 (ASM) in the Snowflake–Mesa Redondo area was a hunting locale (Neily 1988: 257), with little core reduction. Various reductive activities were conducted at habitation settlements, where debitage ranged from primary core reduction and cortical flakes of varying sizes to the small flakes associated with tool manufacture, resharpening, and maintenance (Neily 1988: 245). Lithic analyses support the architectural evidence for the limited use of many small sites in the region and the more diversified use of large sites. The production of cutting and scraping edges occurred at the household level, although some raw material procurement may have been a group activity. Much of the knapping occurred on extramural and ramada surfaces, as at site AZ Q:9:26 (Neily 1988: 257) and at Hough's Great Kiva and Cothrun's Kiva (Kaldahl 1999).

Ceramic Production

Direct evidence for ceramic production is abundant. Scrapers, *pukis*, polishing stones, and plates were left on the floors of houses and discarded with other types of domestic refuse (Table 5.6). Comparisons of the distribution of ceramic tools by context at early and late SCARP sites (Mills, Herr, Stinson, and Triadan 1999) show that ceramics were produced in most Mogollon Rim region households in all time periods, but that during the eleventh and twelfth centuries the context of ceramic production was extensive, with no evidence for specialized production.

An extraordinary sealed assemblage below Floor 1 of Room 13 at Tla Kii Pueblo provided the best evidence of the tools and raw materials used in local ceramic production. As noted on the excavation forms (Haury 1940–1941), the Floor 2 assemblage of Rooms 13/15 included eight fired Black Mesa style Cibola White Ware and Puerco Black-on-white bowls, one Reserve Black-on-white jar, two McDonald Corrugated bowls, one or two unfired pots, two lots of potter's clay, three polishing stones, five pottery scrapers, hematite, and two lots of red paint. Four manos and a trough metate may have been used for processing pigment. In one of the lots of raw clay was a piece that had been rolled into a ball while still wet that fits easily into the palm of the hand. The potter pressed her finger into the clay, and several fingerprints are still visible on the ball. The only other raw clay identified at Tla Kii Pueblo was from a pit under Room 18 (Pit 11), which predates the construction of the pueblo. At another intriguing locus of ceramic production, site AZ Q:9:26 (ASM), Neily (1988: 130–136) reported a ceramic firing area with ash and charcoal deposits and blackened sherds that may have been used as "cover sherds" in a firing episode. Ground stone in the vicinity may have been used for processing clays and tempers.

Compositional data also provide direct evidence of ceramic production (Mills and Crown 1995b: 8). In one study of ceramic variability, using ceramic oxidation analysis, Neily (1988: 169) sampled 76 sherds from different wares and 7 clay samples from a range of geological formations in the Snowflake-Mesa Redondo area in the northern Silver Creek drainage. Mills, Herr, Stinson, and Triadan (1999) summarize ceramic oxidation studies on 270 sherd samples from 2 wares and 11 sites in the Silver Creek drainage and the Forestdale Valley. Another 46 clay samples demonstrate the range of geological variability in the southern portion of the Silver Creek drainage. Results of the two studies provide a regional picture of which wares were locally and nonlocally produced. Brown ware vessels were made with residual yellow-red firing clays. Neily comments that red clays, although available near the volcanic forma-

Table 5.6. Worked Sherds as Evidence of Ceramic Production

Tool	ID No.	Context	Description
Hough's Great Kiva			
Scraper		Ground surface	Undif. Cibola White Ware
Scraper		Ground surface	Undif. Cibola White Ware
Scraper		Ground surface	Undif. Cibola White Ware
Puki		Room 1, surface	16 pieces, Snowflake Black-on-white
Scraper		Great Kiva, fill	P II–P III Cibola White Ware
AZ P:16:160 (ASM)			
Scraper		Midden	2 pieces, P II–P III Cibola White Ware
Cothrun's Kiva			
Scraper		Courtyard	Undif. Cibola White Ware
Scraper		Courtyard	3 pieces, Undif. Cibola White Ware
Scraper		Midden	Undif. P II–P III Cibola White Ware
Scraper		Midden	Plain local brown ware
Puki		Midden	Undif. Cibola White Ware
Scraper		Midden	Sosi Black-on-white
Scraper		Midden	Escavada Black-on-white
Scraper		Midden	Undif. Plain local brown ware
Scraper		Midden	Undif. Cibola White Ware
Scraper		Room 1, roof	P II–P III Cibola White Ware
Scraper		Room 4, wall and roof fall	P II-P III Cibola White Ware
Scraper		Room 6, transect	Undif. Cibola White Ware
Tla Kii Pueblo			
Plate		Unprovenienced	Zoned Corrugated brown ware*
Scraper	A–2042	Unprovenienced	Reserve Black-on-white
Scraper	A–2749	Unprovenienced	Undif. Cibola White Ware
Scraper	A–2752	Unprovenienced	Undif. Showlow Black-on-red
Scraper	A–2850	Pueblo	Holbrook 'B' Black-on-white
Scraper	A–2851	Pueblo	Holbrook 'B' Black-on-white
Plate		Room 2	Indented Corrugated brown ware
Plate	50273	Room 2	Zoned Corrugated brown ware
Plate		Room 3, fill; Rooms 13, 14	Indented Corrugated brown ware
Plate		Room 4, fill	McDonald Corrugated
Scraper		Room 6, fill	Reserve Black-on-white
Scraper		Room 7, fill	Indented Corrugated brown ware
Scraper		Room 7, fill	Escavada Black-on-white
Plate		Room 7, floor	Plain brown ware
Tla Kii Pueblo (continued)			
Plate	50270	Room 12, fill	Exuberant Corrugated brown ware
Scraper	50340	Room 12, fill	Undif. Showlow Black-on-red
Scraper		Room 13	Reserve Black-on-white
Scraper	50341	Room 13, fill	Puerco Black-on-red
Scraper		Room 13, fill	Snowflake Black-on-white
Plate		Room 13, floor	Indented Corrugated brown ware
Scraper		Room 14	Holbrook 'A' Black-on-white
Scraper		Room 14, below floor	P II–P III Cibola White Ware
Plate		Room 16	Indented Corrugated brown ware
Plate		Room 16, floor	Plain brown ware
Plate		Room 16, floor 3	Plain brown ware
Scraper?		Room 18, below floor	Indented Corrugated brown ware*
Plate		Room 20	Plain brown ware
Scraper?		Pit House 1	Plain brown ware
Scraper		Northeast broadside	Reserve or Tularosa Black-on-white
Scraper		Grid C6	P II–P III Tusayan White Ware
Plate		Grid D4	Zoned Corrugated brown ware
Scraper		Storage Pit 1	Black Mesa Black-on-white
Scraper		Storage Pit 1	Black Mesa Black-on-white
Scraper		Storage Pit 1	Reserve Black-on-white
Scraper		Storage Pit 1, 0.5 m - floor	Reserve Black-on-white
Scraper		Storage Pit 1, 0.5 m - floor	Reserve Black-on-white
Scraper		Storage Pit 1, 0.5 m - floor	Sosi Black-on-white
Plate		US2	Clapboard brown ware
Carter Ranch			
Puki		Room 6	St. Johns Black-on-red
Scraper		Room 12, fill	Reserve Black-on-white
Scraper		Room 21, below floor	Escavada Black-on-white
Scraper		Room 23, Level A	Pinedale Black-on-white
Scraper		Room 23, Level B	Snowflake Black-on-white
Scraper		Great Kiva, southeast quadrant	Snowflake Black-on-white
Scrapers		Cataloged artifacts (N = 31)	Unknown

NOTE: Information from Mills, Herr, Stinson, and Triadan 1999; Martin and others 1964: 104; * indicates smudged brown ware.

tions in the Snowflake-Mesa Redondo area, were not commonly used. Decorated and undecorated Puerco Valley Red Ware ceramics have pastes similar to the brown wares and were also produced locally. White Mountain Red Ware vessels were not made in the region until the thirteenth century (Haury 1985b; Triadan and others 2001).

Before refiring, Cibola White Ware ceramic pastes are white, light gray, pink, dark gray, and a mottled red and black. Most of the Cibola White Ware pottery has a light gray paste, with dark gray paste as the most common variant. Dark gray paste Cibola White Ware pottery with Kiatuthlanna and Red Mesa style designs was named Corduroy Black-on-white by Haury (1985d: 75), who identified these vessels as locally produced. After refiring, Cibola White Ware pottery shows high compositional variability, with sherds refiring to color groups from buff to red (Neily 1988: 177). Locally available tempering material is in Cibola White Ware vessels from all color groups (Neily 1988: 178). Oxidized clay samples collected from the Silver Creek drainage (Mills, Herr, Stinson, and Triadan 1999, Table 8.4) demonstrate a range of variability that amply matches the color of refired sherds and indicates that much of the pottery that has been identified on sites in the Silver Creek area could have been locally produced.

Clay sampling in the northern and southern parts of the Silver Creek drainage show a high diversity of locally available "white" clays (Mills, Herr, Stinson, and Triadan 1999; Neily 1988). The variability in vessel pastes probably indicates the use of multiple, locally available clay sources, similar to the use of various raw materials for flaked lithics.

Design styles have been used to bolster some arguments about local production. Locally produced Cibola White Ware ceramics in the southern Silver Creek drainage, Forestdale Valley, and Snowflake-Mesa Redondo areas (Neily 1988: 171) share obvious design affinities with ceramics from the middle Little Colorado, Tusayan, and eastern Cibola areas.

Households probably produced the majority of their own vessels and ceramic specialization was unlikely. Ceramic analysts have commented on the heterogeneity of paste and tempering material (Lombard 1988: 216; Mills, Herr, Stinson, and Triadan 1999; Scholnick 1998) and the diversity of design on vessels from across the region (Hantman and Lightfoot 1978: 56; Haury 1985d: 101; Neily 1988: 161). Ceramic production tools were abandoned on floors or discarded in room fill and extramural trash middens. Permanent features indicative of specialized manufacturing spaces have not been

identified. The manufacture of vessels appears to have been spatially dispersed, and there is no evidence for specialized or centralized production or production for distribution.

Textiles, Basketry, and Hides

Evidence for textile production is sparse. Woven materials found in the Mogollon Rim region are most commonly associated with burials, although a few were recovered from room contexts. Textiles in the Carter Ranch burials included twill plaited mats wrapped around five inhumed individuals and string aprons on two females. Notched sherds from Hough's Great Kiva Site (N = 1) and from Cothrun's Kiva Site (N = 1) may have been used for processing fibers for basketry. Three notched or serrated edged sherds came from Carter Ranch Pueblo (Martin and others 1964: 105, Fig. 47). Grooved bone awls, distinct in shape from other awls, could also have been used for weaving (Martin and others 1964: 99). Perforated ceramic disks (Table 5.7) are often interpreted as spindle whorls (Herr 1998; Kent 1957: 472). Woodbury (1954: 102–104) has suggested that spindles as well as arrows may have been straightened in grooved shaft straighteners. Although occurring at late sites in the area (Mills 1998), evidence of looms, such as weights or loom holes, has not been identified at the early sites, nor have cotton, agave, or other raw textile fibers.

Hematite, a red pigment used for ceramic production and coloring other materials like baskets and textiles, was recovered from five area sites (NA 18,176 and 216, 343, 345, 350). The lead ore (galena) found at Tla Kii Pueblo and NA 17,955 (Hartman 1990; Haury 1985d) may have been used as a black pigment. Bone awls from

Table 5.7. Worked Sherds

Form	Hough's Great Kiva	Tla Kii Pueblo	Carter Ranch
Disk	18	5	82 + 1?
Flaked disk		5	21
Perforated disk	1		14
Jar lid		2?	2
Smooth edge	5	10	63
Beveled edge			3
Mend hole	2	13	28
Geometric			28
Pendant			6
Unknown	51	19	10

Carter Ranch (N = 120) and Tla Kii (N = 29) and lithic scrapers from almost all excavated sites in the region (except NA 18,341 and 349, AZ Q:9:6 ASM) may attest to some hide work.

Ornament Production

Although not common, stone and shell ornaments, especially beads, were collected at Tla Kii and Carter Ranch. Finished ornaments were most common in burials. Ant hills at Tla Kii Pueblo yielded steatite beads and the waste products of manufacture (Haury 1985d: 114). Forty bone shafts used for bone "ring" production were recovered from Carter Ranch (Rinaldo 1964b: 95, Fig. 36*m*, *n*, *o*), and a similar worked deer bone came from Room 13 of Tla Kii Pueblo. These rings and beads represent the few types of ornamentation manufactured locally.

HOUSEHOLD DISTRIBUTION

Household distribution is defined as the disbursement of food and other items among members of the household (Wilk and Netting 1984: 9). It is one of the most difficult variables to examine ethnographically and archaeologically. Here, household distribution is defined as household-initiated participation in exchange relations with local and nonlocal households. Evidence of storage and exchange aid in understanding household distribution practices. Architectural and artifactual data are useful in examining the scale and structure of distribution practices locally and regionally.

Few predictions have been made for patterns of household distribution on the frontier. Extensive social ties created by households are expected to provide a form of risk management. Through daily reciprocal exchanges, occasion-associated redistributive exchanges, and long distance trade, households create relations of obligation within and outside the community. Participation in intracommunity exchange, which likely includes perishable food products, relies in part on the availability of stored resources. Long distance exchanges of mundane or prestige goods create noneconomic, but essential, ties to other areas. Access to information may also be critical for the management of economic risk (Plog and others 1988; Rautman 1993, 1996) and other endeavors.

Storage

Storage and sharing are the means by which households and communities can manage their economic risk.

Sharing evens out the spatial variability of resources across a region and creates relationships of obligation, whereas storage provides a way of dealing with temporal variability caused by climatic or other economic fluctuations (Plog and others 1988; Van West 1993). Computer modeling of data from historic Hopi communities demonstrates that the optimum risk reduction strategy is one in which individual households fill their own storage space first and then contribute the remainder of their resources to the community pool (Hegmon 1991). The context of storage spaces, inside or outside the walls of a single household, provides some measure of the independence or integration of households within a community.

Households try to store resources for more than one year and anticipate participation in ceremonies and feasts. Roasted corn can last up to three years on the cob, whereas shelled corn has a "shelf life" of a single year. However, predictions of storage behavior are complicated by logistical concerns; corn-on-the-cob requires more space and shelled corn is more easily transported and perhaps better protected when stored in pots (Young 1996b: 206). With increasing sedentism and aggregation, individuals spend more time bringing resources from distant fields to their homes; thus, there is more need for field processing and temporary storage facilities close to the fields.

Information from all eleventh- and twelfth-century sites excavated by SCARP, the Snowflake-Mesa Redondo Project, the FLEX projects, and the Corduroy Creek project is used to understand the distribution of habitation and storage rooms and the investment in storage space in the household and community. The 24 sites contained one-room to five-room structures, with a total of 103 rooms. Storage occured in one-room and multiroom structures and in both jacal and masonry structures. Storage in rooms with no other apparent function is interpreted as long-term storage, whereas food stored in small pits, bins, or cists is considered to have been more readily accessible. Most of the food at great kiva settlements and small-structure habitations was stored in the room block or in special storage structures. Few large storage pits were in rooms or in extramural locations. Isolated storage structures, insecure due to their visibility, may have been used for a few weeks or months after the harvest, until the supply was used or moved to more permanent storage in the pueblo.

In the following discussion, one- to five-room structures are considered together and compared to the rooms at great kiva sites. Storage activities account for 25 percent of the rooms at small sites and 23 percent of

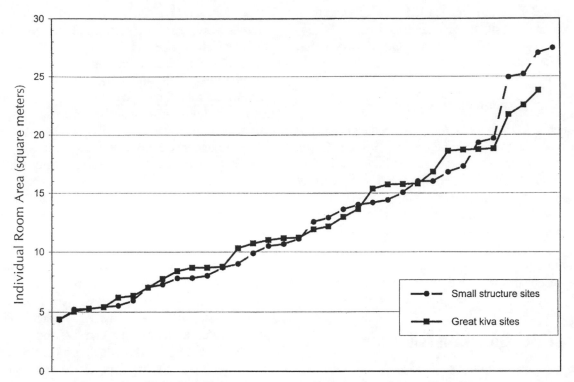

Figure 5.1. Size of habitation rooms at small-structure and great kiva sites.

the rooms at great kiva sites. Storage rooms account for 14 percent of the room block area of small sites and 13 percent of the room block area at great kiva sites (see Appendix A). One exceptionally large storage room (36 square meters) in the Schoens Dam project area was omitted from the small sites calculation; it alone accounted for 5 percent of the storage space at all small sites. The room was in a multiroom structure, and the excavators did not note anything remarkable except its large size (Stebbins and Hartman 1988: 149). Overall, the use of storage and habitation rooms was similar at small-structure and great kiva sites (Figs. 5.1, 5.2).

The distribution of storage rooms reveals no patterns (Fig. 5.3). The majority of the back rooms at Tla Kii Pueblo were storage rooms. No storage rooms were identified at Cothrun's Kiva or Hough's Great Kiva sites, but neither was completely excavated. The five-room structure on Corduroy Creek (AZ P:16:12 ASU) that was completely excavated had no storage rooms. Only one tiny storage room was recorded at the sites in the Snowflake-Mesa Redondo project area. The Scotts Reservoir Project reported six storage rooms, which was more than for many other areas, but all were extremely small and account for only 13.92 square meters of storage space. The largest featureless room in the project area was in a five-room pueblo with small habi-

tation rooms. Most storage spaces were in multiroom masonry structures, but a one-room masonry structure, a one-room jacal structure, and one room in a multiroom jacal structure were used for storage.

In addition to entire rooms used for long-term storage of food and other materials, spaces within habitation rooms were used for more readily accessible storage. Of the 47 habitation rooms excavated at 24 sites, 11 had storage facilities and one had a small external auxiliary wall that was thought by the excavator to enclose a storage area (Feature 15, NA 18,343). Two storage bins were constructed in Room 7 at Tla Kii Pueblo. Elsewhere in the pueblo, partition walls were placed one meter from the back wall of the room, creating areas that may have been used for storage. The interior wall in Room 2 at Hough's Great Kiva Site was non-load bearing. A similar partial wall was noted in Room 9 at site NA 18,216 (Hartman 1990). Interpretation is difficult, because many of the excavators assign this long space, often less than a meter wide, a room number. Table 5.8. summarizes the location and size of storage features. Bushel calculations assume that the whole floor area was used for food storage and that food was stored to a meter high (Plog 1974: 136).

Approximately one room in ten (11 of 103) had internal storage facilities. Identified storage rooms made

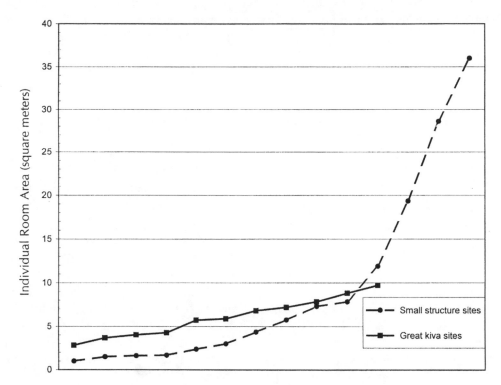

Figure 5.2. Size of storage rooms at small-structure and great kiva sites.

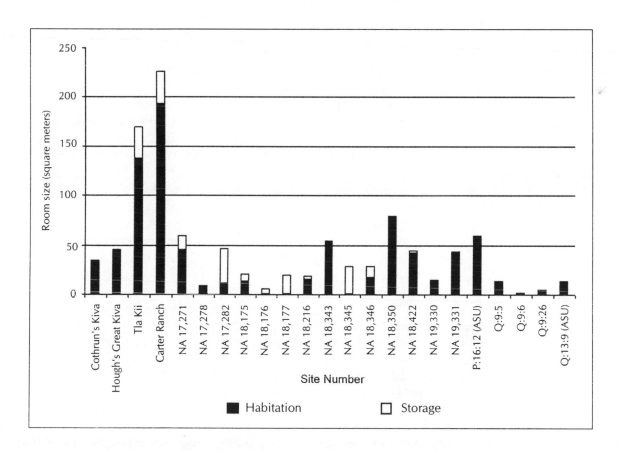

Figure 5.3. Allocation of habitation and storage space in project area sites.

Table 5.8. In-room Storage Areas

Site	Feature, Room	Room Area (m²)	Bushels
NA 18,176	Feature 5	1.35	37.50
NA 18,343	Feature 2	4.00	111.11
NA 18,343	Feature 6	2.03	56.39
NA 18,343	Feature 15	2.03	56.39
NA 18,345	Feature 4	5.21	144.72
NA 18,216	in Room 9	0.56	15.56
NA 18,422	Room 2	1.12	31.11
Hough's G. Kiva	Room 2	5.30	147.22
Tla Kii	Room 7	3.05	84.70
		2.29	63.61
Tla Kii	Room 15	10.32	286.67
Tla Kii	Room 18	10.00	277.78

up about 14 percent of the area (16 percent with the single large room included) and 24 percent of the quantity of rooms and structures in the late eleventh- and early twelfth-century communities. The counts of storage rooms accord well with the estimate that between A.D. 900 and 1150 some 25 percent of the rooms in the Hay Hollow Valley were storage rooms (Plog 1974: 90. This quantification of storage space in the Mogollon Rim region provides some insight into long-term storage activities, but probably underestimates the total amount of storage space in the pueblos. Roofs and partitioned interiors of large habitation rooms may also have been used for the short term storage of shelled or on-the-cob corn. If the wild plants that comprised as much as one-third to one-half the daily diet (Hartman and others 1988: 217) were used more quickly than domesticates, this, too, might account for the limited availability of long-term storage facilities.

As limited as the pueblo storage spaces were, identified communal storage spaces were fewer, if present at all. Independence of households is implied. Shared food was from household stores, not from household contributions to a communal store.

Distribution and Exchange

Exchanges within the household are nearly impossible to reconstruct, but it is possible to examine the distribution relationships in which the household was engaged, especially those relationships created through the exchange of items less perishable than food. Distribution of food and crafts among households within a community has been identified in communities in other regions. When a region has sufficient geological heterogeneity that vessels made in each community could be

compositionally differentiated, the local exchange of vessels could be identified in archaeological contexts (Duff 1993, 1994; Miksa and Heidke 2001). In such places the distribution of cooking and storage vessels can be a proxy measure for lines of food sharing and the movement of information. The results of oxidation studies of brown ware sherds demonstrate that the diversity of alluvial clays in the Mogollon Rim region is not sufficient to compositionally distinguish brown ware production locales.

James Lombard, the petrographer who pioneered what is now known as the petrofacies approach (Miksa and Heidke 1995), conducted a preliminary study in the Snowflake–Mesa Redondo area. In his sample of 39 thin sections from "18 different pottery types and styles," he distinguished six temper categories, but they could not be reliably tied to any one production locale. He concluded that although there are clear geologic differences (the Snowflake–Mesa Redondo area includes a basalt field), potters were using only material from the widespread sedimentary formations in the area (Lombard 1988: 220). The results of ceramic oxidation observations and Lombard's petrographic study suggest that while it may be possible to use trace element analyses to differentiate raw material sources (Lombard 1988: 221), inexpensive methods are of limited use for documenting fine-scale processes of ceramic exchange among households and communities in the Mogollon Rim region.

In contrast, ceramic vessels are useful for approximating some of the relationships between households in the Mogollon Rim region and those outside the region (Herr 1997). Three wares were produced in the region in the eleventh and twelfth centuries: the local brown ware, Cibola White Ware, and Puerco Valley Red Ware. These three wares accounted for 96 percent of the sherd assemblage. Nonlocal wares at the nine-room site of Hough's Great Kiva included Cibola Gray Ware, Little Colorado Gray Ware, Prescott Gray Ware, San Francisco Mountain Gray Ware, Alameda Brown Ware, Tusayan Gray Ware, Tusayan White Ware, Little Colorado White Ware, White Mountain Red Ware, and a single sherd of red-on-buff from the Phoenix Basin area. Cothrun's Kiva Site had a similar diversity of ceramics, minus San Francisco Mountain Gray Ware and plus several sherds of San Juan Red Ware (Fig. 5.4). Surveyors have identified many of these same nonlocal wares at small sites with and without great kivas.

Nonlocally produced vessels in household contexts across the site imply household participation in long dis-

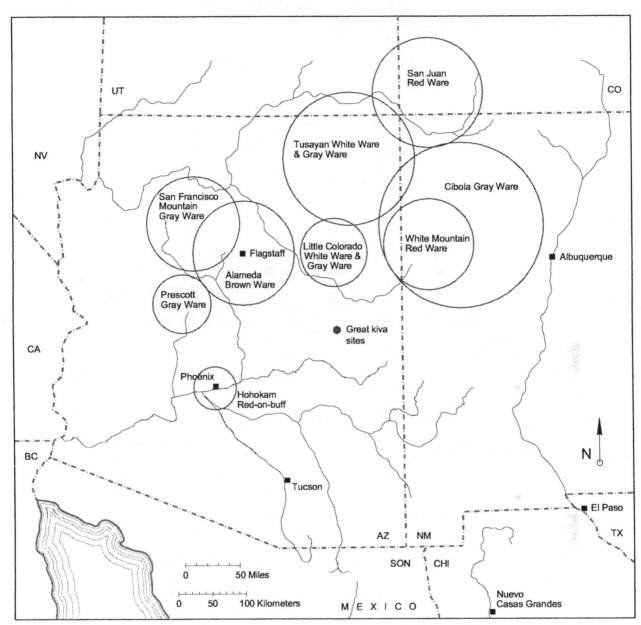

Figure 5.4. Production areas of nonlocal ceramics in great kiva
sites in the Mogollon Rim region. (Graphic by Susan Hall.)

tance social relationships. Three reconstructible nonlocal vessels were on the roof of Room 1 at Cothrun's
Kiva (a Pueblo II–Pueblo III Tusayan White Ware
bowl, a Holbrook 'B' Black-on-white bowl, and a Little
Colorado Indented Corrugated Gray Ware jar), and
approximately half of an Aquarius Orange bowl was on
the roof of Room 1 at Hough's Great Kiva.

This trade in nonlocal ceramics did not fulfill an
economic need, as residents of the Silver Creek
drainage produced more than 95 percent of their
utilitarian and service vessels. Most likely, nonlocal

vessels represented gifts and exchanges used to create
and maintain long-term social ties. The presence of so
many nonlocally produced ceramic wares demonstrates
the importance of varied social connections to community residents.

Other indicators of long-distance trade in the region
are few. Only 12 pieces of turquoise, azurite, quartz
crystal, and shell came from SCARP great kiva sites.
Such materials were similarly lacking at Tla Kii (Haury
(1985d: 131) and Carter Ranch (Rinaldo 1964b: 91–95).
Marine shell, in particular, was extremely sparse at all

Table 5.9. Relationship between Settlement Pattern and Social Organization

	No Ownership	Ownership
Dispersed settlement	Low population density	High population pressure
	Extensive land use	Intensive land use, people live near their fields
	Neolocal residence	Neolocal residence
	No inheritance rules	Inheritance from nuclear family
Aggregated settlement	Unlikely	Higher population density
		Intensive land use
		Lineage organizations
		Lineage based inheritance

NOTE: After Netting 1990.

late eleventh- and early twelfth-century sites in the Silver Creek drainage and was obtained as a manufactured good, not as raw material (Haury 1985d: 131; Vokes 1999).

The limited exchange of prestige materials in the eleventh- and twelfth-century long-distance trade networks was in direct contrast to the more regular long-distance exchange of mundane goods, suggesting that the most important characteristic of these far-flung exchange contacts was not the high value of the ceramics. Instead exchange was a way to create the widespread social ties that evened out spatial variability and provided stability for communities that themselves had few people and resources.

HOUSEHOLD TRANSMISSION

"*Transmission* refers to the transfer of land, property, roles, and rights from one generation to the next" (Lightfoot 1994: 156, emphasis in original). Patterns of inheritance are affected by patterns of ownership (Table 5.9).

Where the conditions of land scarcity and continuous production to support a dense local population are relaxed, rights to resources become less strict and explicit. . . . Where land is plentiful, and exploited by extensive methods, it will have little value for exchange (Netting 1993: 161).

In such situations, movement is expected when natural productivity declines. A cross-cultural study by Adler (1996c) shows that groups with intermediate investment of agricultural labor tend to have patterns of communal rights to land. Individual rights to land were associated with high or low levels of agricultural investment. Proprietary rights were respected while the land was in use, and often fields were marked (Fish and Fish 1984)

with shrines or prayer offerings to ensure the fertility of the land and seeds. In the frontier model, development of the concept of private property is not expected, and thus inheritance rules are not expected to be strong within the household. Personal ornaments and specific tools of trade are likely to be the only items associated with the concept of property. Field boundaries or other proprietary markers are considered evidence for ownership of land. Items taken out of daily circulation and buried are considered "owned" by the individual.

As is common in groups who use land extensively (Netting 1993), usufruct strategies probably governed the use of agricultural fields in the Mogollon Rim region. There is no evidence for investment of labor in field construction, clearing, or demarcation of field boundaries (Stone 1994). There were few water or soil control features in the region during any time period.

Time and labor invested in the construction of field houses is time and labor not expended on agriculture. Although these structures are functional, their elaboration is not. Assuming that full masonry walls indicate a greater labor investment than other walls, field houses with full masonry walls may have been symbolic, if passive, claims to land and associated with the development of land tenure (Kohler 1992; Snead 1995: 44). In the Mogollon Rim region, masonry constituted only the lower portion of the walls of seasonally used, one-room and small structures, implying that the field houses in the region were functional rather than symbolic. Ownership and inheritance of land were probably not an important part of the domestic economy.

Evidence for personal property comes from burials, although some items may be indicative of mortuary ritual. Thirty inhumations were recovered at Carter Ranch Pueblo (Rinaldo 1964c: 59) and four Carrizo phase burials were uncovered at Tla Kii Pueblo (Haury 1985d). Ornaments such as necklaces, collars, and pendants of shell, turquoise, jet, and an unidentified red stone were buried with individuals at both sites. Ceramic vessels were common funerary objects and accompanied every burial at Tla Kii Pueblo. One male at Carter Ranch Pueblo was buried with elaborate grave goods, including a bone club and a bow guard. Grooved bone awls were in the burials of three males (Rinaldo 1964c). Intergenerational transmission of goods was likely limited to the few items of personal property, and possibly ritual paraphernalia, that were not buried with the individual.

HOUSEHOLD REPRODUCTION

Household reproduction occurs if the settlement or region continues to be occupied in the succeeding generation, but the physical reproduction of a single household is nearly impossible to assess when households are mobile. The reproduction of the household includes the socialization of its children. Reproduction is interpreted as the continuity of household relationships and continuity in household division of labor. Architectural remodeling episodes provide evidence of changes in the household through time. Some aspects of the division of labor were addressed in the discussion of household production; here, division of labor is examined as the spatial organization of activities within the domestic space.

Changes to domestic architecture demonstrate changes in the structure of the household through the years (Mindeleff 1989: 647; Stone 1987: 65). Patterns of access, indicated by open and sealed doors, and remodeling of rooms, may indicate changes in the life cycle of the domestic unit. Spatial needs change as children are born, grow, marry, or move away. This means of identifying changing households works best in long occupied houses and settlements (Stone 1987). In the briefly occupied great kiva settlements, remodeling was limited. The one sealed doorway (of three doorways identified) at Cothrun's Kiva Site, the four (of five) at Tla Kii Pueblo, and the five (of 17) at Carter Ranch Pueblo, and construction episodes described in the previous chapter, may represent life-cycle changes in those households. According to architectural, settlement pattern, midden, and chronological data, room blocks at the four southern great kiva settlements were occupied for no more than about two generations, and perhaps for a shorter time.

Changes in the organization of domestic space often coincide with changes in the organization of activities (Rapoport 1990: 11) and may provide a measure for gauging the transmission of learning across generations. As division of labor becomes more rigid, the spatial organization of gendered activities becomes more distinct (Crown 2000). The high ratio of habitation rooms to storage rooms in many of the Mogollon Rim region room blocks suggests that multiple-room household-storage suites were uncommon, as were other types of specialized rooms. Activities that occurred within the prehistoric pueblo were generally habitation, storage, and manufacturing. The definition of space for each activity and the amount of space accorded for each varied through time in the Mogollon Rim region, but in the eleventh and twelfth centuries the use of domestic space in this region was generalized (Reid and Whittlesey 1982: 692).

Despite the large ceremonial structures present in the great kiva settlements, only the remains of domestic production, distribution, and consumption activities were evident in the ceramic assemblages. Artifacts were found in situ (or in primary contexts) in the roof fall of Room 1 and Room 4 at Cothrun's Kiva Site and Room 1 at Hough's Great Kiva Site. Corn was stored on roofs at Cothrun's and whole decorated vessels were either stored in the rafters or on the roofs. A large storage jar and a potter's puki remained on the floor of a room at Hough's, and corn was drying or stored on the roof. Generalized habitation and storage activities occurred in all spaces. At Hough's, Cothrun's, and Tla Kii Pueblo domestic rooms were multifunctional, showing evidence of habitation, storage, food processing, and ceramic production in a single room. The domestic organization into which the child was socialized shows no evidence of strongly marked social differentiation. In the Mogollon Rim region, differentiation of space was a late prehistoric trend whose early expression occurred at places such as Carter Ranch, where more specialization of activities can be discerned.

Exploring the relationship between vessel size and context provided another way to identify the spatial distribution of activities across the settlement, particularly in places where in situ assemblages were not present. Comparisons of the median size (rim radius) of decorated and undecorated bowls and jars from rooms, the great kivas, middens, and extramural surfaces at all great kiva sites produced no evidence of special loci for food processing or storage that might be indicated by concentrations of utilitarian vessels of certain sizes, or for places of increased consumption that might be indicated by increased numbers of decorated bowls. Although both domestic and ritual activities were certainly performed at the great kiva settlements, similar discard

Table 5.10. Habitation and Storage Room Sizes by Site

	Habitation Rooms (square meters)					Storage Rooms (square meters)				
	N	Minimum	Maximum	Median	Sum	N	Minimum	Maximum	Median	Sum
Sites with Great Kivas										
Cothrun's Kiva[a]	2	15.73	18.72	17.22	34.45					
Hough's Great Kiva[a]	2	21.73	23.80	22.77	45.50					
Tla Kii[b]	13	5.04	22.54	8.76	136.91	6	2.82	5.72	3.85	32.90
Carter Ranch[c]	16	6.20	18.80	11.50	192.47	5	4.28	9.72	6.81	33.87
Summary	33	5.04	23.80	11.20	409.35					
Sites with small structures										
NA 17,271[d]	3	8.70	19.31	16.79	44.80	2	7.3	7.84	7.57	15.14
NA 17,278[d]	1			9.00	9.00					
NA 17,282[d]	1			10.60	10.60	1			36.00	36.00
NA 18,175[e]	2	5.22	7.8	6.51	13.02	2	3	4.36	3.68	7.36
NA 18,177[f]		3	1	1.68	1.50	1			19.35	19.35
NA 18,216[e]	1			14.4	14.40	3	1	1.68	1.50	4.18
NA 18,343[f]	3	12.90	25.20	16.00	54.10					
NA 18,345[f]						1			28.60	28.6
NA 18,346[f]	1			17.28	17.28	1			11.90	11.9
NA 18,350[f]	3	24.94	27.44	27.03	79.41	1			5.76	5.76
NA 18,422[e]	4	4.35	15.04	11.21	41.81	1			2.38	2.38
NA 19,330[f]	2	7.28	7.82	7.55	15.10					
NA 19,331[f]	5	5.27	19.69	5.95	43.48					
AZ P:16:12 (ASU)[g]	5	8.00	16.00	11.10	59.20					
AZ Q:9:5 (ASM)[h]	1			14.18	14.18					
AZ Q:9:6 (ASM)[h]						1		1.62		
AZ Q:9:26 (ASM)[h]	1			5.42	5.42					
AZ Q:13:9 (ASU)[g]	1			14.00	14.00					
Summary	34	4.35	27.44	11.82	435.85					

SITE NUMBERS: NA, Museum of Northern Arizona; ASU, Arizona State University; ASM, Arizona State Museum.

SOURCES: a, Herr and others 1999; b, Haury 1985d; c, Martin and others 1964; d, Stebbins and Hartman 1988; e, Hartman 1990; f, Dosh 1988; g, Stafford and Rice 1980; h, Neily 1988.

patterns blur any spatial distinctions that may have existed.

HOUSEHOLD CO-RESIDENCE

Co-residence describes who lives together in the household. For the archaeologist, knowing the exact composition of the household is nearly impossible. A slightly more accessible variable is the size of the household, at least in relationship to household size at other times or in other regions. In the frontier model, strong development of lineages is not postulated (although lineages may develop when the area becomes more settled). Households are likely to be independent and loosely integrated. If labor needs have to be met by the co-residential unit, house size may be larger. If labor availability is flexible within the community, the household may not have to expend its own resources meeting its labor requirements and households would not need to be particularly large.

Although physical characteristics of the prehistoric household are difficult to reconstruct, relative measures of size and structure can be described. Room size indicates either the number of people per room or the number of activities per room. In the Mogollon Rim region, room sizes were highly variable regardless of site type or location (Table 5.10). Hough's and Cothrun's great kiva sites had a larger median room size than the other great kiva sites. Otherwise, there were no significant patterns in habitation room sizes among or within different types of sites. The common occurrence of generalized rooms or large households probably accounts for the large size of rooms.

Vessel sizes can also be used as part of demographic and household size analyses (Mills 1994b: 335–336). Rim diameters are used as proxy measures for vessel siz Rim diameter is more directly related to the vessel capacity of bowls than of jars but, if like vessels (for example, decorated jars, decorated bowls, undecorated

**Table 5.11. Regional Comparison of
Median Vessel Rim Radii**
(In centimeters)

	Decorated Bowl	Undecorated Bowl	Decorated Jar	Undecorated Jar
Mogollon Rim	10	9	4	8
		Bowls		
Upper Puerco*		8		9
Little Colorado*		6		8

* From Mills 1994b

jars) are analyzed separately the differences in orifice diameter may be more meaningful. Vessel capacities have been shown to vary with the size of the consumption group, normally the domestic unit, but on occasions suprahousehold organizations feast together. Those who host feasts are often the wealthier people in the community; thus large vessels may be associated with both larger consumption groups and wealthier households (Nelson 1981; Turner and Lofgren 1966).

There was little internal variation in vessel sizes and forms within the Mogollon Rim region, but comparison with vessels from adjacent regions shows that the median rim radii of undecorated jars were comparable to undecorated jars in the Little Colorado River Valley (Table 5.11). However, the median rim radii of decorated and undecorated bowls (presumably serving-eating vessels) were larger than the median rim radii of all bowls in the nearby Puerco and Little Colorado River valleys (Mills 1994b). Considering that rooms in the Mogollon Rim region were large, it is possible that the households represented by those rooms were also larger than households of nearby areas.

COMMUNITY PRODUCTION

Just as household production is limited by availability of labor, so too, is community production on the frontier. Production outside the household is not a daily event in small-scale agricultural societies, but it does occur regularly, even in frontier situations. People from different households join together in informal and formal organizations to work their fields, build their houses, create and maintain common property, and build and keep ritual structures. Most of the evidence for community production in the Mogollon Rim region is indirect or analogical. The organization of labor can be evaluated by examining the construction methods of communal architecture and other community built features. Many other communal activities are so common

in ethnographic reports of small-scale agricultural societies that their presence can be assumed.

Portions of the agricultural season, particularly planting and harvesting, require more simultaneous tasks than a single household can coordinate. Considering the small size of the sites in the Mogollon Rim region, residents of multiple settlements may have been required for some tasks, "Because at any time anyone may need help, therefore all help one another" (Parsons 1966: 111). Not enough archaeological investigation has occurred in prehispanic agricultural fields to reconstruct specific activities at these locations. However, in modern small-scale agricultural societies, fields that are the primary responsibility of a single household are often planted and harvested by groups of friends and kin. Communal field work is a regular activity in the historic Rio Grande pueblos (Dozier 1983: 127). Hopi men help each other plant and harvest corn fields, and Hopi women help each other plant beans (Beaglehole 1937: 27). The Zuni help each other with planting, hoeing, scaring crows, harvesting, and husking the corn (Green 1979: 257–279). A cross cultural study of nonranked "tribal" societies shows the commonality of agricultural work parties (Table 5.12). Gatherings for labor-intensive planting and complex harvesting and storage tasks play an important role in the seasonal scheduling of labor.

Two lines of evidence suggest that Mogollon Rim communities attempted to attract labor. First, with its abundance of great kivas, a form of communal architecture, the Mogollon Rim region was distinct from other areas of small-scale agriculturalists. The ritual activities held in and around the great kiva attracted people to the settlement at least temporarily. After the ceremony, people probably engaged in feasts, competitions, information sharing, and the coordination of labor. Second, the building of communal architecture (like a great kiva) was an event in itself (Tuzin 1980) and was associated with the same kind of festivities as occurred at other labor-related events, such as "beer farming."

Great Kiva Construction

Great kiva construction was similar at the five excavated Mogollon Rim region great kivas (Table 5.13). SCARP great kivas were situated on an undulating landscape of small hills and drainages. To create an approximately level floor in such a large, fairly shallow, semisubterranean structure, the great kiva was cut into the slope higher on the hillside. The fill was moved to the lower part of the slope to build a level floor, creating a

Table 5.12. Work Groups in a Sample of Twenty-four Tribal Societies

Culture Group	Village Population	Primary plant products	Suprahousehold organization of domestic and agricultural labor	Reference
North America				
Cochiti	486	Corn, beans, pumpkins, watermelon	Communal cleaning of irrigation system. Communal tending of cacique's field. Reciprocal labor among male kin.	Lange 1959
Maidu	175	Acorns, pine nuts, and roots	None.	Bean and Theodoratus 1978; Ridell 1978
Mandan	320	Corn, beans, squash, sunflowers	Village helps with harvest.	Will and Spinden 1906
Owens Valley				
Paiute	100	Acorns, pine nuts, root crops	Village women harvest root crops from irrigated fields.	Liljeblad and Fowler 1986
N. Pomo	150	Acorns, wild seeds, and nuts	None.	Bean 1978
Raramuri	150	Maize, beans	Invited guests help harvest fields of very dispersed households.	Kennedy 1978
Taremuit	100	Wild berries, greens, shrubs, and roots	None.	Burch 1984
Zuni	1,700	Corn	Informal groups of males hoe together, women prepare nightly feast.	Cushing 1979
South America				
Mundurucu	200	Manioc, yams, sweet potatoes, maize, squash, pineapples, and cotton	Women cooperate in fields and in the intensive post-harvest processing of bitter manioc; village men and women help build houses.	Murphy and Murphy 1974
Nambiquara	50?	Maize?	Extended family does all agricultural work together.	Price 1987; Steward 1948
Sherente	200	Maize, root crops, wild plants	Men's society clears land and weeds; wives of men in association harvest.	Nimuendajú 1942
Timbira	400–500	Corn, sweet potato, yam, manioc, horse bean, arrow root, ground nut, squash, cotton, gourds	Junior age-class helps others harvest; members of age-class help each other (e.g., build houses).	Nimuendajú 1946; Gross 1979
Yanomamo	150	Manioc, taro, sweet potatoes, avocado, papaya, hot peppers, wild palm fruit, nuts	Headman's brothers and sons help with this larger garden, but no indications that this is common in individual fields.	Chagnon 1968
Africa				
Dogon	210	Millet, sorghum, po, rice, corn, sesame, bean, squash or gourd, tomato, sweet potato, yam	Junior age-group weeds gardens for others, age-group members help each other. Po is harvested communally.	Griaule and Dieterlen 1954; Palau 1957
Fang	250	Manioc, peanuts, corn, sugarcane, yam	In past, cooperation within minor lineage, government has now introduced "work team."	Balandier 1955; Fernandez 1982
Jola	400–600	Rice, millet, sorghum, ground nuts, palm wine	Non-co-residing kin and paid unisexual groups sow, transplant, and harvest. Work groups organized by residential courtyard or ward. Money is spent communally. Formality of work groups varies by village.	Linares 1997
Kofyar	250	Millet, sorghum, ground nuts, yam, cassava, cocoyam	Two organizations: mar muos invited guests help clear and harvest fields; wuk reciprocal labor group	Netting 1993; Stone 1996
Tallensi	300	Cereals	Lineage members provide help	Fortes 1945

Table 5.12. Work Groups in a Sample of Twenty-four Tribal Societies (continued)

Culture Group	Village Population	Primary plant products	Suprahousehold organization of domestic and agricultural labor	Reference
Oceania				
Arapesh	250	Yams, taro, sago, coconut	Neighbors, spatial proximity may outweigh kinship.	Tuzin 1976, 1980; Mead 1967
Baktaman	250	Taro, sago trees, and wild foods	Sago collection communal with friendly households; men help each other fence adjacent fields.	Barth 1975
Kiwai	250	Yam, taro, sweet potato, banana, coconut, sago, sugar cane	Fellow villagers help with harvest when invited.	Landtman 1927
New Ireland	220	Taro, yams, bananas, coconuts	Men within a hamlet help each other build houses.	Powdermaker 1933
Orokaiva	150	Taro, yams	Male age-mates help, especially with building houses.	Williams 1930
Tsembaga	100	Taro, yams, sweet potatoes, banana, manioc, sugarcane, greens	Generally kept within extended family.	Rappoport 1968; Johnson and Earle 1987

NOTE: Tribes are from a sample of nonranked societies previously selected by Adler (1989) for a study of ritual architecture, with a few added groups.

pattern of cut and fill leveling. On the filled side of the great kiva, the exterior of the earthen core wall was stabilized with massive masonry and the bench was built of construction fill. A broken Reserve Black-on-white bowl in the bench construction materials at site AZ P:16:160 (ASM) may have been placed as part of the construction ritual. At Hough's Great Kiva, the foundation stones of the wall separating the end of the bench from the ramp were built into this fill.

The subterranean walls of Mogollon Rim great kivas were built of earth, and masonry surrounded an earth and rubble core for above-grade walls. Unshaped stones faced the vertical surfaces of the benches, but their horizontal surfaces and the surfaces of the entryways were constructed of packed earth. Large (40–80 cm) stones were minimally shaped before being laid into the great kiva wall in semipatterned courses. The stones were then packed with mud and presumably covered with a mud plaster, although little plaster has been recovered. At Cothrun's Kiva, a small piece of plaster with a line of black paint showed that walls may have been decorated. Some household kivas in the nearby Puerco Valley had simple painted designs.

The shape of the great kiva entryways varied. The ramp at Tla Kii Pueblo descended from the exterior to the interior with the aid of log and stone risers. The ramp at Carter Ranch Pueblo had a high and a low side. The ramps at Hough's Great Kiva and site AZ P:16:160 (ASM) were built of construction fill and appeared U–shaped in cross-section. Internal, single-course walls abutted the main wall of these structures, providing ends to the benches and architecturally separating them from the entryways. A long wall along one side of the ramp at Cothrun's Kiva created a modified keyhole shape for the overall structure.

Was the Great Kiva Roofed?

One of the most labor intensive parts of great kiva construction would have been roofing the structure, and how the superstructures were built in the Mogollon Rim region has not been resolved. Construction of a full roof would have consumed more labor and resources than any other activity associated with a great kiva, and, if roofed, Hough's Great Kiva would have been one of the largest roofed great kivas in the Southwest. There were no visible postholes for primary support posts in the 10 square meters excavated in Hough's Great Kiva or in the 18 square meters excavated in the smaller great kiva at Cothrun's site, where construction of the walls and bench was similar. Exposure of the floor in Cothrun's

Table 5.13. Comparison of Excavated Great Kivas in the Mogollon Rim Region

	Hough's Great Kiva	AZ P:16:160 (ASM)	Cothrun's Kiva	Tla Kii (Kiva 1)	Carter Ranch Great Kiva
Diameter	24 m wall to wall, 20 m below bench	22.6 m wall to wall, 20 m below bench	17.5 m wall to wall, 14.5 m below bench	18.2 m wall to wall, 15.8 m below bench	17.3 m wall to wall, 14.8 m below bench
Estimated floor to roof height	2.3–2.5 m	1.8 m	2.0–2.4 m	2.5 m?	2.5–3.5 m?
Standing wall courses	Interior: 1; Exterior: 2	Interior: 4; Exterior: 2	Interior: 2; Exterior: 2	Interior: 2; Exterior: 1	Exterior: 0.53 m
Wall construction	Double wall of full-coursed sandstone masonry with chinking. Core of earth and rubble. Slight evidence of interior and exterior wall plastering.	Double wall of semi-coursed sandstone masonry with chinking. Core of earth and rubble. Two foundation levels.	Double wall of sandstone masonry with chinking. Core of earth and rubble. Wall incorporates bedrock. Slight evidence of interior wall plastering and painting.	Traces of plaster on interior walls and entrance.	Earthen walls and bench faced with coursed sandstone and igneous masonry with chinking. No traces of plaster.
Wall width	1.05 m	0.65–0.70 m	0.7–1.2 m	At south 1 m, otherwise irregular and narrow	0.24 m
Estimated wall height (above ground surface)	1.0 m	1.3–1.5 m	1.0–1.5 m	Not high, unless stones reused elsewhere	1.5–2.5 m
Structure depth (below ground surface)	0.94 m	0.42 m	1.26 m	1.25 m	1.63 m
Direction of entrance	Southeast	Southeast	Northwest	Southeast	Southeast
Description of entrance	U-shaped ramp descends gradually to end of bench, then steps down to floor.	U-shaped ramp descends gradually to end of bench, then steps down to floor.	Ramp cross-section unknown, cut into sterile, possibly finished with white, flaky loam.	Descending in 3 low risers or steps.	Ramp, divided into two paths.
Bench construction	Earthen bench, masonry slab may define horizontal edge, unshaped stones define vertical face.	Earthen bench with medium, minimally shaped stones defining the vertical face.	Earthen bench with unshaped sandstone defining horizontal edge and small unshaped stones defining the vertical face.	Earthen bench with clay top and coursed stone facing.	Earthen bench with coursed stone facing.
Bench height / Bench width	0.4 m above floor / 1.45 m	0.2 m above floor / 1.28 m	0.5 m above floor / 1.12 m	0.7 m above floor avg. 1.5 m	0.7 m above floor approx. 1 m
Floor preparation	Clean sand on bedrock. Floor slopes gradually from bench to center of structure.	Use-compacted gray clay.	Clean sand on native claystone. Floor slopes gradually from bench to center of structure.	Hard packed clay. Floor slopes from bench to center of structure.	No prepared surface. Floor slopes from bench to center of structure.
Evidence of roofing	Two-step bench, wood impressed daub, evidence of burned beams, small charcoal fragments.	None	Limited charcoal and daub in great kiva fill; 1 small posthole.	Postholes, charcoal fragments.	Masonry pilasters, wood impressed daub, small charcoal fragments.
Floor features	Unknown	Unknown	1 small pit or posthole	3 postholes	Masonry pillars, 3 stone-lined rect. pits and hearth.

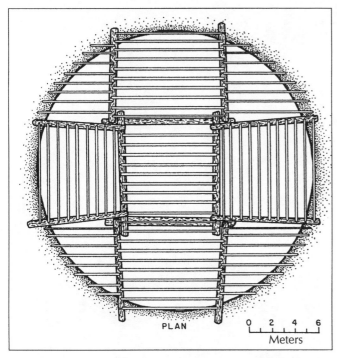

Figure 5.5. Hypothetical reconstruction by Ricky Light-foot of a four-post flat great kiva roof. Adapted from *The Kiva* 53(3), 1988, reprinted by permission of the Arizona Archaeological and Historical Society, Tucson.

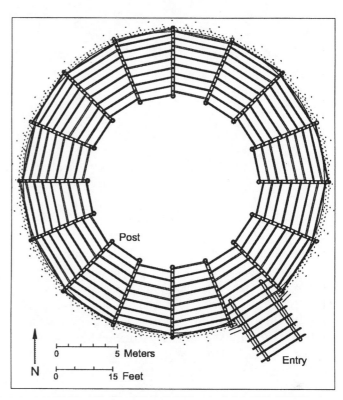

Figure 5.6. Hypothetical reconstruction of partial roofing over a great kiva. (Graphic by Susan Hall.)

great kiva were extensive enough that, if present, a large posthole should have been found, but only a small pit was located. Although charcoal and burnt daub were distributed throughout the fill at both sites and impressed burnt daub was in the fill at Hough's, no large burned beams were present.

Evidence for roofs at Cothrun's Kiva and Hough's Great Kiva includes the presence of charcoal and abundant evidence of burning. The massive, full height walls could have supported some form of roof and were unlike the lower, narrower walls surrounding later Upper Little Colorado region unroofed great kivas at Hinkson Ranch, Los Gigantes, Garcia Ranch, and sites NA 8,013 and NA 8,014 (Herr 1994: 61; Kintigh 1996; Kintigh and others 1996; Marshall and others 1979; Olson 1971). Posts and pilasters were often constructed on benches. Hough's Great Kiva had a double bench that might have provided room for superstructure supports.

Three roofing options are considered. The great kivas at the Hough's and Cothrun's sites may have been fully roofed and excavations in their floors may have missed the large postholes necessary for a flat, four-post roofing plan (Fig. 5.5) like that at Tla Kii. There were

five pillars, presumably roof supports, at Carter Ranch. Elsewhere, domed and corbeled roofs were supported by the walls and pilasters of small kivas, but this type of construction would have been expensive and has not been identified in any great kivas (Lekson 1984: 32).

The least likely possibility is that great kivas remained unroofed. The few, small postholes may indicate that no superstructure was built. However, there is substantial evidence for burning in the great kivas at Hough's and Cothrun's, even if postholes are few.

Another possibility worth considering is that a roof may have been built over the sides, if not the center, of the great kiva (Fig. 5.6). The reconstruction by Rob Ciaccio of a partially roofed kiva (Fig. 5.7) is approximately to scale and illustrates a ramada-like roof, slightly higher on the interior than the exterior (similar to the angled roof hypothesized for Great Kiva 1 at the Village of the Great Kivas; Roberts 1932: 94), covering the walls and bench. The framework illustrated may well have been covered with layers of mud and brush. Moisture would have caused considerable maintenance problems for an unroofed subterranean or semisubterranean structure. The benches of friable sandstone and

Figure 5.7. Cross section of a reconstruction of a typical great kiva in the Mogollon Rim region, with hypothetical partial roofing. (Drawing by Rob Ciaccio.)

construction fill would have eroded quickly in the summer monsoons and spring snowmelt. If no precautions were taken against flooding, considerable bailing of water would have been necessary. Excavation of the "floor zone" at Cothrun's Kiva indicated that although the floor was in good condition near the bench, in the center of the kiva it showed substantial mixing, possibly as a consequence of that portion being exposed to the elements and of the continued maintenance required. A lighter superstructure would have used smaller and fewer posts. It is possible that small postholes situated close to the benches were not uncovered in our excavations, which did not explore the bench or the area immediately adjacent to the bench but focused instead on finding more substantial and centrally located postholes. The small pit in Cothrun's kiva could have held a slender roof support. Depending on the depth of roof coverage, roof support posts could have been located on the bench instead of in, or in addition to, the floor. There was evidence of bench posts in the great kiva at Tla Kii Pueblo. A partial roof would have required regular maintenance, along with the exposed floor, but may have involved less overall labor than the construction and maintenance of a full roof on great kivas.

The Sundown Site (NA 9,093) in the Puerco River valley has a great kiva floor plan (Fig. 5.8) similar to the plans of Mogollon Rim great kivas. In the preliminary report, S. Alan Skinner describes the great kiva as 12.5 m in diameter and 1.2 m deep.

> The walls were constructed by excavating a pit into sterile gray Chinle clay almost to the depth of the underlying yellow sand. The bench was carved out during this work, but the back was unlined except in the SE part of the kiva. The front of the bench was lined almost all around the kiva except in a few spots where a clay wall was constructed. . . . The floor is a layer of gray clay

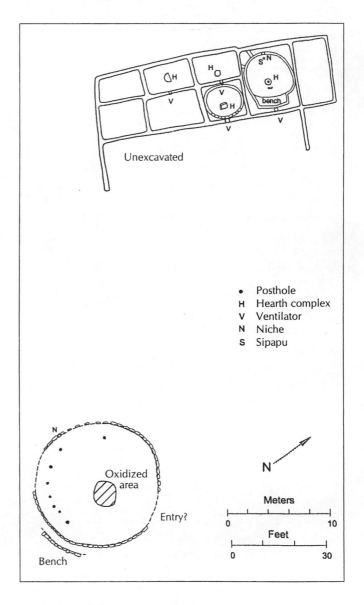

Figure 5.8. Plan of the Sundown Site in the Puerco River valley. (Compiled from site plans by George J. Gumerman, courtesy of the Museum of Northern Arizona; graphic by Susan Hall.)

1 cm to 10 cm thick, plastered over the underlying sterile yellow sand. It is decidedly concave. A central burned area, blackened with charcoal is 2.8 x 3.1 meters in size [similar to Carter Ranch]. A series of postholes located one meter from the wall and encircling the room were dug into the yellow sand. These holes range from 15 to 26 cm in depth and 17 to 20 cm in diameter.

The excavators postulated either a central support post or a four-post plan; they found no indications of roof support even though the entire structure was uncovered. The idea of partial roofing over the large Mogollon Rim great kivas is presented here to stimulate closer examination of great kiva construction in future excavations.

Labor Investment

The Mogollon Rim great kivas were topographically situated and built to be impressive to both the viewer and participant, but they lacked the formality of the great kivas in Chaco Canyon and its outliers. Construction methods used in the Rim region were less labor-intensive than those used elsewhere (Tables 5.13, 5.14). In virtually every major construction task, Mogollon Rim great kivas required less labor: less dirt was excavated for the great kiva pit, stones were not well shaped and were set into greater quantities of mortar, floor preparation and floor features were minimal, raw materials and timber were locally available, and the builders were not as attentive to detail as were Chacoan masons. Although the general morphology of the Chacoan and Mogollon Rim region great kivas was similar, the details of construction and labor investment differed.

Other Evidence for Communal Production

Apart from the great kivas, no community constructions such as irrigation systems (Gregory 1991), roads (Roney 1992; Vivian 1997a, 1997b), or trails (Snead 1995) have been found in the Mogollon Rim region as occurred in other places across the Southwest. No floor assemblages were recovered in any of the excavated great kivas and craft production in the communal structures has not been identified. It is possible groups of crafts people worked together in extramural spaces and ramadas (Dosh 1988; Neily 1988).

The only other evidence for communal production is related to food processing for congregations of people. Although most of the grinding was conducted in the house, finger grooves in manos, a feature designed for comfort, may indicate longer grinding sessions associated with producing food for a large group. Finger grooves were present on approximately half the sample of unifacially used manos, and they appeared on bifacially used manos at Tla Kii (Haury 1985d: 115, 116). At Carter Ranch less than one-fourth of the manos had finger grooves (Rinaldo 1964b: 65). Women did their grinding for communal occasions in their houses, not in a communal work area with women from other households.

Certain animals were likely procured for community ritual practices. In SCARP great kiva assemblages, the only animal interpreted as having ritual use was the kestrel; the fox at Hough's Great Kiva Site was a post-abandonment intrusion (Table 5.3; Horner 1999). Remains of sharp-shinned hawk, harlequin quail, band-tailed pigeon, mourning dove, and black-billed magpie were recovered from Carrizo phase contexts at Tla Kii (Haury 1985d: 68–69). Ethnographic reports show the use of birds in modern pueblos is primarily for feathers and secondarily for food (Hodgetts 1996: 167; Parsons 1966: 29). Evidence from Tla Kii Pueblo may be interpreted accordingly, but a reexamination of this faunal assemblage, enumerating elements present and cut marks, would provide more information.

COMMUNITY DISTRIBUTION

Redistribution is one form of exchange at the community level. Formalized redistribution is not expected in the frontier model, but the exchange and consumption of food and perhaps other materials at festive occasions is likely. In the Mogollon Rim region, these occasions were centered on the great kiva. If formalized redistribution were present, evidence for communal storage would be expected. Trash disposal patterns, vessel size, and reconstruction of vessel function are used to distinguish past ritual and feasting events.

Great kivas and their ancillary rooms are often cited as locations of redistributive activities. Great kiva ceremonies provided occasions for the distribution of stored food. Fred Plog (1974: 125) was specific in his description of the redistributive function of these sites. He suggested that the rings of rooms occasionally built around great kivas in the San Juan Basin, northern San Juan Basin, and Upper Little Colorado were used for storage and that great kivas had a redistributive function. He extrapolated that Mogollon Rim great kivas could be similarly interpreted, even though no similar rings of rooms, and only a few alcove rooms, have been

Table 5.14. Comparison of Labor Investment in Great Kiva Construction in the Chaco and Mogollon Rim Regions

Chaco region, subterranean great kiva	Mogollon region, semisubterranean great kiva	Labor costs
EXCAVATE		
Excavate pit	Dig pit into slope	Estimated excavation cost:[a] 0.46 m³/ph
estimated 1,104 m³ removed from a Pueblo Bonito great kiva	*estimated 212 m³ removed from Hough's great kiva*	
Remove fill	Move fill downslope to create level floor, bench, ramp	
pit depth, Pueblo Bonito Great Kiva I approx. 3.35 m[b]		
WALLS		
Masonry walls built into pits	Subterranean walls of earth	Estimated stone shaping rate:[c] 14.0 ph/m³
	earth walls 0.94 m high at Hough's Great Kiva Site	
	Surface walls of masonry	
	walls more than 1 m high above grade	
Masonry shaped on visible and unseen sides	Masonry minimally shaped on visible side	Estimated mortar mixing rate:[c] 4.4 ph/m³
Quarry stone, locally available	Quarry stone, locally available	Estimated rate for all three tasks and minor stone shaping:[c] 28.25 ph/m³
Set with mortar	Set with mortar	Estimated laying core stones:[c] 7.06 ph/m³
estimate 60% stone, 40% mortar[c]	*Mogollon Rim region walls required more mortar than Chacoan walls, stones not shaped to fit each other as well*	Estimated laying facing stones:[c] 17.65 ph/m³
		Estimated fill transport cost (25 m):[a] 1.25 m³/ph
	Masonry set around an earth and rubble core above ground	Estimated water transport cost (0.5 km):[a] 0.12 m³/ph
Dig earth	Dig earth	Estimated rock transport cost (0.5 km):[a] 127 kg/ph
Acquire water for mixing	Acquire water for mixing	
Walls plastered	Walls plastered	
Transport earth, water, stone, plastering material	Transport earth, water, stone, plastering material	
ROOF		
Postholes or pillars constructed	Postholes or pillars constructed	Primary beam procurement (N = 1):[c] 0.7 ph
Cylindrical disks constructed		Primary beam preparation (N = 1):[c] 2.1 ph
Beam procurement, timber imported from 40+ km distant	Beam procurement — locally available	Primary beam transport (N = 1):[c] 53.4 ph
"roofing of the relatively small Great Kiva at Aztec, when reconstructed by Morris (1921), required fifty 20–30 cm x 3.7 m and eight hundred 1.8 m x 8 cm timbers"[d]		Primary beam installation (N = 1):[c] 0.5 ph
		Secondary beam procurement (N = 15):[c] 3.0 ph
		Secondary beam preparation (N = 15):[c] 9.0 ph
Beam preparation: trimming stripping	Beam preparation: trimming, stripping	Secondary beam transport (N = 15):[c] 45.0 ph
Roof construction	Roof construction	Secondary beam installation (N = 15):[c] 1.0 ph
Fully roofed, flat roof construction	Fully or partially roofed	Closing material: 12.0 ph/roof[c]
FLOOR		
Clay floor	Sand floor	Adobe laying rate, if comparable:[c] 0.23 m³/ph
Bench construction	Bench construction	
horizontal, vertical surfaces faced with shaped masonry	*Vertical edge faced with small unshaped stones*	
Fire box	Hearth?	
Deflector		
Floor vault		
ENTRY		
Antechamber and stair or tunnel construction	Rampway construction	

SOURCES: a, Craig and others 1998, Table 2; b, Vivian and Reiter 1960; c, Lekson 1984, Appendix B; d, Lekson 1984: 52.

found in this region. Although Plog noted that these rooms could have been used primarily for storing ritual material (Vivian 1959), he did not give the idea much credence. Lightfoot (1984: 73) similarly considered redistribution as one of the administrative functions of these central settlements.

Architecture large enough for community level storage is unknown in the Mogollon Rim region. Only the great kiva at Tla Kii Pueblo had auxiliary rooms. They were small, as were the two unit structures detached from the room block. The review of storage facilities above shows that there was little room for anything other than household storage. The few small pits in the great kiva floors could not have held stores of sufficient size to redistribute resources to community residents.

More informal mechanisms for exchange within the community certainly existed, although the evidence is ephemeral. In cross-cultural accounts, food is distributed among households within a community whenever there is occasion for a feast, from work parties to ritual gatherings (Chagnon 1968; Dozier 1966; Fox 1996; Kennedy 1978; Rappaport 1968; Stone 1996; Underhill 1979). Ample opportunity for both occasions would have been present in fields and at great kivas. The cluster of turkey bones deposited in a single dumping event in the midden at Hough's Great Kiva settlement may have been the result of such a feasting event.

Ceramic vessels play an important role in reconstructing ritual aggregations. A study of formation processes at Pueblo Alto showed that utilitarian jars, including many produced in Chuskan communities, far exceeded what would be expected from normal rates of household disposal (Toll and McKenna 1987: 217–218). This result was used to argue that Pueblo Alto was a site of pilgrimage fairs and that items brought into Chaco Canyon were consumed for rituals, not redistributed as other models had postulated (Toll 1985). Not enough information on duration of occupation is available from sites in the Mogollon Rim region to reconstruct such scenarios, but the Chacoan example provides a model that may be applied to other well-sampled sites.

Vessel size information has been used as evidence for feasting. If groups larger than the household eat together, the sizes of associated food processing, cooking, and eating vessels would be larger than the sizes of household vessels. Size modes are apparent in the rim radius histograms of decorated and undecorated bowls and of decorated and undecorated jars in the Mogollon Rim region (Figs. 5.9–5.12, Appendix B), but are not particularly strong when the distribution is multimodal and no obvious large vessel class is indicated. By con-

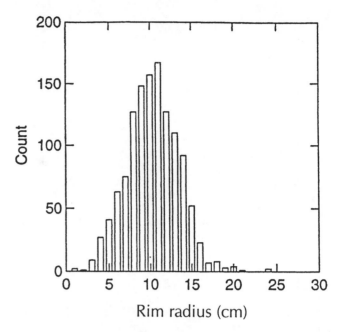

Figure 5.9. Distribution of rim radii of decorated bowls (N = 1,246).

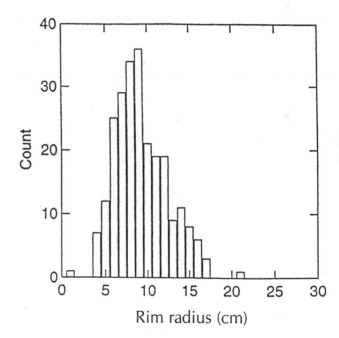

Figure 5.10. Distribution of rim radii of undecorated bowls (N = 241).

trast, studies of assemblages of Tusayan White Ware and Tsegi Orange Ware whole vessels from later sites in the Tusayan area show strong modes, suggesting that there was a real difference between household and communal vessels elsewhere (Mills 1999).

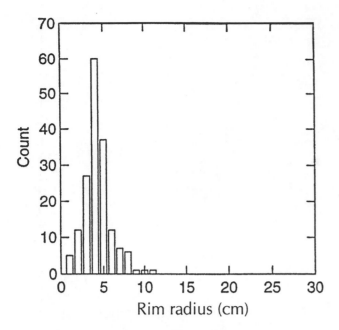

Figure 5.11. Distribution of rim radii of decorated jars (N = 169).

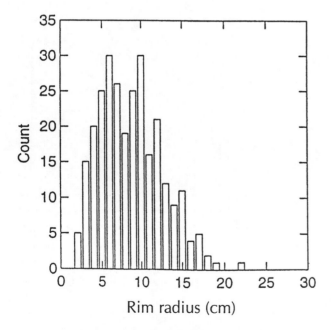

Figure 5.12. Distribution of rim radii of undecorated jars (N = 277).

A few unusually large vessels appear as statistical outliers in the Mogollon Rim region assemblages. The ten outliers to the decorated bowl curve (N = 1,246) have radii of 19, 20, 21, and 24 cm (Fig. 5.9) and one outlier to the undecorated bowl curve (N = 241) has a

radius of 21 cm (Fig. 5.10); three outliers to the decorated jar curve (N = 169) have radii of 9, 10, and 11 cm (Fig. 5.11) and two outliers to the undecorated jar curve (N = 277) have rim radii of 19 and 22 cm (Fig. 5.12). In addition to the lack of evidence for a large vessel class, less than one percent of the ceramic assemblage is statistically identified as "unusually large." Apparently large vessels were needed only occasionally (Blinman 1989: 116).

Feasting and ritual, although present in the eleventh- and twelfth-century Mogollon Rim region, did not leave a strong archaeological signature. Communal architecture indicates that ritual behaviors were performed in groups larger than a single household or settlement, but independent households participated, not organizations of households. Distribution of food and other materials at these events probably occurred, but it was though informal networks, not the institutions that the models of Plog (1974) and Lightfoot (1984) suggest.

COMMUNITY TRANSMISSION

On frontiers, territorial definition of the community is used in competitive situations, overt or not, in which certain resources are closely controlled or identification with a certain sociopolitical entity is advantageous (Graves 1994a, 1994b). Because population is low, land is abundant, and residential mobility is an ample solution to socially stressful situations, community and territory boundary markers are not prevalent on frontiers. Archaeological correlates of defensive settlements and territorial definition are evenly spaced community structures, stretches of uninhabited land, and symbols of self-identification such as petroglyphs (Snead 1995: 49). Marked graves have also been used to legitimate claims to land (Netting 1993: 159). The implication of many of these models is that competition is for limited land resources and that boundaries protect territories.

In the Mogollon Rim region great kivas were the likely focus of community self-identification. Habitation settlements were not evenly spaced across the landscape; they clustered around great kivas. Although some communities have been identified, not enough contiguous area has been surveyed to discuss patterns of the spacing of communities across the landscape. Symbols of self-identification do not appear widely scattered throughout the community or at its borders, as do the shrines and petroglyphs of the Classic period Rio Grande (Snead 1995: 157–159). Neither do "no-man's-lands" appear in the settlement pattern surveys. Limited activity and small-structure sites are distributed continuously across the areas with good resource potential. Formal cemeteries, which also identify person with place, have not been found in this region at this time (Plog 1989: 146). Defensively situated settlements, almost certainly related to perceptions of competition for resources, have not been identified in the Silver Creek drainage, although several thirteenth-century defensive settlements have been reported in the Chevelon drainage to the west (Plog 1978; Solometo 2001).

The community was centered ideologically, if not physically, on the great kiva. It was the community, not the surrounding land, that had value transcending the generations. Great kiva settlements moved occasionally, habitations and small settlements relocated more frequently, but the spatial and social structure of the community remained generally the same throughout the late eleventh and early twelfth centuries. What were transmitted from generation to generation were communal symbols, such as ritual associated with the great kiva. There is no indication of communal investment in long-term maintenance or protection of territory.

COMMUNITY REPRODUCTION

The community is the most ubiquitous organization above the level of the household and is one of the few expected institutions on the frontier. Formal organizations of individuals and households below the level of the community are not present. The expectation is that however weak the community's hold may be over individual households, the community ideal will be reproduced. The material signal of "community centers" is communal architecture and evidence of the social durability of communities with this architecture. The ritual that occurs in this architecture communicates religious beliefs and is an important mechanism for social reproduction (Lipe and Hegmon 1989). The integrative structure is the arena in which people, through ritual, define and redefine themselves (Fox 1996: 484). Societal norms are tested, interpreted, and reinterpreted within the course of an individual life, but community reproduction has occurred if economic, social, and political institutions remain generally unchanged.

For nearly a hundred years, community reproduction in the Mogollon Rim region revolved around the great kiva. Qualitatively, great kiva settlements with their developed middens were among the largest and most occupationally stable of the eleventh- and twelfth-century residential locations. Several of the great kiva communities described in Chapter 4 had two great kivas within their boundaries. In one case I suggest that great

kiva site AZ P:16:160 (ASM), with its poorly developed midden area and possibly incomplete great kiva, was occupied for a short period, and AZ P:16:153 may have preceded or succeeded it as the community center. The multiple great kivas in other communities similarly may have succeeded each other.

In contrast to the enduring symbol of the great kiva as community-level integrative architecture in this period, other architectural features demonstrated a lack of household investment in ritual at levels below that of the community. No small kivas securely dated to the eleventh or early twelfth century have been excavated in the Mogollon Rim region. Haury (1985d) identified a possibly unfinished kiva at Tla Kii. Carter Ranch (Martin and others 1964) had two kivas that were probably associated with the thirteenth-century occupation there. Suprahousehold kivas, so common in the rest of the ancestral Pueblo world, were virtually lacking in the Mogollon Rim region.

A study of ceramic assemblage formation indicates that great kiva settlements were used longer and more intensively than other habitations in the region. A comparison of vessel functional classes among sites shows that assemblages at Cothrun's Kiva and Hough's Great Kiva sites were remarkable similar (Herr 1999). More variability was expressed in assemblages from the shorter occupied sites such as AZ P:16:160 (ASM) and from the small-structure and limited activity sites. A similar pattern appeared with metates at great kiva sites and small sites (above). Mills (1989, 1994a) attributes some differences in ceramic assemblages from small sites to differences in vessel use life and duration of settlement occupation. At a settlement with a long occupation, the discard rates became regularized and the proportions of certain vessel functional classes became more stable (Mills 1989: 141). When small settlements were occupied for a duration shorter than the use life of the vessels, not every form of vessel was discarded, and in the assemblage proportional representation of functional classes is irregular. Regular and similar vessel use and discard behaviors over many years at Cothrun's Kiva and Hough's Great Kiva settlements were responsible for the similar proportional representation of functional classes at the two sites, where assemblages are 97 percent similar. Less regular vessel use and sporadic discard at seasonally occupied habitations resulted in the more disparate assemblages. During the eleventh and early twelfth centuries, frontier residents relocated their domiciles frequently, whereas the great kiva settlements were maintained as the centers of community social, political, and ritual life.

Schlanger's Momentary Population

Momentary Population =

$$\frac{\text{No. of living rooms x Living room lifespan x Rebuilding frequency x People per room}}{\text{Length of period}}$$

Momentary Population of Silver Creek Community Calculation

Momentary Population =

$$\frac{\text{(Rooms at habitation sites)} \times 15 \times 1.32 \times 3}{100}$$

Living room lifespan = 15 (based on Newcomb 1997: 54)

Rebuilding frequency = $\dfrac{\text{Number of floors in excavated rooms at great kiva sites}}{\text{Number of excavated rooms at great kiva sites}}$ = 1.32

People per room = 3 (based on Newcomb 1997: 55)

Community (see Chapter 4)	Rooms at habitation sites	Community Momentary Population
A	133	79
B	155	92
C	63	37

Figure 5.13. The momentary population of Mogollon Rim communities.

On the symbolic landscape of that time, great kiva settlements held the greatest sense of place in the Mogollon Rim region. As "traditional symbols" (Kopytoff 1987b), they provided an interface between the community and the larger, ritual world the great kiva represented. This familiar symbol provided a place in which immigrants could orient themselves in their new life as pioneers. In this role, great kivas attracted and integrated new members into communities (Vivian and others 1978: 63; Stone 1993: 28 recounts a similar situation).

COMMUNITY CO-RESIDENCE

Households cluster around community centers on the frontier, but people are mobile in their production and gathering of resources and move their settlements frequently. Although spatial patterns depend in part on the organization of production (Lansing 1991), the potential hospitality and organizational outcomes of daily encoun-ters make spatial clustering an optimal arrangement. On frontiers, it is likely that this clustering was encouraged for the economic and social benefits of having labor close at hand (Chapter 6).

The scale of co-residence is assessed through population estimates and settlement pattern (Chapter 4). Limited activity and small-structure sites, the loci of seasonal activities, were dispersed across different resource zones on the Mogollon Rim region landscape. Habitations clustered around the one type of communal integrative architecture in the area, the great kiva. The few communities that can be measured with available survey data were no more than 5 km in diameter, comprised 63 to 155 rooms in the more clearly defined communities (A, B, and C), and probably had momentary populations of approximately 37 to 92 people (Fig. 5.13). If the assumptions about larger household size described earlier are considered, population estimates would increase slightly. For example, if the estimate of household size increased to 4 people, estimates of community size would rise to between 50 and 123 people. Excavations at many of the small structures and limited activity sites in the region, both within and outside the community cluster, reveal their seasonal use.

STRONG HOUSEHOLDS AND WEAK COMMUNITIES

Occupation in the Mogollon Rim region in the eleventh and early twelfth centuries was dominated by small habitations, local resource exploitation, a wide range of ceramic variability, expedient and diverse architecture, and limited quantities of trade goods. Settlement pattern, botanical, faunal, ceramic, flaked stone, and ground stone analyses repeatedly show that production was by the household and for the household. Probably every household in the community was conducting the same agricultural and craft production tasks and, although cooperation among households was likely, production ultimately benefitted the household. There is little evidence for community production. The construction of great kivas was a cooperative enterprise and the rituals inside included the members of multiple settlements, but there were no other projects that required shared labor at the community level.

Households appear to have been in charge of their own distribution networks. It is difficult to discern the extent of daily exchanges of food or other perishable items, but storage space was within the house and not in common areas, there is no evidence for communal storage, and large vessels for the preparation and consumption of feasts were uncommon. The presence or absence in domestic contexts of nonlocal artifacts such as traded ceramics and manufactured shell ornaments suggested that households maintained their own exchange relationships with people outside the region.

The pioneers of the Mogollon Rim region were land-rich and labor-poor, and people were valued above resources. The concept of private property was poorly developed at the household level; personal property was confined to personal ornaments. The patterns of extensive production indicate household ownership of fields was unlikely. Although communities had a clear spatial signal on the landscape, there were no boundary markers or defensive positions of territorial communities. Transmission of property did not play an important role in household and community wealth or continuity.

The physical reproduction of household and community definitely occurred during the late eleventh and early twelfth centuries. Population density was always low in the region, but it was at its highest during this 75-to-100-year period. Even so, it is impossible to discern the life cycle of any particular household. Single rooms or even single settlements were rarely occupied for more than one generation. Remodeling or reuse of rooms for new functions appeared only at the settlements with the longest occupations, such as Carter Ranch. However, even if households were mobile, the communities endured. Settlements with communal architecture were occupied longer than those without it. Two communities had two great kivas. Perhaps when a great kiva was no longer used, a second was constructed to ensure community continuity.

The reproduction of household and community values and institutions, as shown by changes in the division of labor demonstrated by the spatial organization of activities, continued for 75 to 100 years. Changes in the division of labor were most visible at Carter Ranch, which was occupied into the thirteenth century. Rituals, such as those held in the great kivas, relayed messages about community values to participants and facilitated the reproduction of community norms.

Based on ceramic and architectural data, there are weak indications that the size of households in the Mogollon Rim region may have been slightly larger than those of adjacent areas. The actual composition of the co-residential household remains unknown. However, it is possible to say that there is no evidence for lineages or any other suprahousehold organizations other than the community. In other parts of the Southwest, such organizations are inferred from the presence of small kivas. Few, if any such structures have been identified in the Mogollon Rim region in the late eleventh and early twelfth centuries. Settlement pattern data and momentary population reconstructions indicate that communities were relatively small, spatially and demographically. Mogollon Rim communities may have been composed of small clusters of slightly larger than usual households.

The weak material patterns of the Mogollon Rim region communities were produced by a situation where the decisions and behaviors of individual households were more evident than those of the community. Households had a great deal of independence, mobility, and flexibility. Institutions above the level of the household were weakly developed. The significance of these behaviors for understanding labor, the social organization of production, leadership, and regional power relationships in the prehistoric Southwest is explored in the final chapter.

CHAPTER SIX

Beyond Chaco: The Frontier Experience

. . . for what people make of their places is closely connected to what they make of themselves as members of society and inhabitants of earth, and while the two activities may be separable in principle, they are deeply joined in practice.

(Basso 1996: 7)

Turning an identified weak archaeological pattern into a behavioral model that explores what people "make of themselves" requires an array of resources. The multiscalar approach of the previous chapters has distinguished weak patterns from strong patterns, place from process, production from reproduction, households from communities and regions, and homelands from destination areas. Comparative anthropological and historical studies identify those characteristics that distinguish the frontier from other areas of strong and weak archaeological patterns. As a place, frontiers are "beyond or between" the dominant regional political organizations of the day. Their spatial marginality has social consequences for the identity of the inhabitants. Processes that distinguish frontiers from homelands include migration, means of integration, and community organization in a situation of low population density. Household and community production, distribution, transmission, reproduction, and co-residence activities affected by these processes are the bases of regional social and political organizations. The frontier model is one way to meet the challenge of archaeology's weak patterns by reintegrating these lines of inquiry in a way that situates the past residents of small settlements in low populated areas on the sociopolitical landscape of prehistory.

CHACO

Chaco Canyon in the San Juan Basin near the Four Corners area in northwest New Mexico was the religious or political center of the most formalized organization in the northern Southwest in the tenth through mid-twelfth centuries. This is the archaeologically strong pattern that best helps us understand the Mogollon Rim weak pattern. Realms of meaning on the Chacoan landscape range from the practical to the ideological, the local to the regional, and the scale of analysis affects the archaeologist's perception of leadership and power.

The Chacoan organization occupied a significant position on the sociopolitical landscape between A.D. 900 and 1150, but the nature of power within the organization changed during this time. The social and political experiences of households and communities *within* the Chacoan organization depended on when and where they were situated: in Chaco Canyon, within approximately 64 km (40 miles) of Chaco Canyon, more than 64 km from the Canyon, and constructed before or after the period of Chacoan expansion in approximately A.D. 1070. Aside from the highly visible and intriguing great houses, the number of excavated structures in Chacoan communities outside of Chaco Canyon are few relative to the scale of the Chacoan organization. Where information is available (Durand and Durand 2000, Gilpin and Purcell 2000; Kendrick and Judge 2000), however, it shows that Chacoan households, like Mogollon Rim households, were responsible for their own production of food and crafts (Hagstrum 2001). Households may also have been in charge of their own distribution networks, as were those at the Cothrun's Kiva and Hough's Great Kiva settlements (Gilpin and Purcell 2000). Such reconstructions are the basis for the interpretation of Chaco as an egalitarian organization.

Examination of the acquisition of wood for the construction of great houses and great kivas provides one instance of the type of anonymity that characterizes corporate leadership strategies. Organizing the harvesting, curing, and transportation of wood from the forested slopes of the Chuska Mountains to Chaco Canyon (approximately 75 km away, some 40 miles) required attention to tree growth and agricultural growing seasons by the residents of communities in both locations. Wood was stockpiled for a decade before the construction of a great house, demonstrating long-term planning. Informal cooperatives of men may have scheduled tree acquisition activities around other yearly events (Windes and McKenna 2001). The Chuska Mountain communities also provided ceramic vessels and flaked stone raw materials to communities in Chaco Canyon and other parts of the San Juan Basin between approximately A.D. 900 and 1200. The economic and ritual implications of this relationship continue to be the subject of much conjecture. However, this example demonstrates that even though households were largely autonomous, communities were not, and in some places within the Chacoan organization the connection between communities was strong and enduring.

Households were integrated into suprahousehold and community organizations through secular and ritual activities. The careful organization needed to procure the wood was just the beginning of the large scale construction of multistoried room blocks. Labor invested in the construction was above the level of what was functional and necessary. Beams and masonry were carefully finished in places that would never be seen by the user of the structure. Construction was probably organized as large seasonal work parties, perhaps motivated by the entitlement of the corporate group, not of an individual leader (Wills 2000).

Kivas in and outside of room blocks may have enclosed secular and ritual activities for groups larger than the household and smaller than the community. Most of the population had access to the community level rituals in the great kivas. Great houses were less accessible on the landscape, had defined access routes, and had a differentiated internal structure, perhaps indicating that use was limited to only a portion of the nearby population.

The "architectural idea" of the great house had adherents across the large Chacoan region (Lekson 2000). The spatial organization of public and private architecture differed between the northern and southern portions of the San Juan Basin, but construction often looked similar. The technology varied; sometimes it was "local" (Kendrick and Judge 2000), other times it was so similar to that at Chaco Canyon that the building designers may have been from Chaco Canyon (Hurst 2000). Local communities may have built their

own great houses to emulate those of Chaco Canyon or great houses and great kivas may have been built for new or existing communities by Chacoan masons. Both construction contexts demonstrate the perceived power gained by association with the "idea" of the great house. Social differentiation within the community may have resulted from unequal access to the great houses and the restricted knowledge with which these structures were associated.

At a "continental scale," the effort taken by residents of Chaco Canyon to acquire the macaws, copper bells, marine shell, obsidian, turquoise, and other rarities cannot be ignored (Lekson 2000). Although these items did not play a role in the daily life of households across the Colorado Plateau, they did play a role, political, ritual, or otherwise, at the center of the Chacoan organization.

These are the data-rich scenarios that can be crafted in regions with abundant artifacts and architectural repetition. Yet areas of strong patterns still need to be explained. Each archaeological reconstruction has implications for understanding the nature of power in the Chacoan organization, whether it was ritual or secular, invested in the individual or the corporate body. The conceptual struggle is how to link ideas about economically autonomous households with those of regional ideologies about identity, power, and leadership. Nowhere is there evidence that authority centered on one person. Information and decision making were not centralized. Complex adaptive systems models show that large numbers of people can participate in extremely flexible organizations by *not* institutionalizing decision making (Wills 2000: 37). Chaco scholars generally agree that the most suitable model will encompass a strong egalitarian ideal among households and communities. Competitive materialism was not rewarded in Chacoan households and communities, but may have played a greater role in regional centers as represented by the construction of great houses (either by Chacoan personnel or by those emulating them) and by the acquisition of rarities. But the competitors are faceless and nameless and thus it is thought that leadership was through the corporate group.

THE MOGOLLON RIM FRONTIER

Although migrants probably came from the southern part of the Chacoan region, they did not recreate Chacoan communities on the Mogollon Rim. They built similar houses, worshiped, feasted, and gathered around similar great kivas, but the social and political organization was not the same. By crossing the boundaries of the Chacoan regional organization and settling in a sparsely populated region beyond, the migrants changed the course of history in the Mogollon Rim region.

Being beyond or between contemporaneous core areas has a transformative effect on individuals and societies that has been identified world wide. In prehispanic times as well, frontier communities were built not only from the history and socialization that the migrants brought with them but also from the liminal political location and processes of migration, integration, and community organization in a situation of low population density. Although the manufacturing techniques used to create their structures, ceramic vessels, and other material products were similar to those of their homeland, the organization of frontier social institutions was different. Contrary to areas in the homeland, where arable land was sparse and labor was abundant, frontier labor was a sought-after commodity. When the context of production changes in such an environment, cultural symbols are revalued and social relationships are reinterpreted.

Reintegrating the many layers of archaeological analyses shows how Mogollon Rim household and community activities can be explained as part of the frontier experience of the late eleventh and early twelfth centuries. Communities were composed of loosely associated households whose spatial association was greater than their degree of formalized social integration. Households were independent production organizations. They used land extensively and invested little in clearing fields or controlling the movement of soil or water. Moving to new fields and building new field structures and residences were more obvious solutions to declining agricultural returns in this area where land was plentiful and other inhabitants were few. The small amount of storage space and the high reliance on wild plants indicate an exploitative approach to food procurement. Minimal reserves of food and other stored items probably limited the ability of households to participate in any formalized restricted sharing relationships like those described as optimal risk-reduction organizations for historic pueblos (Hegmon 1989). When agricultural production and stored foods were not sufficient or predictable enough to support the household, residential mobility to new lands may have been the best means of overcoming periods of scarcity. Because land was abundant, competition for new land was unlikely and boundaries around fields and communities were ephemeral, if even present.

Gendered division of labor is often regulated by cultural norms in core areas, but may be discouraged by circumstances on the frontier. In analogous historically and ethnographically documented small-scale agricultural societies, men and women contribute to agricultural tasks, but the organization of activities can be flexible or gender specific. There is little evidence for a strong gender-based division of labor on the Mogollon Rim frontier. Men, women, and children may have participated in hunting (Szuter 2000) and gathering the large proportions of wild plants consumed. The grinding of food (often a woman's job) was not highly intensive. Evidence for ceramic manufacture (another woman's job), the only craft abundantly represented in the archaeological record, was dispersed throughout room blocks and domestic trash. Crafts were not specialized and production was repetitive, as everyone performed the same types of activities. The low intensity of these tasks suggests some degree of labor flexibility within households. Except for seasonal agricultural tasks and the construction and maintenance of a great kiva, few jobs were complex enough to require simultaneous tasks and thus communal labor.

The egalitarianism evidenced by productive relationships is noticeable in the generalized burial practices. Although some burials, such as those at Carter Ranch (Chapter 5), contained greater quantities and more kinds of funerary objects than others, such distinction is relative. In no way do the Mogollon Rim inhumations approach the rich burials at the sites of Pueblo Bonito (Akins 1986), Winona Ridge (McGregor 1943), Los Hermanos (Clark and Minturn 2001), Grasshopper Pueblo (Whittlesey 1978), and Hawikku (Howell and Kintigh 1996). Personal inequality among individuals is apparent, but unequivocal evidence for institutionalized inequality has not been identified either in the Mogollon Rim region or elsewhere in the northern Southwest.

Households maintained wide-ranging social relationships. Trade of ornaments or prestige items was extremely rare but the exchange of more mundane items reveals a great deal about how households created their own support networks. The relations represented by ceramic vessels show long distances crossed in many directions, but the overall proportion of nonlocal pottery in the ceramic assemblages was low. This type of trade shows that households maintained contacts over long distances, but that these ties had more social than economic importance.

In historical and ethnographic accounts from the Pueblos, suprahousehold organizations such as lineages, clans, and sodalities were responsible for regulation of land, as well as other representative and administrative responsibilities (Eggan 1950; Levy 1992). In the historic aggregated communities of the modern Pueblos, multiple cross-cutting memberships provided community stability in areas where fissioning and residential mobility were not an easy option. Kivas, suprahousehold structures thought to integrate groups of households below the level of community (Lipe 1989; Plog 1989: 148; Steward 1951), were a consistent component of Chacoan area settlements. The variability of public spaces in the Chacoan area suggests that there were a variety of social roles available to individuals in both areas, a situation that often occurs in areas with high populations and mature communities. The eleventh- and twelfth-century Mogollon Rim region settlements, however, lacked the ceremonial rooms and suprahousehold kivas often associated with the presence of suprahousehold organizations in the prehispanic Southwest. The region lacked the intermediary integrative institutions and social roles between those of the household and the community, and Mogollon Rim region households took primary responsibility for their reproduction.

Individual households were flexible and mobile and formalized suprahousehold organizations were essentially nonexistent, but the community, organized around the great kiva, was more durable. On frontiers in particular, the community was only viable to the degree that individuals and households participated in creating shared values and in mediating the tensions created by their diverse backgrounds and new responsibilities as pioneers.

The spatial clustering of habitations around great kivas indicates that households identified with the communal organization architecturally manifested by the great kiva. Circular great kivas were the ritual centers of the migrant communities of the late eleventh and early twelfth centuries in the Mogollon Rim region. The households, responsible for much of their own production and distribution, were loosely articulated into communities. Division of labor in the household was flexible. Specialized tasks did not consume the time of household members. Just as enlarged households are a common response (Netting 1993: 89) to the need for agricultural labor in small-scale agricultural societies around the world, Mogollon Rim households may have been slightly larger than those of nearby regions. Cooperative groups probably helped with specific tasks, agricultural or otherwise, whose simultaneous scheduling could not be met within the organization of the household, but these groups were not formalized. The community, centered on a circular great kiva, was the only recognized organization beyond the household. It, and its residentially flexible and loosely affiliated membership, was a relatively small organization defined by spatial proximity, shared interests, and social needs, including labor, marriage partners, and ritual.

The number of great kivas relative to population in the Mogollon Rim region indicates that a high priority was placed on their construction. The great kivas of the region were similar to those of the Chacoan region, but comparatively lacked the same kind of labor investment. Architectural elements were not finely finished, floor features were not formal, if present at all, and the structures may not have been fully roofed. Great kivas were clearly essential to life on the frontier, but their construction was functionalist. The settlers built a structure that would house their rituals, but because the value of labor was so high in this sparsely populated region they could not or would not replicate the labor-intensive structures of the Chacoan region. These structures served as both ritual places and as a means of attracting people, thus assuring community viability and continuity.

The great kivas housed community ceremonies, but items indicative of the knowledge associated with a strong shared or guarded ritual organization (such as large red ware bowls, ritual fauna, and iconography present at later sites in the region) cannot be identified in the assemblages from great kiva sites. Ideological practices were dispersed, not exclusionary. They were an integral part of community behaviors but were not imposed from a higher regional authority (Magness-Gardiner and Falconer 1994). Domestic and community organizations were mutually served by participation in communal gatherings.

The architectural variability of great kivas and the extensive great kiva communities in the region suggest that the formalized organizations of areas with dense populations were lacking on the frontier. The great kiva focused settlement system of the Little Colorado region, including Hay Hollow Valley, has been described by Longacre (1964b: 209) as:

> probably related to ritual supports underlying community integration . . . . The arrangement would probably have economic overtones in the periodic pooling of labor and other aspects of the economic pattern along the lines created by the corporate mechanisms of solidarity.

Great kivas provided migrant groups with an identity in relation to regional ideologies and provided the space for aggregated households to coordinate and organize their economic and social lives. They may have initially attracted migrants into emerging communities on the Mogollon Rim social and political landscape. An analogous situation in Africa presents a possible model for the early settlements of the Mogollon Rim region. Large *ungwa* (a neighborhood through which labor is organized) settlements on the plain of the Kofyar frontier initially attracted new migrants from the Jos Plateau. Migrants moved toward groups with which they could identify. Only after their households became economically stable did pioneers move again to their own settlements (Stone 1992, 1993, 1996).

In the new environment, the great kiva was a familiar cultural symbol. Migrants who identified with the type of community represented by the great kiva settled nearby. Because of the need for labor and mates in this region of low population density, communities may have competed to recruit members. In the Mogollon Rim region, preparations for domestic and communal gatherings were conducted in the same places and with the same tools and methods. Households provided foods for feasts and great kivas provided opportunities for social encounters. The occasions of feasting associated with ritual were opportunities to establish productive and social relationships, share information, exchange gossip, and compete in games. Community survival and stability depended on acquiring and maintaining a constituency. Those households or leaders who could recruit migrants and maintain the community had "wealth-in-people," that most valuable of resources on the land-rich, labor-poor frontier. Frontier communities endure as long as the population of the region remains low and their organizational flexibility allows them to respond to new challenges brought by changes in the physical and social environment.

One scenario for the reconstruction of the Mogollon Rim frontier begins to the northeast, in the Chacoan region of the Colorado Plateau. The reorganization in Chaco Canyon caused population movement from the heart of the San Juan Basin to its peripheries. In the A.D. 1070s, people began to fill up agricultural niches across the San Juan Basin in an expansion of population from approximately 1070 to 1150, the period of migration into the Mogollon Rim region. Communities across the Colorado Plateau were disrupted as new people moved into previously inhabited communities and constructed new settlements (Vivian 1990). Movements beyond the boundaries of the Chacoan organization to the Mogollon Rim frontier may have been a ripple effect caused by changes in areas to the north and east.

Upon arriving in the Mogollon rim region, some of the firstcomers constructed great kivas. These communal structures functioned both as "traditional symbols" with which other migrants could identify and as an organizational institution, however weak the institutional authority over the population. Later arriving migrants moved into the settlement or community of one of the firstcomers. While gaining access to the resources and rituals of the community, they may also have incurred obligations to the firstcomer families. In this initial social configuration, the families at those great kiva settlements that had successfully recruited new residents to their community would have had an economic and political advantage and would have been locally legitimated through their access to other people, their "wealth-in-people" (Nyerges 1992; Sebastian 1992a: 121). "Wealth-in-people" is a critical asset on frontiers. The acquisition of labor benefits the group more than the individual and thus can be understood as a situation of corporate leadership.

Because "wealth-in-people" may have been more valuable than the products of labor, there was little emphasis placed on the creation or exchange of prestige goods in frontier regions. Instead, trade patterns indicate that lower value items may have been a means of maintaining social connections across the landscape. The lack of structured behaviors implies a lack of leadership with any kind of coercive power. Power was probably exercised on a situational and event specific basis, such as those occasions when households mobilized informal work groups.

CONSEQUENCES OF THE FRONTIER

Frontiers are often temporary social formations, and so too was the Mogollon Rim region frontier. After 75 to 100 years, the frontier organization was no longer successful (Longacre 1970: 17). Between A.D. 1150 to 1170 the settlement pattern changed dramatically. Population began to slowly decline (Newcomb 1997: 80-81), and the widespread social ties of the previous period contracted (Herr 1997) and became oriented toward northeastern Arizona. At the end of the thirteenth century, large movements of Pueblo populations to the Mogollon Rim, the Mogollon highlands south of the Mogollon Rim, Point of Pines, and the Tonto Basin changed the balance of power in the Western Pueblo region. The Mogollon Rim region was no longer spatially or politically a frontier (Clark 2001; Lindsay 1987; Mills 1998; Reid 1989). Population, however, remained low, and some residents may have been pushed out as others moved in or through the region.

After leaving their small habitations in the great kiva communities, the residents of the Mogollon Rim built and occupied aggregated pueblos, such as Roundy Canyon (A.D. 1170–1180) and Pottery Hill (A.D. 1200–1280). At the end of the thirteenth century they dispersed into small settlements (Bryant Ranch) again before aggregating into the largest pueblos in the history of the region between A.D. 1290 and 1390 (Mills 1998), living at places such as Bailey Ruin, Forestdale (pre-1275 to 1325?), and Tundastusa (1275–1390?).

In aggregated pueblos the immediate need for labor was no longer an issue, and communal involvement in its acquisition was less important. Changes in house structure architecturally demarcate the changing spatial organization of activities and the reorganization of domestic labor in aggregated pueblos (Hill 1970; Mills, Van Keuren, and others 1999; Mills, Herr, Kaldahl, and others 1999; Reid and Whittlesey 1982). Agricultural production remained extensive, although organization of field systems likely changed when residents chose not to live alongside their farm land.

Wild plants remained an important supplement to the diet (Huckell 1999) and large fauna became more important. In the late thirteenth century hunting groups may have been organized to procure both large animals for food and other animals for ritual use (Horner 1999). The social power and prestige gained by sharing the products of a successful large animal hunt have implications for the development of gender and social hierarchies (Szuter 2000: 217). Changes in grinding facilities and increased intensity of use (Valado 1999a) indicate that women were spending more time processing wild and domestic plants into flour, potentially for increasing ceremonial obligations. At the same time, craft specialization, although still part time, was practiced. Decorated ceramics, including Cibola White Ware, White Mountain Red Ware, and Roosevelt Red Ware, were likely made by specialists (Mills, Herr, Stinson, and Triadan 1999; Triadan and others 2001), and other part-time specialists manufactured ornaments using a variety of materials. By the Pueblo IV period, exchange networks changed such that not only did the residents of Bailey Ruin have access to shell, they also manufactured shell ornaments (Vokes 1999).

The religious practices of Mogollon Rim residents in the thirteenth and fourteenth centuries also changed. Circular great kivas were no longer used. In the later period, ritual architecture included primarily plazas, either open or within room blocks, square room block kivas, and square plaza kivas. Across the Western Pueblo region during the late thirteenth and fourteenth centuries this suite of ritual architecture was accompanied by changes in ceramic iconography associated with a new panregional cult (Adams 1991; Crown 1994; Mills 1998: 67; Plog and Solometo 1997; Van Keuren 2000). Nothing in the ceramic assemblages from early eleventh and twelfth century sites presupposes the large, elaborately decorated red ware and polychrome vessels associated with later ritual in the area. The diversity of contemporaneous faunal assemblages may be linked to the increased use of animals in ritual (Horner 1999).

The differentiation of both domestic and suprahousehold space and secular and ritual activities reflects the increasingly multifaceted social organization of aggregated pueblos in the Mogollon Rim region. With more social roles at a number of scales of organization, opportunities for personal achievement increased, even if leadership positions were not institutionalized.

Local histories define the particular character of each Pueblo IV period community (Mills 1998). However, by the thirteenth century the local development of the Silver Creek settlement cluster was generally in step with developments of other Pueblo IV clusters and was no longer spatially or socially marginal on the political landscape. The Mogollon Rim region in the fourteenth century was no longer a frontier.

THE SIGNIFICANCE OF THE FRONTIER

The frontier organization had a lasting effect on the long-term history of the Mogollon Rim, but it also holds significance for understanding changes in political organization at the end of the eleventh century and beginning of the twelfth century. Population peaked in the Mogollon Rim region sometime between A.D. 1000 and 1100. At the early end of this time period, the long distance migration to the Mogollon Rim area may have been a response to discontent with the Chacoan status quo as small groups "voted with their feet" (Netting 1993: 276) and headed for "land and freedom" (Nugent 1993). On the other hand, migration could have been spurred by the changing balance of power across the San Juan Basin in the final decades of the eleventh century. Tree-ring dates from the Mogollon Rim region imply the latter, but more are needed to unambiguously confirm this chronological pattern.

The definition of the Chacoan region as a strong pattern and as a core area masks internal patterns of variability in ways that can oversimplify macroregional analyses. Chaco was a multilayered organization with political and ritual institutions powerful enough to affect construction in some outlier communities and to be emulated by local builders in other outlier communities. These institutions enforced the normative behaviors that resulted in creating strong archaeological patterns. Van Dyke (1998: 276) states that, "outlier sociopolitical dynamics, particularly in communities far removed from the canyon environs, might have been quite different from sociopolitical organizations near to or inside the canyon." Understanding the multiple boundaries of economic, political, and ritual action is a complex task in the Chacoan region. Specific understanding of the relationship between the Mogollon Rim region and Chacoan region households and communities depends on where within the Chacoan regions comparisons are made.

At the beginning of this volume I wrote that the occupants of small settlements in areas of weak patterns probably did not behave like the residents of large settlements in areas of strong patterns, but asked if they behaved like the residents of small sites within the areas of strong patterns. The economic organization of households in Chacoan and Mogollon Rim habitations appears similar. It is above the level of the household, at the suprahousehold, community, and intercommunity level, that it becomes clear that residents of the Chacoan region had more social choices than did their Mogollon Rim region contemporaries. Although not at opposite ends of the spectrum by any means, behaviors in the Chacoan region were more controlled by institutions; those in the Mogollon Rim region were more flexible. The degree of control was variable across the Chacoan region. Clearly the egalitarian and economically autonomous households of the Chaco region experienced the Chacoan organization differently than did residents of the great houses, and people outside Chaco Canyon experienced the Chacoan organization differently than did those within.

In modern pueblos, those who hold power within the community are not usually the people who emigrate. If this held true in the past, it could be that it was the residents of the small settlements in the Chacoan region (possibly those of the Puerco Valley), with their limited access to esoteric and technological knowledge, who migrated to the Mogollon Rim region. If institutional knowledge was available to only a portion of the Chacoan population, differences of socialization in the homeland would have had implications for communities on the frontier. Migrants may never have had access to the details of ritual or political orchestration or the material symbols of such except as part of a constituency, further compounding the organizational differences between frontiers and homelands.

The ability to interpret the changes on the Colorado Plateau and the political structure of the northern Southwest in the eleventh and twelfth centuries will come from research in areas adjacent to Chaco Canyon. Recent studies of Chacoan outlier communities and frontier communities, such as the Mogollon Rim region, reveal both local and regional variability on the political landscape. There are portions of the northern Southwest that, in this period, lack virtually all traces of evidence of a relationship with the Chacoan region (Dean 1996b: 40), and they clearly demarcate the bounds of Chacoan influence. A long-term goal of continuing research is to understand the social dynamics of a place and to identify even the short-term social formations that can change the course of local and regional political history. A macroregional perspective that accommodates patterns of repetition as well as patterns of variability will promote a comprehensive understanding of the political and ritual relationships of Chaco Canyon, Chacoan outliers, frontier communities, and regions beyond.

Architectural Details of Excavated Rooms in the Mogollon Rim Region

Architectural details about the rooms at small structure and great kiva sites in the Mogollon Rim region form the basis for the discussions of room size, room function, and room history in Chapter 5. In some cases the excavator provided information about room function; in other cases I interpreted room function based on published maps, photographs, and text descriptions. Following the standard convention in Southwestern archaeology, supported by ethnographic analogy (Adams 1983; Hill 1970), I considered rooms with hearths to be habitation rooms and those with no features to be storage rooms (Lightfoot 1994: 100).

Rooms with unknown functions were often heavily disturbed and I did not consider them in comparative discussions. When possible, rooms are identified in the following table as they were in the original text.

Architectural data are from the Silver Creek Archaeological Research Project (SCARP) great kiva sites (Herr and others 1999), Tla Kii Pueblo (Haury 1985d), Carter Ranch (Martin and others 1964), Corduroy Creek (Stafford and Rice 1980), FLEX—Goodwin (Dosh 1988), FLEX—Show Low II (Dosh 1988), Schoens Dam (Stebbins and Hartman 1988), Snowflake–Mesa Redondo (Neily 1988), and FLEX—Scotts Reservoir (Hartman 1990).

AZ site numbers for the Snowflake–Mesa Redondo area are from the Arizona State Museum Site Survey System. The AZ site numbers listed for the Corduroy Creek Project were recorded by Arizona State University field crews and were not integrated into the official AZ Site Survey System. NA site numbers are designations by the Museum of Northern Arizona.

SCARP Great Kiva Sites

Room	Dimensions (m)	Features	Doors	Remodeling and reuse	Comments
Hough's 1	N: 3.2, S: 4.3 E: 5.4, W: 5.5	Informal hearth	E. wall	None noted	Habitation room; ½ room excavated
Hough's 2	5.3 x 4.1	Slab-lined hearth	None	Non-load-bearing wall for storage and grinding area	Habitation room
Cothrun's 1	N: 3.7, S: 3.7 E: 3.3, W: 4.3	Slab-lined hearth; 3 postholes	S. wall E. wall	Remodeled posthole; subfloor pit	Habitation room; hatch entry; ash from hearth cleaning on floor
Cothrun's 2	N: 4.0, S: 3.6 E: 5.2, W: 4.1	None	None	3 layers of plaster	Unknown; ½ room excavated; severely pothunted
Cothrun's 3	N: 3.7, S: 4.2 E: 6.2, W: 6.0	Unknown	N. wall	Unknown	Unexcavated
Cothrun's 4	N: 3.4, S: 3.9 E: 4.8, W: 4.7	Clay-lined hearth; ash pit	E. wall	Pit below floor	Habitation room; ½ room excavated; small pothunter's hole in floor
Cothrun's 5	W: 3.3	Unknown	W. wall	Unknown	Unexcavated
Cothrun's 6	N: 6.3, S: 5.5 E: 7.1	Unknown	W. wall	Unknown	Unexcavated

Tla Kii Pueblo (Haury 1985d)

Room	Dimensions (m)	Features	Doors	Remodeling and reuse	Comments
1	N: 4.3, S: 4.2 E: 2.3, W: 2.8	None	E. wall	Internal dividing wall removed	Storage
2					Storage
3	N: 1.4, S: 1.8 E: 2.3, W: 2.3	Storage pit in northwest corner	W. wall E. wall	None noted	Storage
4	N: 2.3, S: 2.4 E: 2.3, W: 2.4	Slab-lined hearth; ash pit	W. Wall	None noted	Habitation
5	N: 2.1, S: 2.2 E: 2.8, W: 3.0	None	None	None noted	Habitation
6	N: 2.1, S: 2.5 E: 2.3, W: 2.4	Slab lined hearth	None	None noted	Habitation
7	N: 2.9, S: 2.7 E: 4.4, W: 4.7	3 hearths; ash pit	None	Three floors; storage wall; subterranean wall from earlier pit house?	Habitation; Room 7a added as storage; 7a overlies an earlier pit house
8	N: 3.1, S: 2.6 E: 2.8, W: 2.8	2 hearths, slab-lined and clay; ventilator in E. wall	S. Wall	Subterranean wall from earlier pit house	Habitation; Burial 4 below the floor
9	N: 2.0, S: 2.0 E: 1.6, W: 1.5	None	None	None noted	Storage

Tla Kii Pueblo (Haury 1985d) - *continued*

Room	Dimensions (m)	Features	Doors	Remodeling and reuse	Comments
10	"Small"	None	None	None noted	Storage
11	N: 1.8, S: 2.0, E: 2.1, W: 2.1	None	None	None noted	Storage; Floor unfinished
12	N: 2.5, S: 3.5, E: 3.2, W: 2.8	Slab-lined hearth; ventilator to Room 8 in W. wall	N. wall?	None noted	Habitation; Room 12 built and abandoned before Room 8 was built
13	N: 4.9, S: 4.8, E: 2.4, W: 2.6	Hearth below wall dividing Rooms 13, 15	NE. wall	Rooms 13 and 15 were once one room, later subdivided; trash filled	Habitation; Floor assemblage includes pots with potter's clay, potter's tool kit, and unfired pot; burned roof
14	N: 4.8, S: 4.9, E: 4.7, W: 4.6	Slab-lined hearth; deflector; 3 pits; 3 postholes	NE. wall	None noted	Burial below SW. corner
15	2.2 x 4.8	None	Unknown	Rooms 13 and 15 were once one room, later subdivided; 3 floor levels	Habitation; Floor assemblage includes potter's clay and potter's tool kit; burned roof
16	N: 4.3, S: 4.0, E: 4.2, W: 4.3	2 slab-lined hearths; posthole; slab-lined hearth	SE. wall	2 floors	Habitation; Burned roof; Burial 18 below floor
17	S: 2.5, E: 4.4	Clay hearth	None	Storage pit below W. wall	Habitation
18	S: 2.0, W: 5.0	Slab lined hearth; clay-lined hearth	None	2 floors; storage pit below floor	Storage area for Room 19; Burned roof; potter's clay (on floor?)
19	N: 4.4, S: 2.3, E: 3.9	Slab-lined hearth	None	Storage pit below floor	Habitation; W. wall eroded by Forestdale Creek
20	S: 4.2, E: 2.1	Storage pit	None	Late addition to room block	Habitation, Burned roof
21	S: 4.2, E: 2.1	Clay hearth	None	Late addition to room block	Habitation?
Structure 1	2.3 x 1.7	None	None	None noted	Built above Pit House 3; "menstrual hut"
Structure 2	2.9 x 3.0	Slab-lined hearth; small pits; bench	None	Firepit remodeled	External storage area

Carter Ranch Pueblo (Martin and others 1964)

Room	Dimensions (m)	Features	Doors	Remodeling and reuse	Comments
1	2.4 x 3.0	Hearth?; posthole?	None	None	Storage room? Mano on floor
2	2.6 x 2.7	None	None	None	Storage room
3	3.2 x 3.5	Ventilator; niche; slab-lined hearth; deflector; ladder hole?	None	2 layers of wall plaster; trash filled	Habitation room; manos, hammerstone, and shaped slab on floor
4	2.9 x 3.1	Slab-lined hearth; mealing bin; storage pit	Hatch	2 layers of wall plaster; floor overlies trash	Habitation room; ceramic vessels on floor; room burned

Carter Ranch Pueblo (Martin and others 1964) - *continued*

Room	Dimensions (m)	Features	Doors	Remodeling and reuse	Comments
5	4.1 x 3.9	Ventilator; clay hearth; ash pit; storage pit; posthole	W. wall	2 layers of wall plaster; partly trash filled	Habitation room; black-on-white jar on floor
6	2.4 x 2.5	Flour receptacles?	T-shape; S. wall	2 layers of wall plaster	Storage and grinding room; burned basket, cloth, and jar fragment on floor
7	3.4 x 3.5	Clay hearth; 2 bell-shaped pits	None	3 layers of wall plaster; trash filled	Habitation room; shaped slabs cover pits; plaster on north wall may have been decorated
8	2.9 x 3.4	None	N. wall	2 floors; door sealed; trash filled	Storage room?
9	2.0 x 3.1	Slab-lined hearth	None	None	Habitation room; 2 axes and jar on floor
10	3.6 x 3.6	Slab-lined hearth; mealing bins with receptacles and manos	W. wall	2 floors; door sealed, made into ventilator	Habitation room; corrugated jars on floor; "Burned; occupant caught in fire"
11	2.5 x 3.1	Clay hearth; horseshoe ventilator; pot rest; 3 posts	W. wall	2 floors	Habitation room
12	4.0 x 4.7	Clay hearth; posthole	E. wall	2 layers of plaster	Habitation room; nonflaked lithics on floor
13	1.5 x 2.9	None	W. wall	2 floors?	Storage room
14	2.4 x 3.5	Slab-lined hearth	E. wall	3 layers of plaster; 2 west walls; 2 floors; trash filled	Habitation room; jar on floor
15	3.5 x 4.5	2 slab-lined firepits; storage pit	None	2 layers of plaster; 2 floors	Habitation room?
16	3.5 x 2.4	Horseshoe ventilator; D-shaped slab and clay hearth; slab-lined ash pit?; deflector; benches	N. wall	Benches added	Ceremonial room; some stone slab paving; bowl, axe, and pestle on floor
17	4.8 x 3.2	Ventilator; D-shaped slab and clay hearth; slab-lined ash pit; recessed post	None	2 layers of plaster; 2 floors	Habitation and ceremonial room?
18	3.8 x 3.2	Slab-lined hearth; 7 pits; slab-lined flour receptacle; 2 postholes	S. wall	2 layers of plaster; trash filled	Habitation room
19	3.2 x 3.4	Slab-lined hearth	E. wall	2 layers of plaster	Habitation and manufacturing room; ventilator to Room 10
20	No notes				
21	2.6 x 2.7	Niche; slab-lined hearth; cooking pit; storage pit	W. wall	Trash filled	Habitation room; artifacts on floor

Carter Ranch Pueblo (Martin and others 1964) - continued

Room	Dimensions (m)	Features	Doors	Remodeling and reuse	Comments
22	4.0 x 4.7	Ventilator?; slab-lined hearth; 3 mealing bins; 2 storage pits; ash pit?; postholes	N. wall	2 floors	Habitation room; manos and pecking stones found near mealing bins
23	3.1 x 3.6	Slab-lined hearth; clay-lined hearth; ash pit	N. wall	2 layers of plaster; 2 floors; light trash fill	Habitation room

Corduroy Creek Project (Stafford and Rice 1980)

Site (ASU)	Room	Room dimensions (m)	Room area (square meters)	Features	Comments
AZ Q:13:9	Room 1	3.5 x 4.0	14.0	Cobble-collared hearth	Masonry structure; habitation
AZ P:16:12	Room 1		10.5	Partitioned slab-lined hearth, ½ used as ash bin	Masonry structure; habitation
AZ P:16:12	Room 2		8.0	Slab-lined hearth; subfloor burial	Masonry structure; habitation
AZ P:16:12	Room 3		11.1	Slab-lined hearth; vent; deflector	Masonry structure; habitation
AZ P:16:12	Room 4		16.0	Clay-lined hearth	Masonry structure; habitation
AZ P:16:12	Room 5		13.6	Clay-lined hearth	Masonry structure; habitation

FLEX—Goodwin (Dosh 1988)

Site (MNA)	Room	Dimensions (m)	Features	Comments
NA 18,343	Feature 1	4.0 x 4.0	Slab-lined hearth; clay-lined hearth; walled-in storage area (Feature 2)	Wattle and daub superstructure on masonry foundations; habitation
NA 18,343	Feature 3	6.3 x 4.0	2 mealing bins; 2 slab-lined hearths; shallow pit	Jacal structure; habitation
NA 18,343	Feature 4	5.0 x 3.2	5–7 pits; postholes	Ramada; storage
NA 18,343	Feature 6	4.3 x 3.0	Interior storage area; clay hearth; pit or posthole	One room structure; masonry; habitation
NA 18,343	Feature 10	4.9 x 4.4	Basin hearth; 9 postholes	Pit house
NA 18,343	Feature 12	9.0 x 6.0	6 pits; 116 postholes	Complex series of walls and postholes
NA 18,346	Feature 1, Room 1	4.8 x 3.6	Clay hearth; mealing bin?	Jacal structure with breezeway between Rooms 1 and 2, and 3; large basin found in breezeway; habitation, storage and processing rooms
NA 18,346	Feature 1, Room 2	3.4 x 3.5	None	
NA 18,346	Feature 1, Room 3	8.0 x 3.2	Walled bin; mealing bin?	

FLEX—Goodwin (Dosh 1988) - continued

Site (MNA)	Room	Dimensions (m)	Features	Comments
NA 18,346	Feature 2	9.0 x 4.9	Pit; mealing bin; 14 postholes	Jacal structure; possibly 3 rooms; storage
NA 18,350	Feature 1	5.6 x 4.9	Hearth; 4 corner post sockets	1-room masonry structure; habitation
NA 18,350	Feature 2; Room 1	5.8 x 4.3	Hearth; 2 mealing bins	Bins superimposed; masonry; habitation
NA 18,350	Feature 2; Room 3	5.3 x 5.1	Slab-lined hearth; slab bin	Masonry; habitation
NA 18,350	Feature 1	5.1 x 3.9	Mealing bin	Masonry structure with small storage exterior appendage (Feature 5); processing
NA 18,350	Feature 2	2.4 x 2.4	None	Masonry structure; storage
NA 18,177	Feature 1	4.5 x 4.3	None	1-room masonry structure; storage
NA 18,345	Feature 1	5.5 x 5.2	Clay hearth	Masonry structure; habitation

FLEX—Show Low II (Dosh 1988)

Site (MNA)	Room	Dimensions (m)	Features	Comments
NA 19,330	Feature 2	2.6 x 2.8	Slab-lined hearth; pit?; 19 postholes	Jacal structure; habitation
NA 19,330	Feature 5	3.4 x 2.3	Slab-lined hearth; 14 postholes	Jacal structure; habitation
NA 19,331	Feature 1, Room 1	3.1 x 1.7	Clay-lined hearth; 2 postholes	Jacal structure with patio; habitation
NA 19,331	Feature 1, Room 2	3.5 x 1.7	Clay-lined hearth; posthole	Jacal structure with patio; habitation
NA 19,331	Feature 3a	2.4 x 2.4	Slab-lined hearth	Jacal structure; habitation
NA 19,331	Feature 3b	3.0 x 2.4	Informal hearth; 2 shallow basin pits; bell-shaped pit	Jacal structure; habitation
NA 19,331	Feature 4	7.2 x 5.0	Fire pit; 2 pits; 25 postholes	Brush structure; habitation
NA 19,331	Feature 7	3.2 x 2.1	Clay-lined hearth; 2 shallow pits	Pit house; habitation
NA 19,331	Feature 9	5.3 x 3.8	Clay-lined hearth; 3 shallow pits	Jacal structure; habitation
NA 19,334	Feature 1	4.0 x 2.6	Mealing bin; slab-lined pit	Jacal and masonry structure; processing

Schoens Dam Project (Stebbins and Hartman 1988)

Site (MNA)	Room	Dimensions (m)	Features	Comments
NA 17,271	Comp. 1, Room 1	5.2 x 3.8	Hearth	Masonry structure; internal partition; habitation
NA 17,271	Comp. 1, Room 2	4.3 x 4.0	Hearth; rock-filled cist; small pit	Masonry structure; habitation
NA 17,271	Comp. 1, Room 3	2.9 x 2.8	None	Masonry structure; storage room
NA 17,271	Comp. 1, Room 4	Unknown	None	Masonry structure; storage
NA 17,271	Comp. 2, Room 2	3.7 x 2.4	Hearth; ladder rests?	Masonry structure; habitation
NA 17,271	Comp. 2, Room 3	3.7 x 2.0	None	Masonry and jacal structure; storage

Schoens Dam Project (Stebbins and Hartman 1988) - *continued*

Site (MNA)	Room	Dimensions (m)	Features	Comments
NA 17,278	Room 1	3.0 x 3.0	Small ash pit	Masonry and jacal structure; habitation
NA 17,282	Room 1	2.9 x 2.7	Large pit; mealing area?	Masonry and jacal structure
NA 17,282	Room 2	6.0 x 6.0	None	Masonry structure; storage
NA 17,282	Room 3	4.1 x 2.6	Hearth	Masonry structure; habitation

Snowflake–Mesa Redondo (Neily 1988)

Site (ASM)	Room	Dimensions (m)	Features	Comments
AZ Q:9:5	Structure 1	4.7 x 3.1	Basin hearth; deflector	Seasonal semisubterranean jacal structure; habitation
AZ Q:9:5	Structure 2	2.8 x ?	Slab-lined hearth; 2 shallow pits	Small masonry seasonal structure; habitation
AZ Q:9:6	Structure 1	1.8 x 1.4	Basin hearth; deflector	Pit house; temporary structure; habitation
AZ Q:9:6	Structure 2	3.3 x 2.5	Informal hearth	Unroofed masonry; windbreak; habitation
AZ Q:9:6	Structure 3	1.3 x 1.3	None	Masonry structure; storage
AZ Q:9:26	Structure 1, Room 1	2.9 x 1.9	Basin hearth; posthole	Masonry structure; habitation room
AZ Q:9:26	Structure 1, Room 2	Uncertain	Informal hearth; 2 shallow pits	Masonry structure; habitation room
AZ Q:9:26		2.3 x 3.0	Firepit; deflector; slab-lined bin; 8 shallow pits	Walled ramada
AZ Q:9:26	Structure 2	2.3 x 2.4	Basin firepit; 2 shallow pits	Shallow irregular pit structure; habitation
AZ Q:9:26	Structure 3	3.5 x 2.6	Basin firepit; ash pit; shallow pit; floor holes; mealing pit; 2 postholes; wall niche; interior postholes; 4 exterior postholes	Rectangular pit structure; habitation
AZ Q:9:26	Structure 4	4.0 x 2.7	None	Unfinished pit structure used as ceramic firing area?

FLEX—Scotts Reservoir (Hartman 1990)

Site (MNA)	Room	Dimensions (m)	Features	Comments
NA 17,955	Feature 1	2.0 x 1.7	None	Masonry and jacal structure; function unknown
NA 17,955	Feature 2	Unknown	None	Masonry and jacal structure; function unknown
NA 17,955	Feature 3	4.4 x 2.5	None	Masonry and jacal structure; function unknown
NA 17,955	Feature 4	Unknown	None	Masonry and jacal structure; function unknown
NA 17,955	Feature 5	Unknown	None	Masonry and jacal structure; function unknown
NA 18,175	Feature 2	2.0 x 1.5	Slab-lined cist; South entry	Masonry; vandalized; storage?
NA 18,175	Feature 6	3.9 x 2.0	Hearth (remodeled); vent (remodeled); NW entry	Masonry; habitation initially, then remodeled for storage?
NA 18,175	Feature 9	2.5 x 1.8	None	Masonry and jacal structure; ramada and work area

FLEX—Scotts Reservoir (Hartman 1990) - *continued*

Site (MNA)	Room	Dimensions (m)	Features	Comments
NA 18,175	Feature 12	2.9 x 1.8	Clay-lined hearth; ash pit; West entry	Masonry; 3 battered manos on floor; habitation
NA 18,175	Feature 17	2.2 x 2.0	West entry	Masonry and jacal structure; storage
NA 18,175	Feature 11	2 m diameter		Floor assemblage; processing
NA 18,216	Feature 1	6.8 x 3.6	3 entrys	Masonry and jacal structure; unknown function substantial pothunting
NA 18,216	Feature 4	1.4 x 1.2	None	Jacal structure; storage
NA 18,216	Feature 5	Unknown	None	Jacal structure; unknown
NA 18,216	Feature 9	4.8 x 3.0	2 entrys; posthole	Masonry structure; habitation
NA 18,216		1.0 x 1.0	Unknown	Unexcavated, vandalized; storage facility?
NA 18,216		1.5 x 1.0	Entry	Unexcavated, vandalized; attached to main room block; storage facility?
NA 18,422	Room 1	4.7 x 3.2	3 hearths; posthole	Masonry and jacal structure; metate and ceramic vessels on floor; grinding slab on roof; habitation and processing
NA 18,422	Room 3	1.7 x 1.4	Entry	Masonry and jacal structure; storage
NA 18,422	Room 4	2.9 x 1.5	Hearth?; entry	Masonry and jacal structure; burned corn cluster on floor; habitation
NA 18,422	Room 5	3.8 x 3.3	Hearth	Masonry and jacal structure; ceramic vessels on floor; habitation
NA 18,422	Room 6	3.8 x 2.6	Hearth; entry	Masonry and jacal structure; ceramic vessels on floor; habitation

Ceramic Analyses

Ceramic analyses play an important role in understanding the organization of frontier households and communities. The ceramics collected from surface and excavated contexts at Silver Creek Archaeological Research Project (SCARP) sites (Hough's Great Kiva, AZ P:16:160 ASM, and Cothrun's Kiva) have been fully analyzed. Because the reporting of ceramics by researchers in the Mogollon Rim region has been highly variable, the SCARP ceramic analysis methods were also used to reexamine ceramics from Tla Kii Pueblo and Carter Ranch Pueblo, with a few exceptions described below. The SCARP methods were similar to those used in the Transwestern project (Goetze 1994). Attributes recorded for each sherd included ware, type, vessel form, vessel portion, number of missing surfaces, sherd weight (grams), thickness (mm), and evidence of modification for reuse. Tempering materials were distinguished for each sherd using a 15-to-35 power binocular microscope. Rim radius and rim length were recorded for rim sherds measuring more than 20 mm long. No systematic attempt was made to record joins among sherds. Ceramic studies have been reported fully by Herr (1999).

The analysis of the sherd assemblage from Tla Kii Pueblo (N = 3,466), housed at the Arizona State Museum, includes worked sherds and several reconstructible vessels from the cataloged museum collections, but none of the whole or burial vessels. Analyzed contexts include the room block; Kiva 1; Kiva 2; Unit Structures 1 and 2; Pit Houses 1, 2, and 3; the storage pits; and extramural contexts. Emil Haury recorded 13,322 sherds from these proveniences on his pottery analysis tally sheets (Haury 1941), but only the nonlocal ceramics from the site are published (Haury 1985d: 103). It was necessary to reanalyze the sherds from the site because instead of assigning types to the black-on-white ceramics, Haury assigned design styles: solid, solid and hatch, wavy-hatch, check, scroll, fine line, barbed wire, tick, cross-hatch, and dotting. In the reanalysis it became clear that the designs on these sherds were,

in some cases, unusual. For example, Tusayan styles, such as Black Mesa, appeared on Cibola White Ware pottery. In other instances, the use of negative design was reminiscent of Mimbres ceramics (Anyon and LeBlanc 1984, Plate 27d).

I analyzed approximately one-fourth (N = 9,545) of the sherds from Carter Ranch, housed at the Field Museum of Natural History in Chicago, including all sherds from the room block, great kiva, kiva, and plaza, and a portion of those from Trench B in the midden. Sherds from the remainder of the extramural excavation units were not analyzed. Decorated ceramics subsampled for ceramic design study (Freeman and Brown 1964; Longacre 1964a) were not reanalyzed. Because provenience on these sherds was encoded, I did not analyze them during my study in 1997. Since then the Field Museum has decoded these sherds and context information is again readily available (Nash 2001). I recorded detailed variables on 7,758 of the sherds, but the remaining 1,797 from the great kiva and Trench B were analyzed more quickly, listing only type, form, part, and presence of modification for reuse. The sherd and whole vessel collections from Tla Kii Pueblo and Carter Ranch have been culled, and rims and decorated sherds are overrepresented. The discrepancies between these collections and SCARP's total-ceramic-collection method are taken into account in comparative discussions of ceramics.

Information on ceramic types from the FLEX Goodwin and Show Low II projects is available from published sources (Dosh 1988), but information on vessel size and form is not. To obtain vessel function information from small sites, collections at the Museum of Northern Arizona were examined, including those from the following sites.

NA 18,176	NA 18,341	NA 18,347	NA 19,332
NA 18,177	NA 18,342	NA 18,349	NA 19,333
NA 18,338	NA 18,345	NA 19,330	NA 19,334
NA 18,339			

Table B.1. Division of Ceramic Wares for Determining Minimum Number of Vessels

Wares considered at the ware level	Wares considered at the type level
San Juan Red Ware	Cibola White Ware
Tsegi Orange Ware	Cibola Gray Ware
Little Colorado Gray Ware	Tusayan White Ware
	Tusayan Gray Ware
San Francisco Mountain Gray Ware	Mogollon Brown Ware
	Puerco Valley Red Ware
Alameda Brown Ware	White Mountain Red Ware
Prescott Gray Ware	Little Colorado White Ware
	Miscellaneous wares

Table B.2. Grouping of Ceramic Wares and Types by Surface Treatment

Decorated	Undecorated
Cibola White Ware	Cibola Gray Ware
San Juan Red Ware	Tusayan Gray Ware
Tusayan White Ware	Local Brown Ware
McDonald Corrugated	Little Colorado Gray Ware
White Mountain Red Ware	San Francisco Mtn. Gray Ware
Little Colorado White Ware	Prescott Gray Ware
Showlow Black-on-red, Undif.	Undif. White Ware
	Undif. Red Ware
Showlow Black-on-red, Hatched Style	Undif. Brown Ware
	Undif. Ware, Smudged
Showlow Black-on-red, Bold Style	Undif. Puerco Valley Red Ware
	Showlow Red
Showlow Black-on-red, Corrugated	Showlow Red, Smudged
	Showlow Corrugated

The analysis was slightly more intensive than that used for the Carter Ranch Pueblo sherds. Ware, type, vessel form, vessel portion, number of surfaces missing, weight, and evidence for modification for reuse were recorded.

Sherds were subjected to various analyses for comparisons within and between sites. For discussions of vessel frequency, size, and functional content of the ceramic assemblage, I used the minimum-number-of-vessels (MNV) method. This number was calculated as the circumference of rim sherds of a given ware, type, temper, form, and radius from a specific context divided into the cumulative length of those rim sherds of that ware, type, temper, form, radius, and context. All non-integer answers are then rounded up (1.3 vessel circumferences = 2 MNV). This method underestimates the absolute number of vessels from a site but it regularizes the relative contribution made by large and small vessels. Comparing frequencies of body sherds or rim sherds by form and size without using the MNV technique does not adequately approximate proportions of certain vessel forms and vessel sizes. In this analysis, some MNV calculations of less common wares and mis-

cellaneous sherds were calculated at the ware level (Table B.1).

Four functional classes of vessels were defined based on surface treatment (Table B.2) and vessel form: decorated bowls, undecorated bowls, decorated jars, and undecorated jars. Decorated and undecorated bowls probably functioned as service ware vessels, decorated jars as water storage jars, and undecorated jars as utilitarian cooking or storage vessels. Less common forms included seed jars, plates, ladles, pinch pots, undifferentiated jars, an effigy jar, a straight-walled or cylinder jar, and a flare-rimmed bowl. Considered together, the proportional variation of functional classes and vessel size data provided the best description of any particular ceramic assemblage. In cases where imports were not represented by rim sherds and type and ware information was more useful than functional class and vessel size, vessel body sherds were then included in the analyses; otherwise calculations were based on MNV proportions.

References

Abbott, David R., and Mary-Ellen Walsh-Anduze
1995   Temporal Patterns Without Temporal Variation: The Paradox of Hohokam Red Ware Ceramics. In *Ceramic Production in the American Southwest*, edited by Barbara J. Mills and Patricia L. Crown, pp. 88–114. Tucson: University of Arizona Press.

Adams, E. Charles
1983   The Architectural Analogue of Hopi Social Organization and Room Use, and Implications for Prehistoric Northern Southwestern Culture. *American Antiquity* 48(1): 44–62.
1991   *The Origin and Development of the Pueblo Katsina Cult*. Tucson: University of Arizona Press.

Adams, E. Charles, Miriam T. Stark, and Deborah S. Dosh
1993   Ceramic Distribution and Exchange: Jeddito Yellow Ware and Implications for Social Complexity. *Journal of Field Archaeology* 20(1): 3–21.

Adams, Jenny L.
1994   *The Development of Prehistoric Grinding Technology at Point of Pines, East-Central Arizona*. Doctoral dissertation, University of Arizona, Tucson. Ann Arbor: University Microfilms.
1999   Refocusing the Role of Food-Grinding Tools as Correlates for Subsistence Strategies in the U.S. Southwest. *American Antiquity* 64(3): 475–498.

Adams, Robert McC.
1978   Strategies of Maximization, Stability, and Resilience in Mesopotamian Society, Settlement, and Agriculture. *Proceedings of the American Philosophical Society* 122: 329–335.

Adler, Michael A.
1989   Ritual Facilities and Social Integration in Non-ranked Societies. In "The Architecture of Social Integration in Prehistoric Pueblos," edited by William D. Lipe and Michelle Hegmon. *Occasional Papers of the Crow Canyon Archaeological Center* 1: 35–52. Cortez: Crow Canyon Archaeological Center.
1996a   Fathoming the Scale of Anasazi Communities. In "Interpreting Southwestern Diversity: Underlying Principles and Overarching Patterns," edited by Paul R. Fish and J. Jefferson Reid. *Anthropological Research Papers* 48: 97–106. Tempe: Arizona State University.
1996b   "The Great Period": The Pueblo World During the Pueblo III Period, A.D. 1150 to 1350. In *The Prehistoric Pueblo World, A.D. 1150–1350*, edited by Michael A. Adler, pp. 1–10. Tucson: University of Arizona Press.
1996c   Land Tenure, Archaeology, and the Ancestral Pueblo Social Landscape. *Journal of Anthropological Archaeology* 15: 337–371.

Adler, Michael A., and Richard H. Wilshusen
1990   Large-Scale Integrative Facilities in Tribal Societies: Cross-Cultural and Southwestern US Examples. *World Archaeology* 22(2): 133–146.

Akins, Nancy J.
1986   A Biocultural Approach to Human Burials from Chaco Canyon, New Mexico. *Reports of the Chaco Center* 9. Albuquerque: Branch of Cultural Research, National Park Service.

Akkermans, Peter M. M. G.
1989   Tradition and Social Change in Northern Mesopotamia during the Later Fifth and Fourth Millennium B.C. In "Upon this Foundation: The 'Ubaid Reconsidered," edited by Elizabeth Henrickson and Ingolf Thuessen. The Carsten Nebuhr Institute of Ancient Near Eastern Studies. *CNI Publications* 10: 339–367. Copenhagen: Museum Tusculanum Press.

Alcock, Susan
1999   Imperial Frontiers, Local Frontiers. Paper presented in the Symposium "Frontiers, Interaction, and Identity in Early Europe" at the 64th Annual Meeting of the Society for American Archaeology, Chicago.

Ambler, Richard J., and Alan P. Olson
1977   Salvage Archaeology in the Cow Springs Area. *Technical Series* 15. Flagstaff: Museum of Northern Arizona.

Anthony, David W.
1990   Migration in Archaeology: The Baby and the Bathwater. *American Anthropologist* 92(4): 895–914.

Anyon, Roger, and Steven A. LeBlanc
1984   *The Galaz Ruin: A Prehistoric Mimbres Village in Southwest New Mexico*. Albuquerque: Maxwell Museum of Anthropology and the University of New Mexico Press.

Balandier, Georges
  1955   *Sociologie Actuelle de l'Afrique Noire.* Translatlated by D. Crawford. Paris: Presse Universaire de France.

Bannister, Bryant E., Elizabeth A. M. Gell,
and John W. Hannah
  1966   *Tree-Ring Dates from Arizona N–Q, Verde–Show Low–St. Johns Area.* Tucson: Laboratory of Tree-Ring Research, University of Arizona.

Barth, Fredrik
  1975   *Ritual and Knowledge Among the Baktaman of New Guinea.* New Haven: Yale University Press.

Basso, Keith H.
  1996   *Wisdom Sits in Places: Landscape and Language among the Western Apache.* Albuquerque: University of New Mexico Press.

Bayman, James Morrison
  1994   *Craft Production and Political Economy at the Marana Platform Mound Community.* Doctoral dissertation, Arizona State University, Tempe. Ann Arbor: University Microfilms.

Beaglehole, Ernest
  1937   Notes on Hopi Economic Life. *Yale University Publications in Anthropology* 15. New Haven: Yale University Press.

Bean, Lowell J.
  1978   Social Organization. In *Handbook of North American Indians: California*, Vol. 8 edited by Robert Heizer and William C. Sturtevant, pp. 673–682. Washington: Smithsonian Institution.

Bean, Lowell J., and Dorothea Theodoratus
  1978   Western Pomo and Northeastern Pomo. In *Handbook of North American Indians: California*, Vol. 8 edited by Robert Heizer and William C. Sturtevant, pp. 289-305. Washington: Smithsonian Institution.

Bernbeck, Reinhard
  1995   Lasting Alliances and Emerging Competition: Economic Developments in Early Mesopotamia. *Journal of Anthropological Archaeology* 14: 1–25.

Blanton, Richard E., Gary M. Feinman,
Stephan A. Kowalewski, and Peter N. Peregrine
  1996   A Dual-Processual Theory for the Evolution of Mesoamerican Civilization. *Current Anthropology* 37: 1–14.

Blinman, Eric
  1989   Potluck in The Protokiva: Ceramics and Ceremonialism in Pueblo I Villages. In "The Architecture of Social Integration in Prehistoric Pueblos," edited by William D. Lipe and Michelle Hegmon. *Occasional Papers of the Crow Canyon Archaeological Center* 1: 113–124. Cortez: Crow Canyon Archaeological Center.

Bogucki, Peter I.
  1988   *Forest Farmers and Stockherders: Early Agriculture and its Consequences in North-Central Europe.* New Studies in Archaeology. Cambridge: Cambridge University Press.
  1996   Sustainable and Unsustainable Adaptations by Early Farming Communities of Northern Poland. *Journal of Anthropological Archaeology* 15: 289-311.

Bottomore, Tom, Laurence Harris, V. G. Kiernan,
and Ralph Miliband, Editors
  1991   *A Dictionary of Marxist Thought* (2nd edition). Oxford: Blackwell Publishers.

Bowman, Isaiah
  1931   The Pioneer Fringe. *American Geographical Society Special Publication* 13. New York: American Geographical Society.

Bradfield, Richard Maitland
  1971   The Changing Patterns of Hopi Agriculture. *Occasional Paper* 30. London: Royal Anthropological Institute of Great Britain and Ireland.

Brandt, Elizabeth
  1994   Egalitarianism, Hierarchy, and Centralization in the Pueblos. In *The Ancient Southwestern Community: Models and Methods for the Study of Prehistoric Social Organization*, edited by W. H. Wills and Robert D. Leonard, pp. 9–24. Albuquerque: University of New Mexico Press.

Brumfiel, Elizabeth M.
  1992   Breaking and Entering the Ecosystem: Gender, Class, and Faction Steal the Show. *American Anthropologist* 94(3): 551–567.

Burch, Ernest S.
  1984   Kotzebue Sound Eskimo. In *Handbook of North American Indians: Arctic*, Vol. 5 edited by D. Damas, pp. 300–319. Washington: Smithsonian Institution.

Burton, Jeffery F.
  1993a   [Editor] When is a Great Kiva? Excavations at McCreery Pueblo, Petrified National Park, Arizona. *Publications in Anthropology* 63. Tucson: Western Archeological and Conservation Center, National Park Service.
  1993b   Days in the Painted Desert and the Petrified Forests of Northern Arizona: Contributions to the Archeology of Petrified Forest National Park, 1988-1992. *Publications in Anthropology* 62. Tucson: Western Archeological and Conservation Center, National Park Service.

Calagione, John
  1992   Working in Time: Music and Power on the Job in New York City. In *Worker's Expressions: Beyond Accommodation and Resistance*, edited by John Calagione, Doris Francis, and Daniel Nugent, pp. 12–28. New York: State University of New York Press.

Calagione, John, and Daniel Nugent
1992   Workers' Expressions: Beyond Accommodation and Resistance on the Margins of Capitalism. In *Workers' Expressions: Beyond Accommodation and Resistance*, edited by John Calagione, Doris Francis, and Daniel Nugent, pp. 1–11. New York: State University of New York Press.

Casey, Edward S.
1996   How to Get from Space to Place in a Fairly Short Stretch of Time: Phenomenological Prolegomena. In *Senses of Place*, edited by Steven Feld and Keith H. Basso, pp. 13-52. Santa Fe: School of American Research Press.

Chagnon, Napoleon
1968   *Yanomamo: The Fierce People*. New York: Holt, Rinehart, and Winston.

Chayanov, A. V.
1966   *The Theory of Peasant Economy*. Homewood, Illinois: Richard D. Irwin.

Ciolek-Torrello, Richard S.
1981   Archaeological Survey of the Stott Timber Sale. Museum of Northern Arizona, Flagstaff. MS submitted to USDA Forest Service, Panatella Ranger District, Apache-Sitgreaves National Forests, Navajo County, Arizona.

Clark, Jeffery J.
2001   Tracking Prehistoric Migrations: Pueblo Settlers among the Tonto Basin Hohokam. *Anthropological Papers of the University of Arizona* 65. Tucson: University of Arizona Press.

Clark, Jeffery J., and Penelope Minturn, Editors
2001   Life and Death along Tonto Creek. Draft Report. *Anthropological Papers* 24. Tucson: Center for Desert Archaeology.

Clark, Jeffery J., M. Kyle Woodson, and Mark C. Slaughter
2000   Those Who Went to the Land of the Sun: Puebloan Migrations into Southeastern Arizona. MS prepared for *Between the Hohokam and the Mimbres: Archaeology of a Land Between*, edited by Henry D. Wallace. Amerind New World Studies Series, forthcoming.

Coombs, Jan
1993   Frontier Patterns of Marriage, Family, and Ethnicity: Central Wisconsin in the 1880s. *Journal of Family History* 18(3): 265–282.

Costin, Cathy Lynne
1991   Craft Specialization: Issues in Defining, Documenting, and Explaining the Organization of Production. In *Archaeological Method and Theory*, Vol. 3, edited by Michael B. Schiffer, pp. 1–56. Tucson: University of Arizona Press.

Cowgill, George L.
1975   On Causes and Consequences of Ancient and Modern Population Changes. *American Anthropologist* 77(3): 505–525.

Craig, Douglas B., James P. Holmlund, and Jeffery J. Clark
1998   Labor Investment and Organization in Platform Mound Construction: A Case Study from the Tonto Basin of Central Arizona. *Journal of Field Archaeology* 25(3): 245–259.

Crown, Patricia L.
1994   *Ceramics and Ideology: Salado Polychrome Pottery*. Albuquerque: University of New Mexico Press.
2000   Gendered Tasks, Power, and Prestige in the Prehispanic American Southwest. In *Women and Men in the Prehispanic Southwest: Labor, Power, and Prestige*, edited by Patricia L. Crown, pp. 3-41. School of American Research Advanced Seminar Series. Santa Fe: School of American Research Press.

Cummings, Linda Scott
1988   Pollen Analysis. In "Subsistence and Settlement along the Mogollon Rim, A.D. 1000-1150," edited by Steven G. Dosh, pp. 256–299. *MNA Research Paper* 39. Flagstaff: Museum of Northern Arizona.

Cushing, Frank Hamilton
1979   Corn Raising: The Regeneration of the Seed. In *Zuñi: Selected Writings of Frank Hamilton Cushing*, edited by Jesse Green, pp. 270-281. Lincoln: University of Nebraska Press.

Cutler, Hugh C.
1964   Plant Remains from the Carter Ranch Site. In "Chapters in the Prehistory of Eastern Arizona, II," by Paul S. Martin, John B. Rinaldo, William A. Longacre, Leslie G. Freeman, Jr., J. A. Brown, R. H. Hevly, and M. E. Cooley. *Fieldiana: Anthropology* 55: 227–234. Chicago: Chicago Natural History Museum.

Dean, Jeffrey S.
1988   Dendrochronology and Paleoenvironmental Reconstruction on the Colorado Plateaus. In *The Anasazi in a Changing Environment*, edited by George J. Gumerman, pp. 119–167. Cambridge: Cambridge University Press.
1996a   Demography, Environment and Subsistence Stress. In "Evolving Complexity and Environmental Risk in the Prehistoric Southwest: Proceedings of the Workshop 'Resource Stress, Economic Uncertainty, and Human Response in the Prehistoric Southwest,' Held February 25–29, 1992 in Santa Fe, New Mexico," edited by Joseph A. Tainter and Bonnie Bagley Tainter. *Santa Fe Institute Studies in the Sciences of Complexity* 24: 25-56. Reading: Addison-Wesley.
1996b   Kayenta Anasazi Settlement Transformations in Northeastern Arizona, A.D. 1150-1350. In *The Prehistoric Pueblo World, A.D. 1150–1350*, edited

Dean, J. S. (*continued*)
by Michael A. Adler, pp. 29–47. Tucson: University of Arizona Press.

Dean, Jeffrey S., William H. Doelle, and Janet D. Orcutt
1994   Adaptive Stress, Environment, and Demography. In *Themes in Southwest Prehistory*, edited by George J. Gumerman, pp. 53–86. Santa Fe: School of American Research Press.

Dean, Jeffrey S., George J. Gumerman, Joshua M. Epstein, Robert Axtell, Alan C. Swedlund, Miles T. Parker, and Steven McCarroll
2000   Understanding Anasazi Culture Change Through Agent-Based Modeling. In *Dynamics in Human and Primate Societies: Agent-Based Modeling of Social and Spatial Processes*, edited by Timothy A. Kohler and George J. Gumerman, pp. 179–207. Santa Fe Institute Studies in the Sciences of Complexity. New York: Oxford University Press.

Dennell, Robin W.
1994   The Hunter-Gatherer/Agricultural Frontier in Prehistoric Temperate Europe. In *The Archaeology of Frontiers and Boundaries*, edited by Stanton W. Green and Stephen M. Perlman, pp. 163–211. Orlando: Academic Press.

Dosh, Deborah S., and Gigi Maloney
1991   The Fence Area Cultural Resource Assessment, Lakeside Ranger District, Apache-Sitgreaves National Forests, Navajo County, Arizona. *Kinlani Archaeological Project Technical Report* 6. Flagstaff.

Dosh, Deborah S., and Linda Neff
1996a   The Lewis Canyon Heritage Resource Survey, Lakeside Ranger District, Apache-Sitgreaves National Forests, Navajo County, Arizona. MS on file, Kinlani Archaeology, Flagstaff.
1996b   The South Sundown Heritage Resource Survey, Heber Ranger District, Apache-Sitgreaves National Forests, Navajo County, Arizona. Kinlani Archaeology. MS submitted to USDA Forest Service. Copies available from Project No. 95-13.

Dosh, Steven G., Editor
1988   *Subsistence and Settlement Along the Mogollon Rim Region, A.D. 1000–1150*. Flagstaff: Museum of Northern Arizona.

Douglas, John E., and Carol Kramer
1992   Interaction, Social Proximity, and Distance: A Special Issue. *Journal of Anthropological Archaeology* 11(2): 103–110.

Doyel, David E.
1980   [Editor] Prehistory in Dead Valley, East Central Arizona: The TG&E Springerville Report. *Arizona State Museum Archaeological Series* 144. Tucson: Arizona State Museum, University of Arizona.
1992   Exploring Chaco. In "Anasazi Regional Organization and the Chaco System," edited by David E. Doyel. *Maxwell Museum of Anthropology Anthropological Papers* 5: 3–14. Albuquerque: University of New Mexico.

Doyel, David E., and Stephen H. Lekson
1992   Regional Organization in the American Southwest. In "Anasazi Regional Organization and the Chaco System," edited by David E. Doyel. *Maxwell Museum of Anthropology Anthropological Papers* 5: 15–22. Albuquerque: University of New Mexico.

Dozier, Edward P.
1966   *Hano: A Tewa Indian Community in Arizona*. New York: Holt, Rinehart, and Winston.
1983   *The Pueblo Indians of North America*. Prospect Heights, Illinois: Waveland Press.

Duff, Andrew I.
1993   An Exploration of Post-Chacoan Community Organization through Ceramic Sourcing. MS, Master's thesis, Department of Anthropology, Arizona State University, Tempe.
1994   The Structure of Economic Interaction Through Ceramic Sourcing: Implications for Social Organization. In "Exploring Social, Political and Economic Organization in the Zuni Region," edited by Todd L. Howell and Tammy Stone. *Anthropological Research Papers* 46: 25–45. Tempe: Arizona State University.

Durand, Stephen R., and Kathy Roler Durand
2000   Notes from the Edge: Settlement Pattern Changes at the Guadalupe Community. In "Great House Communities Across the Chacoan Landscape," edited by John Kantner and Nancy M. Mahoney. *Anthropological Papers of the University of Arizona* 64: 101–109. Tucson: University of Arizona Press.

Eggan, Fred
1950   *Social Organization of the Western Pueblos*. Chicago: University of Chicago Press.

Eidt, Robert C.
1971   *Pioneer Settlement in Northeast Argentina*. Madison: University of Wisconsin Press.

Feinman, Gary M.
1995   The Emergence of Inequality: A Focus on Strategies and Processes. In *Foundations of Social Inequality*, edited by T. Douglas Price and Gary M. Feinman, pp. 255–279. New York: Plenum Press.

Feld, Steven, and Keith H. Basso
1996   Introduction. In *Senses of Place*, edited by Steven Feld and Keith H. Basso, pp. 3–11. Santa Fe: School of American Research Press.

Fernandez, James
1982   *Bwiti: An Ethnography of the Religious Imagination in Africa*. Princeton: Princeton University Press.

Fish, Paul R., and Suzanne K. Fish
1984   Agricultural Maximization in the Sacred Mountain Basin, Central Arizona. In "Prehistoric Agricultural Strategies in the Southwest," edited by Suzanne K. Fish and Paul R. Fish. *Anthropological Research Papers* 33: 147–159. Tempe: Arizona State University.
1994   Multisite Communities as Measures of Hohokam Aggregation. In *The Ancient Southwestern Community: Models and Methods for the Study of Prehistoric Social Organization*, edited by W. H. Wills and Robert D. Leonard, pp. 119–130. Albuquerque: University of New Mexico Press.

Flannery, Kent V., Editor
1976   *The Early Mesoamerican Village*. Orlando: Academic Press.

Fortes, Meyer
1945   *The Dynamics of Clanship among the Tallensi*. London: Oxford University Press.

Fowler, Andrew P., and John R. Stein
1992   The Anasazi Great House in Space, Time and Paradigm. In "Anasazi Regional Organization and the Chaco System," edited by David E. Doyel. *Maxwell Museum of Anthropology Anthropological Papers* 5: 15–22. Albuquerque: University of New Mexico.

Fox, John Gerard
1996   Playing with Power: Ballcourts and Political Ritual in Southern Mesoamerica. *Current Anthropology* 37(3): 483–509.

Freeman, Leslie G., Jr., and James A. Brown
1964   Statistical Analysis of Carter Ranch Pottery. In "Chapters in the Prehistory of Eastern Arizona, II," by Paul S. Martin, John B. Rinaldo, William A. Longacre, Leslie G. Freeman, Jr., James A. Brown, Richard H. Hevly, and M. E. Cooley. *Fieldiana: Anthropology* 55: 126–154. Chicago: Chicago Natural History Museum.

Gilpin, Dennis
1998   Historic Pueblos Colonization of the Northern Chaco Plateau, Northwestern New Mexico. In "Diné Bikeyah: Papers in Honor of David M. Brugge," edited by Meliha S. Duran and David T. Kirkpatrick, pp. 99–108. *New Mexico Archaeological Society Papers*. Albuquerque: New Mexico Archaeological Society.

Gilpin, Dennis, and David E. Purcell
2000   Peach Springs Revisited: Surface Recording and Excavation on the South Chaco Slope, New Mexico. In "Great House Communities Across the Chacoan Landscape," edited by John Kantner and Nancy M. Mahoney. *Anthropological Papers of the University of Arizona* 64: 28–38. Tucson: University of Arizona Press.

Gluckman, Max
1955   *Custom and Conflict in Africa*. Glencoe: The Free Press.

Goetze, Christine E.
1994   Introduction and Methods of Analysis. In *Across the Colorado Plateau: Anthropological Studies for the Transwestern Pipeline Expansion Project, Vol XVI: Interpretation of Ceramic Artifacts*, by Barbara J. Mills, Christine E. Goetze, and María Nieves Zedeño, pp. 1–20. Albuquerque: Office of Contract Archaeology and the Maxwell Museum of Anthropology, University of New Mexico.

Graves, Michael W.
1994a   Community Boundaries in Late Prehistoric Puebloan Society: Kalinga Ethnoarchaeology as a Model for the Southwestern Production and Exchange of Pottery. In *The Ancient Southwestern Community: Models and Methods for the Study of Prehistoric Social Organization*, edited by W. H. Wills, and Robert D. Leonard, pp. 149–169. Albuquerque: University of New Mexico Press.
1994b   Kalinga Social and Material Culture Boundaries: A Case of Spatial Convergence. In *Kalinga Ethnoarchaeology: Expanding Archaeological Method and Theory*, edited by William A. Longacre and James M. Skibo, pp. 12–49. Washington: Smithsonian Institution Press.

Graves, William M., and Suzanne L. Eckert
1998   Decorated Ceramic Distributions and Ideological Developments in the Northern and Central Rio Grande Valley, New Mexico. In "Migration and Reorganization: The Pueblo IV Period in the American Southwest," edited by Katherine A. Spielmann. *Anthropological Research Papers* 51: 263–283. Tempe: Arizona State University.

Green, Jesse, Editor
1979   *Zuni: Selected Writings of Frank Hamilton Cushing*. Lincoln: University of Nebraska Press.

Green, Margerie
1984   The Aztec Timber Sale Cultural Resource Survey. Archaeological Consulting Services, Ltd, Tempe. MS submitted to USDA Forest Service, Heber Ranger District, Apache-Sitgreaves National Forests, Navajo County, Arizona.

Green, Stanton W.
1991   Foragers and Farmers on the Prehistoric Irish Frontier. In "Between Bands and States," edited by Susan A. Gregg. *Southern Illinois University at Carbondale Occasional Paper* 9: 216–244. Carbondale: Center for Archaeological Investigations.

Green, Stanton W., and Stephen M. Perlman
1985   Frontiers, Boundaries, and Open Social Systems. In *The Archaeology of Frontiers and Boundaries,*

Green, S. W., and S. M. Perlman (*continued*)
        edited by Stanton W. Green and Stephen M.
        Perlman, pp. 3-29. Orlando, Academic Press.

Greenwald, Dawn M.
    1988   Lithic Analysis. In "Subsistence and Settlement
            along the Mogollon Rim, A.D. 1000–1150," ed-
            ited by Steven G. Dosh. *MNA Research Paper*
            39: 202–255. Flagstaff: Museum of Northern
            Arizona.

Greenwald, David H., Kirk C. Anderson,
and Mark L. Chenault
    1990   Cultural Resource Survey of the Colbath Timber
            Sale. SWCA, Inc., Flagstaff. MS submitted to
            USDA Forest Service, Lakeside District, Apache-
            Sitgreaves National Forests, Navajo County,
            Arizona.

Gregory, David A.
    1989a   Mullen Unit, Wolf/Mullen/North Cultural Re-
            source Survey. DAG Enterprises, Tucson. MS
            submitted to USDA Forest Service, Springerville
            Ranger District, Apache-Sitgreaves National
            Forests, Navajo County, Arizona.
    1989b   Wolf II Cultural Resource Survey. DAG Enter-
            prises, Tucson. MS submitted to USDA Forest
            Service, Springerville Ranger District, Apache-
            Sitgreaves National Forests, Navajo County,
            Arizona.
    1991   Form and Variation in Hohokam Settlement Pat-
            terns. In *Chaco & Hohokam: Prehistoric Regional
            Systems in the American Southwest*, edited by Pa-
            tricia L. Crown, and W. James Judge, pp. 159–193.
            Santa Fe: School of American Research Press.
    1992a   Burton Areas Cultural Resource Survey, Lakeside
            District. DAG Enterprises, Tucson. MS sub-
            mitted to USDA Forest Service, Lakeside Ranger
            District, Apache-Sitgreaves National Forests,
            Navajo County, Arizona.
    1992b   Red Knoll Area Cultural Resource Survey, Heber
            Ranger District, Apache-Sitgreaves National For-
            ests, Navajo County, Arizona. DAG Enterprises.

Gregory, David A., and Fred L. Nials
    1985   Observations Concerning the Distribution of
            Classic Period Hohokam Platform Mounds. In
            "Proceedings of the 1983 Hohokam Symposium,"
            edited by Alfred E. Dittert, Jr., and David E.
            Doyel. *Arizona Archaeological Society Occa-
            sional Paper* 2: 373–388. Phoenix.

Gregory, David A., and David R. Wilcox
    1999   Adaptation of Man to the Mountains: Revising
            the Mogollon Concept. Paper presented at the
            64th Annual Meeting of the Society for Amer-
            ican Archaeology, Chicago, Illinois.

Griaule, Marcel, and G. Dieterlen
    1954   The Dogon. In *African Worlds*, edited by D. Forde,
            pp. 83–110. London: Oxford University Press.

Gross, Daniel
    1979   Central Brazilian Social Organization. In *Brazil:
            Anthropological Perspectives: Essays in Honor of
            Charles Wagley*, edited by M. L. Margolis and
            W. E. Carter, pp. 321–343. New York: Colum-
            bia University Press.

Gumerman, George J.
    1988   The Archaeology of the Hopi Buttes District,
            Arizona. *Center for Archaeological Investigations
            Research Paper* 49. Carbondale: Southern Illinois
            University.

Gumerman, George J., and Alan P. Olson
    1968   Prehistory in the Puerco Valley, Eastern Arizona.
            Plateau 40(4): 113–127.

Gumerman, George J., and S. Alan Skinner
    1968   A Synthesis of the Prehistory of the Central Little
            Colorado Valley, Arizona. *American Antiquity*
            33(2): 185–199.

Gupta, Akhil, and James Ferguson
    1992   Beyond "Culture": Space, Identity and the Poli-
            tics of Difference. *Cultural Anthropology* 7 (1):
            6–23.

Guy, Donna J., and Thomas E. Sheridan
    1998   On Frontiers: The Northern and Southern Edges
            of the Spanish Empire in the Americas. In *Con-
            tested Ground: Comparative Frontiers on the
            Northern and Southern Edges of the Spanish Em-
            pire*, edited by Donna J. Guy and Thomas E.
            Sheridan, pp. 3–15. Tucson: University of Ari-
            zona Press.

Hack, John T.
    1942   The Changing Physical Environment of the Hopi
            Indians of Arizona. *Papers of the Peabody Muse-
            um of American Archaeology and Ethnology,
            Harvard University* 35(1). Cambridge: Harvard
            University.

Hagstrum, Melissa
    2001   Household Production in Chaco Canyon Society.
            American Antiquity 66(1): 47–55.

Hammack, Laurens C.
    1984   Cultural Resource Inventory of the Bailey Timber
            Sale. Complete Archaeological Service Assoc.,
            Cortez, Colorado. MS submitted to USDA Forest
            Service, Heber Ranger District, Apache-Sitgreaves
            National Forests, Navajo County, Arizona.

Hantman, Jeffrey L.
    1984   Regional Organization of the Northern Mogollon.
            American Archeology 4(3): 171–180.

Hantman, Jeffrey L., and Kent Lightfoot
    1978   An Analysis of Ceramic Design: A New Meth-
            od for Chronological Seriation. In "An Analyti-
            cal Approach to Cultural Resource Management:
            The Little Colorado Planning Unit," edited by
            Fred Plog. *Arizona State University Anthropolog-
            ical Research Papers* 13: 38–62, and *USDA For-*

est Service Cultural Resource Report 19. Tempe: Arizona State University.

Harrill, Bruce G.
1973   The DoBell Site: Archaeological Salvage near the Petrified Forest. *The Kiva* 39(1): 35–67.

Hartman, Dana, Editor
1990   Small Site Utilization Along the Mogollon Rim. *MNA Research Paper* 41. Flagstaff: Museum of Northern Arizona.

Hartman, Dana, and Donald R. Keller
1990   Site Descriptions. In "Small Site Utilization Along the Mogollon Rim," edited by Dana Hartman, pp. 25–112. *MNA Research Paper* 41. Flagstaff: Museum of Northern Arizona.

Hartman, Dana, Carl D. Habirt,
and Robert E. Gasser
1988   Human Remains, Nonartifactual Bone, and Botanical Analyses. In "Archaeological Investigations along Show Low Creek: The Schoens Dam Flood Control Project, Navajo County, Arizona, Apache-Sitgreaves Forest, Taylor, Navajo County, Arizona," prepared by Sara T. Stebbins and Dana Hartman. *Museum of Northern Arizona Department of Anthropology Report* A–84–38: 210–224. Flagstaff: Museum of Northern Arizona.

Hassan, Fekri
1981   *Demographic Archaeology*. New York: Academic Press.

Haury, Emil W.
1940–   Pueblo Excavation Record Forms. Material on
1941   file in the Arizona State Museum Archives (Folder A–1210B). Tucson: University of Arizona.
1941   AZ P:16:2, Pottery Analysis, 1941. Material on file in the Arizona State Museum Archives (Folder A–1210C), Tucson: University of Arizona.
1985a   Excavations in the Forestdale Valley, East-central Arizona. In *Mogollon Culture in the Forestdale Valley, East-central Arizona*, by Emil W. Haury, pp. 135–279. Tucson: University of Arizona Press.
1985b   The Forestdale Valley Cultural Sequence. In *Mogollon Culture in the Forestdale Valley, East-central Arizona*, by Emil W. Haury, pp. 375–407. Tucson: University of Arizona Press.
1985c   *Mogollon Culture in the Forestdale Valley, East-central Arizona*. Tucson: University of Arizona Press.
1985d   Tla Kii Ruin, Forestdale's Oldest Pueblo. In *Mogollon Culture in the Forestdale Valley, East-Central Arizona*, by Emil W. Haury, pp. 1–133. Tucson: University of Arizona Press.

Haury, Emil W., and E. B. Sayles
1985   An Early Pit House Village of the Mogollon Culture, Forestdale Valley, Arizona. In *Mogollon Culture in the Forestdale Valley, East-central Ari-*

zona, by Emil W. Haury, pp. 281–371. Tucson: University of Arizona Press.

Hegmon, Michelle
1989   Social Integration and Architecture. In "The Architecture of Social Integration in Prehistoric Pueblos," edited by William D. Lipe and Michelle Hegmon. *Occasional Papers of the Crow Canyon Archaeological Center* 1: 5–14. Cortez: Crow Canyon Archaeological Center.
1991   Risks of Sharing and Sharing as Risk Reduction: Interhousehold Food Sharing in Egalitarian Societies. In "Between Bands and States," edited by Susan A. Gregg. *Center for Archaeological Investigations Occasional Paper* 9: 309–332. Carbondale: Southern Illinois University.

Hegmon, Michelle, and William D. Lipe
1989   Introduction. In *The Architecture of Social Integration in Prehistoric Pueblos*, edited by William D. Lipe and Michelle Hegmon, pp. 1-4. Cortez: Crow Canyon Archaeological Center.

Hegmon, Michelle, Margaret C. Nelson,
and Susan M. Ruth
1998   Abandonment and Reorganization in the Mimbres Region of the American Southwest. *American Anthropologist* 100(1): 148–162.

Heidke, James M.
1998   Utilitarian Ceramic Production and Distribution in the Prehistoric Tonto Basin. In "Tonto Creek Archaeological Project: A Tonto Basin Perspective on Ceramic Economy," edited by James M. Vint and James M. Heidke. Draft Report. *Anthropological Papers* 23: 101–166. Tucson: Center for Desert Archaeology.

Herr, Sarah A.
1994   Great Kivas as Integrative Architecture in the Silver Creek Community. MS, Master's thesis, Department of Anthropology, University of Arizona, Tucson.
1995   1995 Excavations at Hough's Great Kiva (AZ P: 16:112 [ASM]), and Ceramic Analyses. In "Silver Creek Archaeological Research Project: 1995 Field Report," by Barbara J. Mills, Sarah A. Herr, Eric J. Kaldahl, Joanne M. Newcomb, Susan L. Stinson, and Scott Van Keuren, pp. 10–25, 82–89. MS on file, University of Arizona Archaeological Field School, Department of Anthropology, University of Arizona, Tucson.
1997   The Organization of Migrant Communities on the Chacoan Frontier. Paper presented at the 62nd Annual Meeting of the Society for American Archaeology, Nashville.
1998   Sherd Disks and Other Worked Sherds. In "Tonto Creek Archaeological Project: A Tonto Basin Perspective on Ceramic Economy," edited by James M. Vint and James M. Heidke. *Anthropo-*

Herr, S. A. (*continued*)
    logical Papers 23: 299–308. Tucson: Center for Desert Archaeology.
1999   *The Organization of Migrant Communities on a Pueblo Frontier*. Doctoral dissertation, University of Arizona, Tucson. Ann Arbor: University Microfilms.

Herr, Sarah A., Elizabeth M. Perry, and Scott Van Keuren
1999   Excavations at Three Great Kiva Sites. In "Living on the Edge of the Rim: Excavations and Analysis of the Silver Creek Archaeological Research Project, 1993-1998," edited by Barbara J. Mills, Sarah A. Herr, and Scott Van Keuren. *Arizona State Museum Archaeological Series* 192: 53–115. Tucson: University of Arizona.

Hill, James N.
1970   Broken K Pueblo: Prehistoric Social Organization in the American Southwest. *Anthropological Papers of the University of Arizona* 18. Tucson: University of Arizona Press.

Hine, Robert V.
1980   *Community on the American Frontier: Separate but not Alone*. Norman: University of Oklahoma Press.

Hodgetts, Lisa M.
1996   Faunal Evidence from El Zurdo. *Kiva* 62(2): 149–170.

Hohmann, John W., and Deborah S. Johnson
1989   McNeil Area Cultural Resource Inventory. DSHJ Research Associates, Inc., Tempe. MS submitted to USDA Forest Service, Lakeside Ranger District, Apache-Sitgreaves National Forests, Navajo County, Arizona.

Horne, Lee
1994   *Village Spaces: Settlement and Society in Northeastern Iran*. Washington: Smithsonian Institution Press.

Horner, Jennifer Z.
1999   Aggregation and the Silver Creek Faunal Record. In "Living on the Edge of the Rim: Excavations and Analysis of the Silver Creek Archaeological Research Project, 1993-1998," edited by Barbara J. Mills, Sarah A. Herr, and Scott Van Keuren. *Arizona State Museum Archaeological Series* 192: 433–457. Tucson: University of Arizona.

Hostetler, John A.
1980   *Amish Society*. 3rd ed. Baltimore: John Hopkins University Press.

Hough, Walter W.
1903   Archaeological Field Work in Northeastern Arizona, The Museum-Gates Expedition of 1901. *Report of the U.S. National Museum, 1901*. Washington.

Howell, Todd L., and Keith W. Kintigh
1996   Archaeological Identification of Kin Groups Us-
    ing Mortuary and Biological Data: An Example from the American Southwest. *American Antiquity* 61(3): 537–554.

Huckell, Lisa W.
1999   Paleoethnobotany. In "Living on the Edge of the Rim: Excavations and Analysis of the Silver Creek Archaeological Research Project, 1993-1998," edited by Barbara J. Mills, Sarah A. Herr, and Scott Van Keuren. *Arizona State Museum Archaeological Series* 192: 459–504. Tucson: University of Arizona.

Hudson, John C.
1976   Migration to an American Frontier. *Annals of the Association of American Geographers* 66(2): 242–265.
1979   The Study of Western Frontier Populations. In *The American West: New Perspectives, New Dimensions*, edited by Jerome O. Steffen, pp. 35–60. Norman: University of Oklahoma Press.

Hurst, Winston B.
2000   Chaco Outlier or Backwoods Pretender? A Provincial Great House at Edge of the Cedars Ruin, Utah. In "Great House Communities Across the Chacoan Landscape," edited by John Kantner and Nancy M. Mahoney. *Anthropological Papers of the University of Arizona* 64: 63–78. Tucson: University of Arizona Press.

Jeffrey, J. R.
1998   *Frontier Women: "Civilizing" the West? 1840-1880* (Revised Edition). New York: Hill and Wang.

Johnson, Allen W., and Timothy Earle
1987   *The Evolution of Human Societies: From Foraging Group to Agrarian State*. Palo Alto: Stanford University Press.

Johnson, Gregory A.
1975   Locational Analyses and the Investigation of Uruk Local Exchange Systems. In *Ancient Civilization and Trade*, edited by Jeremy A. Sabloff and C. C. Lamberg-Karlovsky. Albuquerque: School of American Research and University of New Mexico Press.

Jordan, Terri G., and Matti Kaups
1989   *The American Backwoods Frontier: An Ethnic and Ecological Interpretation*. Baltimore: Johns Hopkins University Press.

Judge, W. James
1989   Chaco Canyon—San Juan Basin. In *Dynamics of Southwest Prehistory*, edited by Linda S. Cordell and George J. Gumerman, pp. 209-261. Washington: Smithsonian Institution Press.
1991   Chaco: Current Views of Prehistory and the Regional System. In *Chaco & Hohokam: Prehistoric Regional Systems in the American Southwest*, edited by Patricia L. Crown and W. James Judge,

pp. 11-30. Santa Fe: School of American Research Press.

Kaldahl, Eric J.
1995   Ecological and Consumer Group Variation in Expedient Chipped Stone Technology in the Pueblo Period: An Exploratory Study in the Silver Creek Drainage, Arizona. MS, Master's thesis, Department of Anthropology, University of Arizona, Tucson.

1999   Chipped Stone. In "Living on the Edge of the Rim: Excavations and Analysis of the Silver Creek Archaeological Research Project, 1993-1998," edited by Barbara J. Mills, Sarah A. Herr, and Scott Van Keuren. *Arizona State Museum Archaeological Series* 192: 325-372. Tucson: University of Arizona.

Kaldahl, Eric J., and Jeffrey S. Dean
1999   Climate, Vegetation, and Dendrochronology. In "Living on the Edge of the Rim: Excavations and Analysis of the Silver Creek Archaeological Research Project, 1993-1998," edited by Barbara J. Mills, Sarah A. Herr, and Scott Van Keuren. *Arizona State Museum Archaeological Series* 192: 11-29. Tucson: University of Arizona.

Kantner, John
1996   Political Competition among the Chaco Anasazi of the American Southwest. *Journal of Anthropological Archaeology* 15(1): 41-105.

Kantner, John, and Nancy M. Mahoney, Editors
2000   Great House Communities across the Chacoan Landscape. *Anthropological Papers of the University of Arizona* 64. Tucson: University of Arizona Press.

Kendrick, James W., and W. James Judge
2000   Household Economic Autonomy and Great House Development in the Lowry Area. In "Great House Communities Across the Chacoan Landscape," edited by John Kantner and Nancy M. Mahoney. *Anthropological Papers of the University of Arizona* 64: 113-129. Tucson: University of Arizona Press.

Kennedy, John G.
1978   *Tarahumara of the Sierra Madre*. Arlington Heights, Illinois: AHM Publishing Corp.

Kent, Katherine P.
1957   The Cultivation and Weaving of Cotton in the Prehistoric Southwestern United States. *Transactions of the American Philosophical Society* 47(3).

Kintigh, Keith W.
1996   The Cibola Region in the Post-Chacoan Era. In *The Prehistoric Pueblo World, A.D. 1150-1350*, edited by Michael A. Adler, pp. 131-144. Tucson: University of Arizona Press.

Kintigh, Keith W., Todd L. Howell, and Andrew I. Duff
1996   Post-Chacoan Social Integration at the Hinkson Site, New Mexico. *Kiva* 61(3): 257-274.

Kohler, Timothy A.
1992   Field Houses, Villages, and the Tragedy of the Commons in the Early North Anasazi Southwest. *American Antiquity* 57(4): 617-635.

Kopytoff, Igor
1987a   [Editor] *The African Frontier: The Reproduction of Traditional African Societies*. Bloomington: Indiana University Press.

1987b   The Internal African Frontier: The Making of African Political Culture. In *The African Frontier: The Reproduction of Traditional African Societies*, edited by Igor Kopytoff, pp. 2-84. Bloomington: Indiana University Press.

Kroeber, Alfred
1917   Zuni Kin and Clan. *Anthropological Papers* 18(2): 41-204. New York: American Museum of Natural History.

Lancaster, Chet S.
1987   Political Structure and Ethnicity in an Immigrant Society: The Goba of Zambezi. In *The African Frontier: The Reproduction of Traditional African Societies*, edited by Igor Kopytoff, pp. 102-119. Bloomington: Indiana University Press.

Landtman, Gunnar
1927   *The Kiwai Papuans of British New Guinea*. London: Macmillan.

Lange, Charles
1959   *Cochiti*. Albuquerque: University of New Mexico Press.

Lange, Richard C.
1989   Survey of the Homolovi Ruins State Park. *Kiva* 54(3): 195-216.

Lansing, J. Stephen
1991   *Priests and Programmers: Technologies of Power in the Engineered Landscape of Bali*. Princeton: Princeton University Press.

Lattimore, Owen
1940   *Inner Asian Frontiers of China*. New York: American Geographical Society.

Leach, Edmund R.
1977   Political Systems of Highland Burma: A Study of Kachin Social Structure. *London School of Economics Monographs on Social Anthropology* 44. London: The Athlone Press.

Lechtman, Heather
1977   Style in Technology—Some Early Thoughts. In *Material Culture: Styles, Organization, and Dynamics of Technology*, edited by Heather Lechtman and Robert S. Merrill, pp. 3-20. New York: West Publishing.

Lekson, Stephen H.
1984   Great Pueblo Architecture of Chaco Canyon, New

Lekson, S. H. (*continued*)

Mexico. *Chaco Canyon Studies, Publications in Archeology* 18B. Albuquerque: National Park Service. [Published in 1986 by the University of New Mexico Press, Albuquerque.]

1988   The Idea of the Kiva in Anasazi Archaeology. *The Kiva* 53(3): 213–234.

1991   Settlement Patterns and the Chaco Regional System. In *Chaco & Hohokam: Prehistoric Regional Systems in the American Southwest*, edited by Patricia L. Crown and W. James Judge, pp. 31–55. Santa Fe: School of American Research Press.

2000   Great! In "Great House Communities Across the Chacoan Landscape," edited by John Kantner and Nancy M. Mahoney. *Anthropological Papers of the University of Arizona* 64: 157–163. Tucson: University of Arizona Press.

Levi-Strauss, Claude

1969   *The Elementary Structures of Kinship.* Boston: Beacon Press.

Levy, Jerrold E.

1992   *Orayvi Revisited: Social Stratification in an "Egalitarian" Society.* Santa Fe: School of American Research Press.

Lewis, Kenneth E.

1984   *The American Frontier: An Archaeological Study of Settlement Pattern and Process.* Orlando: Academic Press.

Liffman, Paul M.

2000   Gourdvines, Fires, and Wixárika Territoriality. *Journal of the Southwest* 42(1): 129–165.

Lightfoot, Kent G.

1984   *Prehistoric Political Dynamics: A Case Study from the American Southwest.* DeKalb: Northern Illinois University Press.

Lightfoot, Kent G., and Roberta Jewett

1986   The Shift to Sedentary Life: A Consideration of the Occupation Duration of early Mogollon Pithouse Villages. In "Mogollon Variability," edited by Charlotte Benson and Steadman Upham. *University Museum Occasional Papers* 15: 9–43. Las Cruces: New Mexico State University.

Lightfoot, Kent G., and Antoinette Martinez

1995   Frontiers and Boundaries in Archaeological Perspective. *Annual Review of Anthropology* 24: 471–492.

Lightfoot, Ricky R.

1988   Roofing an Early Anasazi Great Kiva: Analysis of an Architectural Model. *The Kiva* 53(3): 253–272.

1994   The Duckfoot Site: Archaeology of the House and Household. *Occasional Papers of the Crow Canyon Archaeological Center* 3-4. Cortez: Crow Canyon Archaeological Center.

Liljeblad, Sven, and Catherine S. Fowler

1986   The Owens Valley Paiute. In *Handbook of North American Indians: Great Basin*, Vol. 11 edited by Warren D'Azevedo, pp. 412–434. Washington: Smithsonian Institution.

Limerick, Patricia N.

1994   The Adventures of the Frontier in the Twentieth Century. In *The Frontier in American Culture*, edited by J. R. Grossman, pp. 67–102. Berkeley: University of California Press.

Linares, Olga F.

1976   "Garden Hunting" in the American Tropics. *Human Ecology* 4: 331–349.

1997   Diminished Rains and Divided Tasks: Rice Growing in Three Jola Communities of Casamance, Senegal. In "The Ecology of Practice: Studies of Food Crop Production in Sub-Saharan West Africa," edited by A. Endre Nyerges. *Food and Nutrition in History and Anthropology* 12: 39–76. Amsterdam: Gordon and Breach.

Lindsay, Alexander J., Jr.

1987   Anasazi Population Movements to Southeastern Arizona. *American Archeology* 6(3): 190–198.

Lipe, William D.

1989   Social Scale of Mesa Verde Anasazi Kivas. In "The Architecture of Social Integration in Prehistoric Pueblos," edited by William D. Lipe and Michelle Hegmon. *Occasional Papers of the Crow Canyon Archaeological Center* 1: 53–72. Cortez: Crow Canyon Archaeological Center.

Lipe, William D., and Michelle Hegmon

1989   Historical Perspectives on Architecture and Social Integration in the Prehistoric Pueblos. In "The Architecture of Social Integration in Prehistoric Pueblos," edited by William D. Lipe and Michelle Hegmon. *Occasional Papers of the Crow Canyon Archaeological Center* 1: 15-34. Cortez: Crow Canyon Archaeological Center.

Lipe, William D., and Scott Ortman G.

2000   Spatial Patterning in Northern San Juan Villages, A.D. 1050–1300. *Kiva* 66(1): 91-122.

Logan, Noel

1993   An Archaeological Survey of a Proposed Construction Site for Navajo County Buildings, Show Low, Arizona. Southwestern Environmental Consultants, Sedona, Arizona. MS submitted to Clint Shreve, Navajo County.

Lombard, James

1988   Ceramic Petrography. In "Archaeological Investigations in the Snowflake-Mesa Redondo Area, East-Central Arizona: The Apache-Navajo South Project," by Robert B. Neily. *Arizona State Museum Archaeological Series* 173: 203–221. Tucson: University of Arizona.

Longacre, William A.
1964a The Sociological Implications of the Ceramic Analysis. In "Chapters in the Prehistory of Eastern Arizona, II," by Paul S. Martin, John B. Rinaldo, William A. Longacre, Leslie G. Freeman, Jr., James A. Brown, Richard H. Hevly, and M. E. Cooley. *Fieldiana: Anthropology* 55: 155–170. Chicago: Chicago Natural History Museum.
1964b A Synthesis of Upper Little Colorado Prehistory, Eastern Arizona. In "Chapters in the Prehistory of Eastern Arizona, II," by Paul S. Martin, John B. Rinaldo, William A. Longacre, Leslie G. Freeman, Jr., James A. Brown, Richard H. Hevly, and M. E. Cooley. *Fieldiana: Anthropology* 55: 201–215. Chicago: Chicago Natural History Museum.
1966 Changing Patterns of Social Integration: A Prehistoric Example from the American Southwest. *American Anthropologist* 68(1): 94–102.
1970 Archaeology as Anthropology: A Case Study. *Anthropological Papers of the University of Arizona* 17. Tucson: University of Arizona Press.
Lyneis, Margaret
1984 The Western Anasazi Frontier: Cultural Processes Along a Prehistoric Boundary. In "Exploring the Limits: Frontiers and Boundaries in Prehistory," edited by S. P. DeAtley and F. J. Findlow. *BAR International Series* 223: 81–92. Oxford.
Magness-Gardiner, Bonnie, and Steven E. Falconer
1994 Community, Polity, and Temple in a Middle Bronze Age Levantine Village. *Journal of Mediterranean Archaeology* 7(2): 127–164.
Marshall, Michael P., David E. Doyel, and Cory Dale Breternitz
1982 A Regional Perspective on the Late Bonito Phase. In "Bis'sani: A Late Bonito Phase Community on Escavada Wash, Northwest New Mexico," edited by Cory Dale Breternitz, David E. Doyel, and Michael P. Marshall. *Navajo Nation Papers in Anthropology* 14(3): 1227–1240. Window Rock: NNCRMP.
Marshall, Michael P., John R. Stein, Richard W. Loose, and Judith E. Novotny
1979 *Anasazi Communities of the San Juan Basin*. Albuquerque and Santa Fe: Public Service Company of New Mexico and New Mexico Historic Preservation Bureau.
Martin, Paul S., John B. Rinaldo, William A. Longacre, Leslie G. Freeman, Jr., James A. Brown, Richard H. Hevly, and M. E. Cooley
1964 Chapters in the Prehistory of Eastern Arizona, II. *Fieldiana: Anthropology* 55. Chicago: Chicago Natural History Museum.

Marx, Karl
1906 *Capital: A Critique of Political Economy*. Translated by Samuel Moore and Edward Aveling. New York: The Modern Library.
1973 *Grundisse*. Translated by Martin Nicholaus. New York: Vintage Publications. (Reprint of 1857–1858 publication.)
Mauss, Marcel
1967 *The Gift: Forms and Functions of Exchange in Archaic Societies*. Translated by Ian Cunnison. New York: W. W. Norton.
McGregor, John C.
1943 Burial of an Early American Magician. *Proceedings of the American Philosophical Society* 86(2): 270–298.
McNeill, William Hardy
1983 *The Great Frontier: Freedom and Hierarchy in Modern Times*. Princeton: Princeton University Press.
Mead, Margaret
1967 *Sex and Temperament in Three Primitive Societies*. New York: Morrow Quill.
Merchant, Carolyn
1989 *Ecological Revolutions: Nature, Gender, and Science in New England*. Chapel Hill and London: University of North Carolina Press.
Meyer, Dan
1998 Social Variability and the Chaco System. Paper presented in session, "Beyond Normative Boundaries" at the Sixth Biennial Southwest Symposium, Hermosillo, Sonora, February 7.
Miksa, Elizabeth, and James M. Heidke
1995 Drawing a Line in the Sands: Models of Ceramic Temper Provenance. In "The Roosevelt Community Development Study, Vol. 2: Ceramic Chronology, Technology, and Economics," edited by James M. Heidke and Miriam T. Stark. *Anthropological Papers* 14(2): 133–204. Tucson: Center for Desert Archaeology.
2001 It all Comes Out in the Wash: Actualistic Petrofacies Modeling of Temper Provenance, Tonto Basin, Arizona, USA. *Geoarchaeology: An International Journal* 16(2): 177–222.
Mills, Barbara J.
1989 Integrating Functional Analyses of Vessels and Sherds Through Models of Ceramic Assemblage Formation. *World Archaeology* 21(1): 133–147.
1994a Community Dynamics and Archaeological Dynamics: Some Considerations of Middle-Range Theory. In *The Ancient Southwestern Community: Models and Methods for the Study of Prehistoric Social Organization*, edited by W. H. Wills and Robert D. Leonard, pp. 55–65. Albuquerque: University of New Mexico Press.
1994b Functional Variation in the Ceramic Assemblages.

Mills, B. J. (*continued*)

In *Across the Colorado Plateau: Anthropological Studies for the Transwestern Pipeline Expansion Project, Vol 16: Interpretation of Ceramic Artifacts*, by Barbara J. Mills, Christine E. Goetze, and María Nieves Zedeño, pp. 301–346. Albuquerque: Office of Contract Archeology and the Maxwell Museum of Anthropology, University of New Mexico.

1998   Migration and Pueblo IV Community Reorganization in the Silver Creek Area, East-Central Arizona. In "Migration and Reorganization: The Pueblo IV Period in the American Southwest," edited by Katherine A. Spielmann. *Anthropological Research Papers* 51: 65–80. Tempe: Arizona State University.

1999   Ceramics and the Social Contexts of Food Consumption in the Northern Southwest. In *Pottery and People: Dynamic Interactions*, edited by James M. Skibo and Gary Feinman, pp. 99–114. Salt Lake City: University of Utah Press.

2000   Alternative Models, Alternative Strategies: Leadership in the Prehispanic Southwest. In *Alternative Leadership Strategies in the Prehispanic Southwest*, edited by Barbara J. Mills, pp. 3–18. Tucson: University of Arizona Press.

Mills, Barbara J., and Patricia Crown

1995a   [Editors] *Ceramic Production in the American Southwest*. Tucson: University of Arizona Press.

1995b   Ceramic Production in the American Southwest: An Introduction. In *Ceramic Production in the American Southwest*, edited by Barbara J. Mills and Patricia L. Crown, pp. 1–29. Tucson: University of Arizona Press.

Mills, Barbara J., and Sarah A. Herr

1999   Chronology of the Mogollon Rim Region. In "Living on the Edge of the Rim: Excavations and Analysis of the Silver Creek Archaeological Research Project, 1993-1998," edited by Barbara J. Mills, Sarah A. Herr, and Scott Van Keuren. *Arizona State Museum Archaeological Series* 192: 269–293. Tucson: University of Arizona.

Mills, Barbara J., Sarah A. Herr, and Scott Van Keuren, Editors

1999   Living on the Edge of the Rim: Excavations and Analysis of the Silver Creek Archaeological Research Project, 1993–1998. *Arizona State Museum Archaeological Series* 192. Tucson: University of Arizona.

Mills, Barbara J., Sarah A. Herr, Susan L. Stinson, and Daniela Triadan

1999   Ceramic Production and Distribution. In "Living on the Edge of the Rim: Excavations and Analysis of the Silver Creek Archaeological Re-

search Project, 1993–1998," edited by Barbara J. Mills, Sarah A. Herr, and Scott Van Keuren. *Arizona State Museum Archaeological Series* 192: 295–324. Tucson: University of Arizona.

Mills, Barbara J., Sarah Herr, Eric Kaldahl, Joanne Newcomb, and Scott Van Keuren

1994   Silver Creek Archaeological Research Project: 1994 Field Report. MS on file, Department of Anthropology, University of Arizona, Tucson. Submitted to USDA Forest Service and National Science Foundation.

Mills, Barbara, Tom Fenn, Kristen Hagenbuckle, Shannon D. Plummer, Susan Stinson, and Raphael Vega-Centeno

1999   Silver Creek Archaeological Research Project: 1999 Annual Report. MS on file, Department of Anthropology, University of Arizona, Tucson. Submitted to USDA Forest Service.

Mills, Barbara J., Sarah A. Herr, Eric J. Kaldahl, Joanne M. Newcomb, Charles R. Riggs, and Ruth Van Dyke

1999   Excavations at Pottery Hill. In "Living on the Edge of the Rim: Excavations and Analysis of the Silver Creek Archaeological Research Project, 1993-1998," edited by Barbara J. Mills, Sarah A. Herr, and Scott Van Keuren. *Arizona State Museum Archaeological Series* 192: 117–148. Tucson: University of Arizona.

Mills Barbara J., Scott Van Keuren, Susan L. Stinson, William M. Graves, III, Eric J. Kaldahl, and Joanne M. Newcomb

1999   Excavations at Bailey Ruin. In "Living on the Edge of the Rim: Excavations and Analysis of the Silver Creek Archaeological Research Project, 1993–1998," edited by Barbara J. Mills, Sarah A. Herr, and Scott Van Keuren. *Arizona State Museum Archaeological Series* 192: 149–242. Tucson: University of Arizona.

Mindeleff, Cosmos

1989   Appendix I: Localization of Tusayan Clans. In *A Study of Pueblo Architecture: Tusayan and Cibola*, by Victor Mindeleff, pp. 635–653. Classics of Smithsonian Anthropology. Washington: Smithsonian Institution Press.

Mitchell, Mark, Sarah Herr, and Mark Elson

2000   Current Trends in Frontier Research. Paper presented in the symposium "Social Perspectives on Anthropological and Historical Frontiers" at the 65th Annual Meeting of the Society for American Archaeology, Philadelphia.

Moore, James A.

1985   Forager/Farmer Interactions: Information, Social Organization, and the Frontier. In *The Archaeology of Frontiers and Boundaries*, edited by Stanton W. Green and Stephen M. Perlman, pp. 93–112. Orlando: Academic Press.

Most, Rachel
1987 *Reconstructing Prehistoric Subsistence Strategies: An Example from East-Central Arizona.* Doctoral dissertation, Arizona State University, Tempe. Ann Arbor: University Microfilms.

Murdock, George Peter
1949 *Social Structure.* New York: Macmillan.

Murphy, Yolanda, and Robert F. Murphy
1974 *Women of the Forest.* New York: Columbia University Press.

Nash, Stephen E.
2001 Carter Ranch Pueblo. http://www.fmnh.org/research_collections/anthropology/anthro_sites/paul_martin/martin_web/Carter/carter.html

Neily, Robert B.
1984 The Snowflake-Mesa Redondo Project: An Intensive Archaeological Survey in The Upper Little Colorado River Area of East-Central Arizona. MS on file, Arizona State Museum Cultural Resource Management Division, University of Arizona, Tucson. Prepared for the Indian Projects Office, Bureau of Land Management.
1988 Archaeological Investigations in the Snowflake-Mesa Redondo: The Apache-Navajo South Project. *Arizona State Museum Archaeological Series* 173. Tucson: University of Arizona.
1991 Bagnal Area Cultural Resource Survey, Lakeside Ranger District, Apache-Sitgreaves National Forests, Navajo County, Arizona. *Archaeological Consulting Services, Cultural Resources Report* 43. Submitted to USDA Forest Service, Lakeside Ranger District, Apache-Sitgreaves National Forests, Navajo County, Arizona.

Nelson, Ben A.
1981 Ethnoarchaeology and Paleodemography: A Test of Turner and Lofgren's Hypothesis. *Journal of Anthropological Research* 37(2): 107–129.

Nelson, Margaret C.
1999 *Mimbres during the Twelfth Century: Abandonment, Continuity, and Reorganization.* Tucson: University of Arizona Press.

Nelson, Margaret C., and Michelle M. Hegmon
1996 Regional Social and Economic Reorganization: The Mimbres. MS on file, Department of Anthropology, Arizona State University, Tempe. Submitted to the Turner Foundation and National Geographic Society (#5213-94).

Netting, Robert, McC.
1990 Population, Permanent Agriculture, and Polities: Unpacking the Evolutionary Portmanteau. In *The Evolution of Political Systems: Sociopolitics in Small-Scale Sedentary Societies*, edited by Steadman Upham, pp. 21–61. School of American Research. New York: Cambridge University Press.
1993 *Smallholders, Householders: Farm Families and the Ecology of Intensive, Sustainable Agriculture.* Palo Alto: Stanford University Press.

Netting, Robert McC., M. Priscilla Stone, and Glenn D. Stone
1989 Kofyar Cash-Cropping: Choice and Change in Indigenous Agricultural Development. *Human Ecology* 17(3): 299–319.

Newcomb, Joanne M.
1997 Prehistoric Population Movements in the Silver Creek Area, East-Central Arizona. MS, Master's thesis, Department of Anthropology, University of Arizona, Tucson.
1999 Silver Creek Settlement Patterns and Paleodemography. In "Living on the Edge of the Rim: Excavations and Analysis of the Silver Creek Archaeological Research Project, 1993–1998," edited by Barbara J. Mills, Sarah A. Herr, and Scott Van Keuren. *Arizona State Museum Archaeological Series* 192: 31–52. Tucson: University of Arizona.

Newcomb, Joanne M., and Donald E. Weaver, Jr.
1992 An Archaeological Survey of a 120 Acre Parcel along Silver Creek, North of Snowflake, Navajo County, Arizona. MS submitted to East Side Pigs, Inc., Navajo County, Arizona. Plateau Mountain Desert Research, Flagstaff.

Nightengale, Christian B., and John A. Peterson
1990a Clay Springs Cultural Resource Survey. MS submitted to USDA Forest Service, Heber Ranger District, Apache-Sitgreaves National Forests, Navajo County, Arizona. New World Consultants, Albuquerque.
1990b Sackett Area Cultural Resource Survey. MS submitted to USDA Forest Service, Heber Ranger District, Apache-Sitgreaves National Forests, Navajo County, Arizona. New World Consultants, Albuquerque.
1991a Colbath II Area Cultural Resource Survey. MS submitted to USDA Forest Service, Lakeside Ranger District, Apache-Sitgreaves National Forests, Navajo County, Arizona. New World Consultants, Albuquerque.
1991b Fools Hollow Area Cultural Resource Survey. MS submitted to USDA Forest Service, Lakeside Ranger District, Apache-Sitgreaves National Forests, Navajo County, Arizona. New World Consultants, Albuquerque.

Nimuendajú, Curt
1942 *The Serente.* Translated by Robert H. Lowie. Los Angeles: Publications of the Frederick Webb Hodge Anniversary Publication Fund, Vol. 4.
1946 *The Eastern Timbira.* Berkeley: University of California Press.

Nugent, Daniel
1991 Revolutionary Posturing, Bourgeois Land "Reform:" Reflections on the Agrarian Reform in

Nugent, D. (*continued*)
    Northern Mexico. *Labour, Capital and Society* 24(1): 90–108.
1993   *Spent Cartridges of Revolution: An Anthropological History of Namiquipa, Chihuahua*. Chicago: University of Chicago Press.

Nugent, Walter
1989   Frontiers and Empires in the Late Nineteenth Century. *The Western Historical Quarterly* 20: 393–408.

Nyerges, A. Endre
1992   The Ecology of Wealth-in-People: Agriculture, Settlement, and Society on the Perpetual Frontier. *American Anthropologist* 94(4): 860–881.

Odess, Daniel
1998   The Archaeology of Interaction: Views from Artifact Style and Material Exchange in Dorset Society. *American Antiquity* 63(3): 417–435.

Oliver, Theodore J., and Deborah S. Dosh
1992   The Lons Area Cultural Resource Assessment. MS submitted to USDA Forest Service, Lakeside Ranger District, Apache-Sitgreaves National Forests, Navajo County, Arizona. Kinlani Archaeology, Flagstaff.

Olson, Alan P.
1971   Archaeology of the Arizona Public Service Company 345KV Line. *Museum of Northern Arizona Bulletin* 46. Flagstaff: Northern Arizona Society of Science and Art.

Orcutt, Janet D.
1991   Environmental Variability and Settlement Changes on the Pajarito Plateau, New Mexico. *American Antiquity* 56(2): 315–332.

Ostergren, Robert C.
1998   Prairie Bound: Migration Patterns to a Swedish Settlement on the Dakota Frontier. In *European Immigrants in the American West: Community Histories*, edited by Frederick Luebke, pp. 15-31. Albuquerque: University of New Mexico Press.

Palau, Montserrat
1957   *Les Dogon*. Institut International Africain. Vendome: Presses Universitaires de France.

Parsons, Elsie Clews
1966   *Pueblo Indian Religion*. Lincoln: University of Nebraska Press.

Peterson, John A., and Christian B. Nightengale
1991   Dodson Area Cultural Resource Survey. MS submitted to USDA Forest Service, Lakeside Ranger District, Apache-Sitgreaves National Forests, Navajo County, Arizona. New World Consultants, Albuquerque.

Pierson, George W.
1973   *The Moving American*. New York: Knopf.

Plog, Fred T.
1974   *The Study of Prehistoric Change*. New York: Academic Press.

1978   An Analysis of Variability in Site Locations in the Chevelon Drainage, Arizona. In "Investigations of the Southwestern Anthropological Research Group: An Experiment in Archaeological Cooperation: The Proceedings of the 1976 Conference," edited by Robert C. Euler and George J. Gumerman. *Museum of Northern Arizona Bulletin* 50: 53–71. Flagstaff: Museum of Northern Arizona.

1983   Political and Economic Alliances on the Colorado Plateaus, A.D. 400–1450. In *Advances in World Archaeology*, Vol. 2, edited by Fred Wendorf and Angela E. Close, pp. 289–330. New York: Academic Press.

1984   Exchange, Tribes and Alliances: The Northern Southwest. *American Archeology* 4(3): 217–223.

Plog, Fred T., George J. Gumerman, Robert C. Euler, Jeffrey S. Dean, Richard H. Hevly, and Thor N. V. Karlstrom
1988   Anasazi Adaptive Strategies: The Models, Predictions, and Results. In *The Anasazi in a Changing Environment*, edited by George J. Gumerman, pp. 230–276. School of American Research Advanced Seminar Series. Cambridge: Cambridge University Press.

Plog, Stephen
1989   Ritual, Exchange, and the Development of Regional Systems. In "The Architecture of Social Integration in Prehistoric Pueblos," edited by William D. Lipe and Michelle Hegmon. *Occasional Papers of the Crow Canyon Archaeological Center* 1: 143–154. Cortez: Crow Canyon Archaeological Center.

Plog, Stephen, and Julie Solometo
1997   The Never-Changing and the Ever-Changing: The Evolution of Western Pueblo Ritual. *Cambridge Archaeological Journal* 7(2): 161–182.

Powdermaker, Hortense
1933   *Life in Lesu: The Study of a Melanesian Society in New Ireland*. New York: W. W. Horton.

Powers, Robert P., William B. Gillespie, and Stephen H. Lekson
1983   The Outlier Survey: A Regional View of Settlement in the San Juan Basin. *Reports of the Chaco Center* 3. Albuquerque: Division of Cultural Research, National Park Service.

Prescott, J. R. V.
1978   *Boundaries and Frontiers*. London: Croom Helm.

Preucel, Robert Washington, Jr.
1988   *Seasonal Agricultural Circulation and Residential Mobility: A Prehistoric Example from the Pajarito Plateau, New Mexico*. Doctoral dissertation, University of California, Los Angeles. Ann Arbor: University Microfilms.

Price, David
    1987   Nambiquara Geopolitical Organization. *Man* 22:
            1–24.
Ramsey, Christopher Bronk
    1995   *OxCal Program 2.18.*
Rapoport, Amos
    1990   Systems of Activities and Systems of Settings. In
            *Domestic Architecture and the Use of Space: An
            Interdisciplinary Cross-Cultural Study*, edited by
            Susan Kent, pp. 9–20. Cambridge: Cambridge
            University Press.
Rappaport, Roy A.
    1968   *Pigs for the Ancestors: Ritual in the Ecology of a
            New Guinea People.* New Haven: Yale Univer-
            sity Press.
Rautman, Alison E.
    1993   Resource Variability, Risk, and the Structure of
            Social Networks: An Example from the Prehis-
            toric Southwest. *American Antiquity* 58(3): 403–
            424.
    1996   Risk, Reciprocity, and the Operation of Social
            Networks. In "Evolving Complexity and Environ-
            mental Risk in the Prehistoric Southwest: Pro-
            ceedings of the Workshop 'Resource Stress, Eco-
            nomic Uncertainty, and Human Response in the
            Prehistoric Southwest,' Held February 25–29,
            1992 in Santa Fe, NM," edited by Joseph A.
            Tainter and Bonnie Bagley Tainter. *Santa Fe In-
            stitute Studies in the Sciences of Complexity* 24:
            197–222. Reading: Addison-Wesley.
Rawlings, Marjorie Kinnan
    1942   *Cross Creek.* New York: Charles Scribner's
            Sons.
Reagan, Albert B.
    1930   Archaeological Notes on the Fort Apache Region,
            Arizona. *Transactions Kansas Academy of Sci-
            ence* 33: 111–132.
Reid, J. Jefferson
    1989   A Grasshopper Perspective on the Mogollon of
            the Arizona Mountains. In *Dynamics of Southwest
            Prehistory*, edited by Linda S. Cordell and
            George J. Gumerman, pp. 65–97. Washington:
            Smithsonian Institution Press.
Reid, J. Jefferson, and Stephanie M. Whittlesey
    1982   Households at Grasshopper Pueblo. *American
            Behavioral Scientist* 25(6): 687–703.
Rice, Glen E.
    1980   Archaeological Sites in the Corduroy Creek Val-
            ley. In *Studies in the Prehistory of the Forestdale
            Region, Arizona*, edited by C. Russell Stafford
            and Glen E. Rice, pp. 119–250. Tempe: Office
            of Cultural Resource Management, Arizona State
            University.
Rice, Prudence M.
    1998   Contexts of Contact and Change: Peripheries,

Frontiers, and Boundaries. In "Studies in Culture
            Contact: Interaction, Culture Change, and Ar-
            chaeology," edited by James G. Cusick. *Center
            for Archaeological Investigations Occasional Pa-
            per* 25: 44–66. Carbondale: Southern Illinois
            University.
Ridell, Francis A.
    1978   Maidu and Konkow. In *Handbook of North Amer-
            ican Indians: California*, Vol. 8 edited by Robert
            Heizer and W. C. Sturtevant, pp. 370–387. Wash-
            ington: Smithsonian Institution.
Rinaldo, John B.
    1964a   Architectural Details, Carter Ranch Pueblo. In
            "Chapters in the Prehistory of Eastern Arizona,
            II," by Paul S. Martin, John B. Rinaldo, William
            A. Longacre, Leslie G. Freeman, Jr., James A.
            Brown, Richard H. Hevly, and M. E. Cooley.
            Fieldiana: Anthropology 55: 15–58. Chicago:
            Chicago Natural History Museum.
    1964b   Artifacts. In "Chapters in the Prehistory of East-
            ern Arizona, II," by Paul S. Martin, John B. Ri-
            naldo, William A. Longacre, Leslie G. Freeman,
            Jr., James A. Brown, Richard H. Hevly, and M.
            E. Cooley. *Fieldiana: Anthropology* 55: 63–109.
            Chicago: Chicago Natural History Museum.
    1964c   Burials and Mortuary Customs. In "Chapters in
            the Prehistory of Eastern Arizona, II," by Paul S.
            Martin, John B. Rinaldo, William A. Longacre,
            Leslie G. Freeman, Jr., James A. Brown, Rich-
            ard H. Hevly, and M. E. Cooley. *Fieldiana: An-
            thropology* 55: 59–62. Chicago: Chicago Natural
            History Museum.
Roberts, Frank H. H., Jr.
    1932   The Village of the Great Kivas on the Zuni Res-
            ervation, New Mexico. *Bureau of American Eth-
            nology Bulletin* 111. Washington: Smithsonian
            Institution.
Roney, John R.
    1992   Prehistoric Roads and Regional Integration in the
            Chacoan System. In "Anasazi Regional Organiza-
            tion and the Chaco System," edited by David E.
            Doyel. *Maxwell Museum of Anthropology Anthro-
            pological Papers* 5: 123–132. Albuquerque: Uni-
            versity of New Mexico.
Roseberry, William
    1988   Political Economy. *Annual Review of Anthropol-
            ogy* 17: 161–185.
Rozen, Kenneth
    1988   Letter Report to the Arizona State Land Depart-
            ment, Phoenix, Arizona, regarding the East Side
            Pigs Land Exchange. MS on file, Arizona State
            Museum, University of Arizona, Tucson.
Ruppé, Patricia A.
    1988   Flotation Analysis. In "Subsistence and Settle-
            ment along the Mogollon Rim, A.D. 1000–1150,"

Ruppé, P. A. (*continued*)
    edited by Steven G. Dosh. *MNA Research Paper* 39: 300–323. Flagstaff: Museum of Northern Arizona.

1990   Flotation Sample Analysis. In "Small Site Utilization Along the Mogollon Rim," edited by Dana Hartman. *MNA Research Paper* 41: 160–185. Flagstaff: Museum of Northern Arizona.

Sahlins, Marshall D.
1981   Historical Metaphors and Mythical Realities: Structure in the Early History of the Sandwich Islands Kingdom. *Association for Social Anthropology in Oceania Special Publications* 1. Ann Arbor: University of Michigan Press.

1985   *Islands of History*. Chicago: University of Chicago Press.

1994   Cosmologies of Capitalism: The Trans-Pacific Sector of the "World System." In *Culture/Power/History: A Reader in Contemporary Social Theory*, edited by Nichola B. Dirks, Geoff Eley, and Sherry B. Ortner, pp. 412–455. Princeton: Princeton University Press.

Saitta, Dean J.
1997   Power, Labor, and the Dynamics of Change in Chacoan Political Economy. *American Antiquity* 62(1): 7–26.

Salzer, Matthew
2000   Temperature Variability and the Northern Anasazi: Possible Implications for Regional Abandonment. *Kiva* 65(4): 295-318.

Schlanger, Sarah H.
1987   Population Measurement, Size, and Change, A.D. 600–1175. In *Dolores Archaeological Program Supporting Studies: Settlement and Environment*, compiled by K. L. Petersen and Janet D. Orcutt, pp. 568–613. Denver: Bureau of Reclamation, Engineering and Research Center.

1988   Patterns of Population Movement and Long-Term Population Growth in Southwestern Colorado. *American Antiquity* 53(4): 773–793.

Schlegel, Alice
1992   African Political Models in the American Southwest: Hopi as an Internal Frontier Society. *American Anthropologist* 94(2): 376–397.

Scholnick, Jonathon
1998   Examining Interaction in the Apache-Sitgreaves Region: A Compositional Analysis of Cibola Whiteware. MS, BA thesis, Department of Anthropology, University of Virginia, Richmond.

Sebastian, Lynne
1992a   *The Chaco Anasazi: Sociopolitical Evolution in the Prehistoric Southwest*. New York: Cambridge University Press.

1992b   Chaco Canyon and the Anasazi Southwest: Changing Views of Sociopolitical Organization. In "Anasazi Regional Organization and the Chaco System," edited by David E. Doyel. *Maxwell Museum of Anthropology Anthropological Papers* 5: 23–34. Albuquerque: University of New Mexico.

Senior, Louise M, and Linda J. Pierce
1989   Turkeys and Domestication in the Southwest: Implications from Homol'ovi III. *Kiva* 54(3): 245–259.

Sewastynowicz, James
1986   "Two-Step" Migration and Upward Mobility on the Frontier: The Safety Valve Effect in Pejibaye, Costa Rica. *Economic Development and Cultural Change* 34(4): 731–754.

Seymour, Deni J.
1989   Habitat 89 Cultural Resource Inventory. MS submitted to USDA Forest Service, Lakeside Ranger District, Apache-Sitgreaves National Forests, Navajo County, Arizona. SWCA, Tucson.

Snead, James E.
1995   *Beyond Pueblo Walls: Community and Competition in the Northern Rio Grande, A.D. 1300–1400*. Doctoral dissertation, University of California at Los Angeles, Los Angeles. Ann Arbor: University Microfilms.

Solometo, Julie
2001   Tactical Sites of the Chevelon and Clear Creek Drainages. In "The Archaeology of Ancient Tactical Sites," edited by John R. Welch and Todd W. Bostwick. *The Arizona Archaeologist* 32: 21–36. Phoenix: Arizona Archaeological Society.

Spalding, Nathanael E., and David R. Michelson
1993   An Archaeological Survey of a 120 Acre Parcel along Silver Creek, North of Snowflake, Navajo County, Arizona. MS submitted to East Side Pigs, Inc., Snowflake, Arizona. Plateau Mountain Desert Research, Flagstaff.

Speth, John D., and Susan L. Scott
1989   Horticulture and Large-Mammal Hunting: The Role of Resource Depletion and the Constraints of Time and Labor. In *Farmers as Hunters: The Implications of Sedentism*, edited by Susan Kent, pp. 71–79. Cambridge: Cambridge University Press.

Spielmann, Katherine A., Editor
1991   *Farmers, Hunters, and Colonists: Interaction between the Southwest*. Tucson: University of Arizona Press.

Spier, Leslie
1918   Notes on Some Little Colorado Ruins. *Anthropological Papers of the American Museum of Natural History* 18(4). New York: American Museum of Natural History.

Stafford, Barbara D.
1980   Prehistoric Manufacture and Utilization of Lithics from Corduroy Creek. In *Studies in the Prehistory of the Forestdale Region, Arizona*, edited

by C. Russell Stafford and Glen E. Rice, pp. 251–297. Tempe: Office of Cultural Resource Management, Arizona State University.

Stafford, C. Russell
1980 GBU:P:16:12 (ASU). In *Studies in the Prehistory of the Forestdale Region, Arizona*, edited by C. Russell Stafford and Glen E. Rice, pp. 94–118. Tempe: Office of Cultural Resource Management, Arizona State University.

Stafford, C. Russell, and Glen E. Rice
1980 *Studies in the Prehistory of the Forestdale Region, Arizona*. Tempe: Office of Cultural Resource Management, Arizona State University.

Stebbins, Sara T.
1988 Ground Stone. In "Archaeological Investigations along Show Low Creek: The Schoens Dam Flood Control Project, Navajo County, Arizona, Apache-Sitgreaves Forest, Taylor, Navajo County, Arizona," prepared by Sara T. Stebbins and Dana Hartman. *Museum of Northern Arizona Department of Anthropology Report* A–84–38: 175–195. Flagstaff: Museum of Northern Arizona.

Stebbins, Sara T., and Dana Hartman
1988 Archaeological Investigations along Show Low Creek: The Schoens Dam Flood Control Project, Navajo County, Arizona, Apache-Sitgreaves Forest, Taylor, Navajo County, Arizona. *Museum of Northern Arizona Department of Anthropology Report* A–84–38. Flagstaff: Museum of Northern Arizona.

Steffen, Jerome O.
1979 Insular *v.* Cosmopolitan Frontiers: A Proposal for the Comparative study of American Frontiers. In *The American West: New Perspectives, New Dimensions*, edited by Jerome O. Steffen, pp. 94–123. Norman: University of Oklahoma Press.
1980 *Comparative Frontiers: A Proposal for Studying the American West*. Norman: University of Oklahoma Press.

Steward, Julian
1948 Tropical Forest Tribes. In "Handbook of South American Indians," Vol. 3. *Bureau of American Ethnology Bulletin* 143. Washington.
1951 Levels of Sociocultural Integration: An Operational Concept. *Southwest Journal of Anthropology* 7: 374–391.

Stewart, Yvonne
1980 An Archeological Overview of Petrified Forest National Park. *Publications in Anthropology* 10. Tucson: Western Archeological Center, National Park Service.

Stinson, Susan L.
1996 Roosevelt Red Ware and the Organization of Ceramic Production in the Silver Creek Drainage.

MS, Master's thesis, Department of Anthropology, University of Arizona, Tucson.

Stoddart, Simon
1999 Frontiers in First Millennium B.C. Central Italy. Paper in symposium "Frontiers, Interaction, and Identity in Early Europe," 64th Annual Meeting of the Society for American Archaeology, Chicago.

Stone, Elizabeth
1987 Nippur Neighborhoods. *Studies in Ancient Oriental Civilization* 44. Chicago: The Oriental Institute of the University of Chicago.

Stone, Glenn D.
1992 Social Distance, Spatial Relations, and Agricultural Production among the Kofyar of Namu District, Plateau State, Nigeria. *Journal of Anthropological Archaeology* 11(2): 152–172.
1993 Agrarian Settlement and the Spatial Disposition of Labor. In *Spatial Boundaries and Social Dynamics: Case Studies from Food-Producing Societies*, edited by Augustin Holl and Thomas E. Levy, pp. 25–38. Ann Arbor: International Monographs in Prehistory.
1994 Agricultural Intensification and Perimetrics: Ethnoarchaeological Evidence from Nigeria. *Current Anthropology* 35(3): 317–323.
1996 *Settlement Ecology: The Social and Spatial Organization of Kofyar Agriculture*. Tucson: University of Arizona Press.

Stone, Glenn D., Robert McC. Netting, and M. Priscilla Stone
1990 Seasonality, Labor Scheduling, and Agricultural Intensification in the Nigerian Savanna. *American Anthropologist* 92(1): 7–23.

Stuiver, M., and R. S. Kra, Editors
1986 *Radiocarbon* 28(2B): 805–1030.

Sullivan, Alan P., III
1994 Frontiers, Barriers, and Crises Today: Colton's Methods and the Wupatki Survey Data. In *The Ancient Southwestern Community: Models and Methods for the Study of Prehistoric Social Organization*, edited by W. H. Wills and Robert D. Leonard, pp. 191–207. Albuquerque: University of New Mexico Press.

Szuter, Christine R.
2000 Gender and Animals: Hunting Technology, Ritual, and Subsistence in the Greater Southwest. In *Women and Men in the Prehispanic Southwest: Labor, Power, and Prestige*, edited by Patricia L. Crown, pp. 197–220. School of American Research Advanced Seminar Series. Santa Fe: School of American Research Press.

Szuter, Christine R., and William B. Gillespie
1994 Interpreting Use of Animal Resources at Prehistoric American Southwest Communities. In *The Ancient Southwestern Community: Models and*

Szuter, C. R., and W. B. Gillespie (*continued*)
    Methods for the Study of Prehistoric Social Organization, edited by W. H. Wills and Robert D. Leonard, pp. 67–76. Albuquerque: University of New Mexico Press.

Tainter, Joseph A., and Fred T. Plog
    1994   Strong and Weak Patterning in Southwestern Prehistory: The Formation of Puebloan Archaeology. In *Themes in Southwest Prehistory*, edited by George J. Gumerman, pp. 165–181. Santa Fe: School of American Research Press.

Toll, H. Wolcott
    1985   *Pottery Production, Public Architecture, and the Chaco Anasazi System.* Doctoral dissertation, University of Colorado, Boulder. Ann Arbor: University Microfilms.

Toll, H. Wolcott, and Peter J. McKenna
    1987   The Ceramography of Pueblo Alto. In "Investigations at the Pueblo Alto Complex, Chaco Canyon, Artifactual and Biological Analyses," Vol. 3, Pt. 1, edited by Frances Joan Mathien and Thomas C. Windes. *Chaco Canyon Studies, Publications in Archeology* 18F: 19–230. Santa Fe: National Park Service.

Triadan, Daniela, Barbara J. Mills,
and Andrew I. Duff
    2001   From Analytical to Anthropological: 14th Century Red Ware Circulation and Its Implications for Pueblo Reorganization. In *Ceramic Compositional Modeling in the American Southwest*, edited by Donna Glowacki and Hector Neff. Los Angeles: UCLA Institute of Archaeology Publications, in press.

Turner II, Christy G., and Laurel Lofgren
    1966   Household Size of Prehistoric Western Pueblo Indians. *Southwestern Journal of Anthropology* 22(2): 117–132.

Turner, Frederick J.
    1972   The Significance of the Frontier in American History. In "The Turner Thesis: Concerning the Role of the Frontier in American History," edited by G. R. Taylor, pp. 3–28. *Problems in American Civilization*, 3rd ed., E. C. Rozwenc, general editor. Lexington: D. C. Heath.

Tuzin, Donald F.
    1976   *The Ilahita Arapesh: Dimensions of Unity.* Berkeley: University of California Press.
    1980   *The Voice of the Tambaran.* Berkeley: University of California Press.

Underhill, Ruth M.
    1979   *Papago Woman.* Prospect Heights: Waveland Press.

Upham, Steadman, Patricia L. Crown,
and Stephen Plog
    1994   Alliance Formation and Cultural Identity in the American Southwest. In *Themes in Southwest Pre-*

history, edited by George J. Gumerman, pp. 183–210. Santa Fe: School of American Research Press.

Valado, Trenna
    1999   Ground Stone Technology. In "Living on the Edge of the Rim: Excavations and Analysis of the Silver Creek Archaeological Research Project, 1993–1998," edited by Barbara J. Mills, Sarah A. Herr, and Scott Van Keuren. *Arizona State Museum Archaeological Series* 192: 373–403. Tucson: University of Arizona.

Van Dyke, Ruth M.
    1997   The Andrews Great House Community: A Ceramic Chronometric Perspective. *Kiva* 63(2): 137–154.
    1998   *The Chaco Connection: Bonito Style Architecture in Outlier Communities.* Doctoral dissertation, University of Arizona, Tucson. Ann Arbor: University Microfilms.

Van Keuren, Scott
    1999   Ceramic Design Structure and the Organization of Cibola White Ware Production in the Grasshopper Region, Arizona. *Arizona State Museum Archaeological Series* 191. Tucson: University of Arizona.
    2000   Ceramic Decoration as Power: Late Prehistoric Design Change in East-Central Arizona. In *Alternative Leadership Strategies in the Prehispanic Southwest*, edited by Barbara J. Mills, pp. 79–94. Tucson: University of Arizona Press.

Van West, Carla R.
    1993   Modeling Prehistoric Streamflow, Climatic Variability, Productive Strategies and Human Settlement in the Middle Little Colorado River Valley. Paper presented at the Anasazi Symposium, Farmington, New Mexico, October 21-24.

Vickery, Parke E.
    1941   Architectural Details of the Construction of Surface Pueblo Ruin Arizona P:16:2. MS on file, Arizona State Museum Archives, University of Arizona, Tucson.

Vint, James M.
    1998   Functional Aspects of the TCAP Ceramics. In "Tonto Creek Archaeological Project: A Tonto Basin Perspective on Ceramic Economy," edited by James M. Vint and James M. Heidke. *Anthropological Papers* 23: 247–298. Draft Report. Tucson: Center for Desert Archaeology.

Vivian, Gordon
    1959   *The Hubbard Site and Other Tri-wall Structures.* Washington: U.S. National Park Service.

Vivian, Gordon, and Paul Reiter
    1960   The Great Kivas of Chaco Canyon and Their Relationships. *Monographs of the School of American Research* 22. Santa Fe: School of American Research.

Vivian, R. Gwinn
1990 *The Chacoan Prehistory of the San Juan Basin.* San Diego: Academic Press.
1997a Chacoan Roads: Function. *Kiva* 53(2): 35–67.
1997b Chacoan Roads: Morphology. *Kiva* 63(1): 7–34.

Vivian, R. Gwinn, Dulce N. Dodgen, and Gayle H. Hartmann
1978 Wooden Ritual Artifacts from Chaco Canyon, New Mexico: The Chetro Ketl Collection. *Anthropological Papers of the University of Arizona* 32. Tucson: University of Arizona Press.

Vokes, Arthur W.
1999 Shell. In "Living on the Edge of the Rim: Excavations and Analysis of the Silver Creek Archaeological Research Project, 1993–1998," edited by Barbara J. Mills, Sarah A. Herr, and Scott Van Keuren. *Arizona State Museum Archaeological Series* 192: 405–432. Tucson: University of Arizona.

Waldrop, M. Mitchell
1992 *Complexity: The Emerging Science at the Edge of Order and Chaos.* New York: Simon and Schuster.

Warburton, Miranda, and Donna K. Graves
1992 Navajo Springs, Arizona: Frontier Outlier or Autonomous Great House? *Journal of Field Archaeology* 19(1): 51–69.

Weaver, Donald E., Jr.
1989 An Archaeological Survey of a Materials Pit and Haul Road near Show Low, Navajo County, Arizona. MS submitted to the Arizona Department of Transportation, Highways Division, Phoenix. Plateau Mountain Desert Research, Flagstaff.

Whittlesey, Stephanie M.
1978 *Status and Death at Grasshopper Pueblo: Experiments Toward an Archaeological Theory of Correlates.* Doctoral dissertation, University of Arizona, Tucson. Ann Arbor: University Microfilms.

Wilcox, David R.
1999 A Peregrine View of the Macroregional Systems in the North American Southwest. In *Great Towns and Regional Polities in the Prehistoric American Southwest and Southeast*, edited by Jill E. Neitzel, pp. 115–141. Amerind Foundation Publication. Albuquerque: University of New Mexico Press.

Wilk, Richard R., and Robert McC. Netting
1984 Households: Changing Forms and Functions. In *Households: Comparative and Historic Studies of the Domestic Group*, edited by Robert McC. Netting, Richard R. Wilk, and Eric J. Arnould, pp. 1–28. Berkeley: University of California Press.

Wilkinson, Leland
1997 Systat 7.0 for Windows: Statistics. Chicago: SYSTAT products, SPSS, Inc.

Wilkinson, T. J.
1982 The Definition of Ancient Manured Zones by Means of Extensive Sherd-sampling Techniques. *Journal of Field Archaeology* 9(3): 323–333.
1989 Extensive Sherd Scatters and Land-use Intensity: Some Recent Results. *Journal of Field Archaeology* 16(1): 31–46.

Will, George F., and H. J. Spinden
1906 *The Mandans*, Vol. 3, No. 4. Cambridge: Harvard University.

Williams, F. E.
1930 *Orokaiva Society.* London: Oxford University Press.

Wills, W. H.
2000 Political Leadership and the Construction of Chacoan Great Houses, A.D. 1020–1140. In *Alternative Leadership Strategies in the Prehispanic Southwest*, edited by Barbara J. Mills, pp. 19–44. Tucson: University of Arizona Press.

Windes, Thomas C.
1987 Investigations at the Pueblo Alto Complex, Chaco Canyon, New Mexico, 1975–1979. *Chaco Canyon Studies, Publications in Archeology* 18F. Santa Fe: National Park Service.

Windes, Thomas C., and Peter J. McKenna
2001 Going against the Grain: Wood Production in Chacoan Society. *American Antiquity* 66(1): 119–140.

Winter, Joseph C.
1994 *Across the Colorado Plateau: Anthropological Studies for the Transwestern Pipeline Expansion Project: Synthesis and Conclusions—Communities, Boundaries, and Cultural Variation*, Vol. 20. Albuquerque: Office of Contract Archeology.

Woodbury, Richard B.
1954 Prehistoric Stone Implements of Northeast Arizona. Reports of the Awatovi Expedition 6. *Papers of the Peabody Museum of American Archaeology and Ethnography* 34. Cambridge: Harvard University.
1979 Prehistory: Introduction. In *Handbook of North American Indians: Southwest*, Vol. 9 edited by Alfonso Ortiz, pp. 22–30. Washington: Smithsonian Institution.

Young, Lisa C.
1994 Lithics and Mobility: The Homol'ovi Chipped Stone Assemblage. In "Middle Little Colorado River Archaeology: From the Parks to the People," edited by Anne Trinkle Jones and Martyn D. Tagg. *The Arizona Archaeologist* 27: 47–56. Phoenix: Arizona Archaeological Society.
1996a *Mobility and Farmers: The Pithouse-to-Pueblo Transition in Northern Arizona.* Doctoral dissertation, University of Arizona, Tucson. Ann Arbor: University Microfilms.
1996b Pits, Rooms, Baskets, Pots: Storage among South-

Young, L. C. (*continued*)

western Farmers. In "Interpreting Southwestern Diversity: Underlying Principles and Overarching Patterns," edited by Paul R. Fish and J. Jefferson Reid. *Anthropological Research Papers* 48: 201–210. Tempe: Arizona State University.

1998   Early and Late Pithouses in the Middle Little Colorado River Valley. Paper prepared for working group "Why do Pit Structures Vary" at the 63rd Annual Meeting of the Society for American Archaeology, Seattle.

Index

Abstract

A rchaeological, ethnographic, and historical accounts demonstrate that both individuals and societies are transformed by processes common to frontiers: migration, integration, and the organization of communities in a situation of low population density. These processes and the sense of being in a marginal place affect societies at all scales and can be used to identify frontiers in the archaeological past. The Mogollon Rim region in east-central Arizona was such a frontier, situated beyond or between larger organizations such as Chaco, Hohokam, and Mimbres, and eleventh- and twelfth-century settlement there poses a contradiction to those who study it. On this southwestern edge of the Puebloan world, population density was low and land abundant, yet the region was overbuilt with great kivas, a form of community level integrative architecture.

In this study, a frontier model is used to evaluate five excavated community centers in the Mogollon Rim region: Cothrun's Kiva, Hough's Great Kiva, site AZ P:16:160 (ASM), Tla Kii Pueblo, and Carter Ranch Pueblo. Five large excavation projects and 27 surveys provide additional information about household and community production, distribution, transmission, reproduction, and co-residence. When household, community, and regional scale data are integrated, they show that the weak archaeological pattern of the Mogollon Rim region was created by the flexible and creative behaviors of small-scale agriculturalists who lived in a land-rich and labor-poor environment where expediency, variability, mobility, and fluid social organization were the rule and rigid structures and normative behavior the exception.

The eleventh- and twelfth-century inhabitants of the Mogollon Rim region appear to have been recent migrants from the southern portion of the Chacoan region. The early settlers built houses and ceremonial structures and made ceramic vessels that resembled those of their homeland, but their social and political organizations were not those of their ancestral communities. The Mogollon Rim communities reflect the cultural backgrounds of the migrants, their new marginal position on the political landscape, and the unique processes associated with frontiers. Whereas arable land was sparse and labor was abundant in the homeland, on the frontier labor, not land, was the primary constraint

Resumen

L as narrativas arqueológicas, etnográficas e históricas demuestran que los procesos comunes en fronteras, tales como la migración, la integración, y la organización de comunidades de baja densidad demográfica, transforman tanto a individuos como a sociedades. Estos procesos, además de la sensación de habitar un lugar marginal, afectan a las sociedades de toda escala y pueden ser utilizados para identificar fronteras en el pasado arqueológico. La región del altiplano de Mogollón en Arizona centro-este, fue una de estas fronteras, situada más allá o entre organizaciones mayores como Chaco, Hohokam y Mimbres, y sus asentamientos de los siglos XI y XII de esta era presentan una contradicción para quienes los estudian. En esta frontera suroeste del mundo Pueblo, la densidad demográfica fue baja; sin embargo, la región exhibió una sobreabundancia de grandes kivas, los cuales son una forma de arquitectura integrativa comunitaria.

En este estudio se utiliza un modelo de frontera para evaluar cinco centros comunitarios excavados en el altiplano de Mogollón: Cothrun's Kiva, Hough's Great Kiva, AZ P:16:160 (ASM), Pueblo Tla Kii, y Pueblo Carter Ranch. Cinco proyectos de excavación y 27 prospecciones proveen información adicional sobre la producción, distribución, transmisión, reproducción, y co-residencia a nivel de unidad doméstica y comunidad. Cuando se integran los datos a escala doméstica, comunitaria, y regional, se demuestra que el débil patrón arqueológico del altiplano de Mogollón fue generado por las actividades flexibles y creativas de agricultores a pequeña escala quienes vivieron en un medioambiente de abundante tierra y poca mano de obra, donde la eficiencia, variabilidad, mobilidad, y organización social fluida fueron la regla y las estructuras rígidas y comportamientos normativos la excepción.

Los habitantes del altiplano de Mogollón durante los siglos XI y XII parecen haber sido inmigrantes recientes de la porción sur de la región de Chaco. Estos inmigrantes construyeron casas y estructuras ceremoniales y fabricaron cerámica semejantes a aquellas de su región de origen, pero su organización social y política no replicó la de las comunidades ancestrales. Las comunidades del altiplano de Mogollón reflejan el bagaje cultural de los inmigrantes, su nueva posición marginal en el paisaje político, y los procesos unicamente asociados

to production. This reversal in the relative proportions of land to labor from core to frontier dramatically changed the social relations of production. When the context of production changes in this way, wealth-in-people becomes more valuable than material wealth, and cultural symbols (such as the great kiva) and social relationships are reinterpreted accordingly.

con fronteras. Mientras que la tierra arable fue escasa y la mano de obra abundante en el lugar de origen, en la frontera fue la mano de obra la que principalmente constriñó la producción. Este cambio en las proporciones relativas de tierra y mano de obra del centro a la frontera transformó dramaticamente las relaciones sociales de producción. Cuando el contexto de la producción cambia de esta manera, la riqueza laboral se vuelve más importante que la riqueza material, y los símbolos culturales (así como el gran kiva) y las relaciones sociales son reinterpretados de acuerdo a estos cambios.

ANTHROPOLOGICAL PAPERS OF THE UNIVERSITY OF ARIZONA

Anthropological Papers listed as O.P., D are available as Docutech reproductions (high quality xerox) printed on demand. They are tape or spiral bound and nonreturnable.